PROGRESS IN SELF PSYCHOLOGY
Volume 2

PROGRESS IN SELF PSYCHOLOGY
Editor: Arnold Goldberg, MD

PROGRESS IN SELF PSYCHOLOGY
Volume 2

Edited by
ARNOLD GOLDBERG

THE GUILFORD PRESS
New York   *London*

Copyright © 1986 The Guilford Press
A Division of Guilford Publications, Inc.
200 Park Avenue South, New York, N.Y. 10003

Printed in the United States of America

Library of Congress Catalog Card No. 85–21875
ISBN 0–89862–301–4

Contributors

Michael Franz Basch, MD
Chicago, Illinois

Bernard Brandchaft, MD
Beverly Hills, California

Homer C. Curtis, MD
Philadelphia, Pennsylvania

Douglas W. Detrick, PhD
Portola Valley, California

Arnold Goldberg, MD
Chicago, Illinois

Jerald Kay, MD
Cincinnati, Ohio

Joshua Levy, PhD
Ottawa, Ontario, Canada

Joseph Lichtenberg, MD
Washington, D.C.

Elliott Markson, MD
Toronto, Ontario, Canada

Hyman L. Muslin, MD
Chicago, Illinois

Anna Ornstein, MD
Cincinnati, Ohio

David E. Reiser, MD
Denver, Colorado

William H. Rickles, MD
Los Angeles, California

Estelle Shane, PhD
Los Angeles, California

Morton Shane, MD
Los Angeles, California

John A. Sloane, MD
Toronto, Ontario, Canada

Robert D. Stolorow, PhD
Los Angeles, California

Peter G. Thomson, MD
Toronto, Ontario, Canada

Marian Tolpin, MD
Chicago, Illinois

Paul H. Tolpin, MD
Chicago, Illinois

Harry Trosman, MD
Chicago, Illinois

Robert S. Wallerstein, MD
San Francisco, California

Ernest S. Wolf, MD
Chicago, Illinois

Preface

Several years after the publication of the second of Heinz Kohut's books on psychoanalytic self psychology (Kohut, 1977), he asked a group of colleagues to join with him in compiling a book of a series of essays that would focus on answers to the critics of his work. I clearly remember the initial meeting, which, because of the group's size, took place in a small meeting room in a hotel. I do not remember all of the attendees, but they were those of his friends and students who had long been interested in and associated with Kohut's work. Our first meeting was noteworthy because of the extensive discussion about whether we should indeed devote the time and energy required to answer all of the many and varied criticisms. There were those of us who felt that it would profit us more to direct attention to advancing further the tenets of self psychology and so ignore the opposing voices. There were others who felt that self psychology faced a danger of being further alienated from the mainstream of psychoanalysis, and thus its proponents must devote themselves to responding to those many worthwhile critical examinations that called attention to weaknesses or errors in the concepts of self psychology. And there was Kohut himself who thought we should do both.

Over the years the group met regularly with the avowed aim of compiling a list of criticisms and questions that we would discuss at length. We would then prepare, in turn, a series of position papers on the varied topics. Not surprisingly the discussion and the papers took on lives of their own, and our hoped-for book of responses seems still to be percolating on the stove. One of the reasons for this unfulfilled promise was that every question seemed to invite a plethora of associated questions to come along with it, and soon we found ourselves questioning anything and everything about psychoanalysis itself.

In order to gain some perspective on the more outstanding questions and criticisms about self psychology we decided to make it the focus of a conference, and many of the papers in this volume derive from that meeting held in Toronto in the fall of 1984. Our subject was the broad one of questions and controversies in self psychology; and we aimed for a format involving a critic, a respondent, and several discussants. Although many authors have had occasion to take self psychology to task, there have been but a few who have taken the time to read all the relevant literature and to detail and map out their critical positions carefully. We were extremely fortunate to have invitations accepted by Homer Curtis and Robert Wallerstein on the three primary areas for critical inquiry: theory, clinical practice, and developmental issues.

A brief overview of each of these areas will prepare the reader for the aforementioned sections in this volume. The discussion of theory was clearly an outgrowth of Kohut's early ideas whose fate at the time of first appearance was unpredictable. His original contributions were primarily clinical and were placed firmly within classical psychoanalytic concepts. The theoretical modifications that he made were modest; and the most salient one, that of a separate line of development for narcissism, was openly debated and discussed. But new ideas take on a life of their own, and there seemed no easy way to constrain the debate or the implications that derived from that early position. Once narcissism could be seen in its own right it was necessary to reconsider many other concepts including those of the drives, the nature of transference, and, eventually, the nature of cure. One way to handle the problem of self psychology seemingly breaking the bounds of classical analytic theory was simply to declare that it was not psychoanalysis. I suspect that this is more of an administrative than a scientific solution. There may be a few fortunate individuals who really know what psychoanalysis is and is not, but most scientific pursuits are characterized by open-ended curiosity that needs have no boundaries. Whatever questions arise must be answered by investigation and not by legislation. Thus our first panel struggles with the issue of just how self psychology fits within the boundaries of psychoanalysis. It necessarily challenges many of the accepted notions of psychoanalysis, but the reader will recognize that the holes in the fabric of analytic theory were there long before self psychology came upon the scene and need repair regardless of one's commitment to the psychology of the self. Our major papers are by Homer Curtis and Michael Basch. They are discussed by Robert Stolorow, Elliott Markson, and Peter Thomson. The last word is a rejoinder by Dr. Curtis.

The next section on clinical practice stems from our many hours of discussion about the difference in the doing of analysis between self psychologists and classical analysts. For many years much of self psychology has been dismissed by saying it was what every good analyst did anyway. This came as a surprise only to those hearty souls who changed what they did when they learned about self psychology; but this position was insisted upon by, for instance, the critics of Kohut's report of the case of Mr. Z, which was condemned as being a poor first analysis and a subsequent correct second analysis. This stance was a real puzzle for our discussions since we were never sure how people really did conduct an analysis, nor could we see what the rationale would be for a classical analyst doing pretty much the same as a self psychologist does. Those of us who did reanalyses of individuals were impressed by the marked discrepancies between the two, but this could possibly be said of many reanalyses. If it were the case that self psychology really offers nothing new to the practitioner then there seemed no point to its pursuit. There is perhaps no more eloquent spokesman for the incorporation of the ideas of self psychology into the totality of psychoanalysis than Robert Wallerstein who begins our next section with this very question of just how and whether self psychology differs in practice. The reader may then compare Ernest Wolf's position on this issue in order to decide if the broad spectrum of analytic practice easily incorporates that of self psychology or if there is something special about it. The discussions by Paul Tolpin and Joshua Levy are meaningful accompaniments to the problem.

Our group's discussions about development were perhaps the most unsatisfactory ones, not because of our own lack of interest, but rather due to the scarcity of experts in child development who chose to address the problems posed by self psychology. On the one hand we found those students of developmental psychology who found self psychology to be perfectly compatible with their own findings, while on the other hand we continued to read of the usual and familiar ideas of psychoanalytic development with a total dismissal of self psychological contributions. We were unsuccessful in stimulating a real debate on the issues but our offering to the readers is a worthy alternative. Marian Tolpin continues her ideas on the fundamental distinctions of development in self psychology. This paper is then discussed by Anna Ornstein and Joseph Lichtenberg. Estelle and Morton Shane present their reformulated idea for an integrated model of development to complete this section.

It is difficult to give organization to the many other remaining contributions to this volume that range from abstract theoretical to specific clinical inquiries. The papers are thus rather loosely divided into two sections dealing with applied psychoanalysis and theory. The first contains a psychoanalytic interpretation of *The Bacchae* of Euripides by Jerald Kay with a discussion by Harry Trosman. Other essays in this section include John Sloane's paper on the empathic vantage point in supervision, a chapter on self psychology and somatization by William Rickles, and David Reiser's paper on self psychology and the problem of suicide. Our final section is more involved with the theoretical stance of self psychology. It begins with Bernard Brandchaft's review of self psychology and British object relations theory and goes on to Robert Stolorow's brief but trenchant essay, "On Experiencing an Object." The two papers that follow are, "On Working Through in Self Psychology" by Hyman Muslin and Douglas Detrick's continuing investigation of alterego phenomena and alterego transferences. This final section perhaps most adequately represents the work of our group and especially the wishes of Heinz Kohut who wanted both answers for our critics as well as a progressive research investigation.

The volume, as a whole, is by no means meant to be a final answer to the critics and criticisms of self psychology. That, of course, is the ongoing effort of any scientific activity. It certainly is meant as an indicator that we take criticism seriously and, at times, gladly. It probably also is testament to Heinz Kohut's own solution to our group's quandary about where we should direct our energies, since there is little doubt that the work of answering our critics cannot help but contribute to further progress in self psychology: and that is the title of our volume.[1]

Arnold Goldberg, MD

REFERENCE

Kohut, H. (1977). *The Restoration of the Self.* New York: International Universities Press.

---

1. The preparation of this book was financed by funds from the Harry and Hazel Cohen Research Fund. Ms. Chris Susman provided secretarial and editorial assistance.

Contents

THEORETICAL ISSUES

1

Clinical Consequences of the Theory of Self Psychology

HOMER C. CURTIS

In this chapter, I would like to address some of the questions that have been raised about self psychology and to participate in a constructive dialogue with its proponents. In the *Random House Dictionary of the English Language* (1966), dialogue is defined as "an exchange of ideas between two or more persons on a particular issue, especially political or religious, with a view of reaching an amicable agreement or settlement." There are two aspects of this definition that we should not follow: We do not want our dialogue to have political or religious overtones, nor do we expect to reach agreement. In the words of Godfrey Turton (1967), "Harmony is a great good but there are others greater for whose sake it must in the last resort be renounced." (p. 2) If we do not set harmony as our goal, we should at least strive for communication.

I have assumed that anyone sufficiently interested in reading this chapter will likely have a general grasp of the main propositions and concepts of self psychology as developed by Kohut and his coworkers. For that reason I will dispense with any introductory summary and immediately state the premise of my exposition, namely, that if applied exclusively and literally, the theoretical concepts of self psychology lead to a clinical approach that departs in certain important ways from essential elements of the psychoanalytic situation and process. Further, while such an approach may achieve demonstrable therapeutic change, it may be questioned whether such change can be considered as derived from the same personality processes and alterations as are set in motion in psychoanalytic treatment conducted along classical lines.

In order to demonstrate this point of view, I present two case vignettes offered in the literature by proponents of self psychology that offer an opportunity to examine some of the consequences of using that frame of reference. The first case (Basch, 1980) provides a springboard to a discussion of some of the major points of controversy between self psychology and psychoanalysis as usually conceptualized and practiced.

The patient, a social worker with prior psychotherapy, sought further treatment because of problems in her relationships with men. She approached the therapy in a challenging and critical way. The therapist was able to tolerate her attacks and over a period of time engaged her interest in examining her unhappy experiences with her previous therapist and with her father, both of whom had seriously disappointed her. Considerable work on her feelings for her father made her realize that his anger with her disguised anxious, insecure feelings about his roles as father and physician. This knowledge helped her give up the childhood hope that she would be able to win his approval and through him become satisfied with herself. As she worked through this insight into her relationship with her father, she became more trusting of the therapist, mobilizing a long-dormant wish for a trusted parent with whom she could share her ideas and hopes.

She was able to delineate her manner of dealing with men—she would encourage and flatter them, only to make deflating comments under the guise of frank discussion. The therapist states,

> Once she could see clearly what she had been doing, the patient lost interest in men as suitors. Her work preoccupied her, and she was reluctant to invest the time and effort required to play the dating game; instead she signed up for extra evening courses in clinical psychology to supplement her training. (Basch, 1980, p. 84)

A likely explanation for such a shift in interest follows, when the author writes,

> When for a brief time the patient sexualized the transference and became frightened by her thoughts, the therapist pointed out to her that she was mistakenly attributing genital motives to the love and affection she felt for him who was, through his work, giving her a chance to achieve satisfactions heretofore closed to her. She was helped to understand that her emotions were appropriate to the child who stands in awe of and wants to unite with the powerful, giving parent, and were not those of a sexually excited woman. The resolution of the transference was embodied in her going beyond the stage of working for the therapist–parent's implicit or explicit approval and praise and, instead, forming her own concept of an ideal self that she then set out to fulfill. (Basch, 1980, p. 86).

The practical solution the patient reached was to decide to become a psychiatrist. She was able to enlist the support of her father, who after an initial concern that this would undermine their newfound closeness, was proud of her ambition and initiative. The therapist also supported this decision and agreed to her wish to terminate in order to devote herself singlemindedly to her premedical studies.

The therapist considered the possibility that the patient's wish to become a physician was an identification with both the father and therapist and an attempt to resolve a conflict through action rather than through psychological insight. He rejected this possibility on the grounds that the patient proceeded with her plans thoughtfully, with no awareness of being driven. He did not concern himself over whether genital sexuality would ever play a part in her life, and likened her renunciation of sexuality to latency, wondering whether there might be a later "pubertal" phase and a recapitulation or first awakening of an oedipal phase after she had consolidated her self.

In view of the patient's major difficulty in her relationships with men and the significant conflict about her father, it is difficult to understand how the erotic transference could be so easily dismissed. To diagnose her as having a "selfobject disturbance" seems to assume that she had no important sexual conflicts needing exploration, yet her history, behavior, and the transference indicated otherwise. The patient, who was frightened by her sexual feelings for the therapist, was apparently only too glad to accept his denial of her sexual experience and to turn her attention to nonsexual interests and achievement. The therapist's comparison of this development with that of a latency child is apt, but this was a woman in her late 20s who not only did not have the luxury of time, but also was not given the opportunity of making an informed decision. This was denied her when the therapist told her that, contrary to her actual experience, her feeling were not those of a sexually excited woman, but of a child wishing to unite with a powerful parent. In so doing, he was indeed acting out the role of the powerful parent forcing her, in collusion with her own resistance to her sexual urges, to renounce sexuality and, like a good latency child, "singlemindedly" attend to her studies. His comments appear to have functioned as an "inexact interpretation," as described by Edward Glover (1931), in which a new displacement or compromise formation can relieve anxiety and symptoms, especially, as in this case, when supported by powerful suggestion and buttressed by a ready identification. The author's disclaimer of this possibility on the basis of an absence of awareness of conflict in the patient's renunciation of sex and her choice of medical school overlooks that just such an outcome is the common experience with defensive identifications. A case can be made for the knowing and planned use of such inexact interpretations in selected cases of psychotherapy when further exploration and insight are judged to be impossible or undesirable. However, interpretation in this case seems rather to have been based on a presumption that the patient had a "selfobject disturbance" and therefore could not have significant structural conflict of a sexual nature.

Examination of this clinical vignette uncovers imbalance and reductionism. As a consequence of reducing the complexities of neurosogenesis to the relative simplicity of failures in parental empathy, self psychology offers an appealing but misleading model. In a sense, it is regressive in that it retards the growing complexity and range of psychoanalytic theory, which from its beginnings in Freud's early seduction theory has steadily expanded our knowledge of every aspect of mental functioning. To the early focus on drive vicissitudes have been added empirical data and valuable theories on defense, transference, narcissism, superego and ego development and function, character, and so forth. The study of preoedipal issues, of increasing interest over the past 50 years, has been given added impetus by research in child observation and by clinical work and sicker patients. Valuable work in the areas of object relations and adaptation has illuminated the interface between the individual and his environment. Some aspects of Kohut's (1959, 1971) work have added perspectives to our view of narcissism and the self experience, although, paradoxically, his (1977) broad view of the self as supraordinate leads to a narrowing of theoretical range and a widening gulf from psychoanalysis.

While current psychoanalytic theory is far from complete, it does provide for a more balanced view of past and present, trauma and fantasy, oedipal and preoedipal, and reality and unconscious motivation than any other psychological theory. For example, it has the conceptual means to take into account the contributions of both the real traumatic experience and the drive-motivated fantasy elaboration of such crucial events as the primal scene. Here the traumatic effects of surprise, confusion, and overstimulation are mixed with arousal of sexual and aggressive impulses and the child's need to explain and gain mastery. The resulting synthesis can lead to idiosyncratic fantasy views of the sexual act as sadistic attack, and to neurotic symptoms and character sequelae.

As in the case of the social worker who renounced men in favor of medicine, current psychoanalytic theory can offer a more balanced, comprehensive explanation of the clinical data than self psychology. The claim that some narcissistic or self-disordered patients do not have significant oedipal conflict has been seriously questioned by many who work with patients of every type (e.g., Eagle, 1984; Kernberg, 1967; Singer, in press). Failure to find evidence of a crucial, normal developmental and organizing psychic constellation suggests a use of preconceptions that lead to overlooking or minimizing such material, or that encourage the material to develop along other lines. One place this can occur is in the paradoxical effect of the effort to establish ideal emphatic responses. While this effort is said to demonstrate respect and to build up a cohesive self through transmuting internalizations, the assumption that the patient is defective due to maternal failures in empathy not only can collude with a regressive defense, but also minimizes the patient's autonomy. It overvalues the mother–analyst and external experience at the expense of the patient's more mature needs and capacities, and gives the analyst the responsibility for the patient's feelings. Thus the analyst's empathic successes or failures dictate the patient's self-esteem rather than granting him a sense of individuality. In addition it encourages dependent regressive material at the expense of more advanced object related conflictual material, which, when and if it emerged, would be treated as "disintegration products." What is thus validated is the patient's experiential deficit and dependent vulnerability to mother and analyst, while the genuineness of his drives and separateness are minimized.

What then are we to make of the challenge of self psychology to psychoanalysis? Certainly, that challenge has contributed to further evaluation of current theory (Blum, 1982), the results of which at this point are increased doubt about the usefulness of the concept of the supraordinate self as the primary psychic agency and motivator (Rangell, 1982). This change in the conceptualization of the self has a number of significant ramifications. As usually defined, the self is understood not as an agency, but as content, the product of the functioning of the mental agencies (e.g., Spruiell, 1981). It is a subjective constellation of reflexive images and views of the body, memories and attributes that differentiate a person from others, containing elements of wishful fantasy and personal myth as well as objective self-observations. As such, its composition and genesis may be analyzed. To broaden this into a supraordinate self that is the seat of both experience and motivation equates the self with the total personality, Freud's "Gesamt-Ich" (1915). It also entails certain conceptual problems such as the use of the concept of self before a self has been differentiated, and the self as motivator for the self.

The hypothesis (Kohut, 1971) of a separate line of development of narcissism or the self seems a minor issue, especially in the light of observational and clinical data pointing to the complex interweaving and interdependence of drive vicissitudes and transformations, and the development of self and object representations. The same mother–child interactions that provide drive gratification also help structure the child's inner and outer reality, his differentiation of self and object, and establishment of self and object representations. Viewing the development of the self as separate from that of the drives suggests that the former seeks regulation and control of tensions and ultimately structural cohesion, while the latter seeks drive gratification through relationships with objects. Yet, such a distinction between drive needs and regulatory needs seems artificial, since it is primarily from drive pressures that the need for control and regulatory structures arise. Thus defenses as they mature, in part out of drive vicissitudes, are important contributors to building regulatory structures. The self experience is inevitably bound up with the object experience since they both occur in the context of mother–child interactions. What is described as mirroring is one aspect of the mother's loving care of the child, who experiences this care as gratifying the need for both object love and self love leading eventually to regulatory structure. The child's feeling of being loved and admired is sustained by internalizing and structuralizing the concomitants of drive satisfaction and optimal regulation. It has been my clinical experience that narcissistic problems do not occur unless there have been disturbances in the object relationships of childhood.

Of importance is Kohut's formulation of selfobject transferences, which after starting as "narcissistic transferences" in rather apologetic quotation marks have become a central fact of the whole life span. Kohut (1980) stated, "Man lives in a matrix of selfobjects from birth to death. He needs selfobjects for his psychological survival, just as he needs oxygen in his environment throughout his life for physiological survival" (p. 478). This claim seems to run counter to his concept that selfobjects are needed to build up a cohesive self that eventually has joyful, independent initiative and creativity, at which time dependence on the gleam in the mother's eye must surely have diminished. More importantly, the concept of selfobjects seems too broad, having been extended beyond any reasonable connection with autistic and symbiotic states to include more advanced developmental phases in which self and object are well delineated. Not all attachments or needs for the mother or other people have the aim of merger, or of use of an object as a part of the function of an undifferentiated self. The selfobject concept tends to deemphasize the whole range of needs served by the object, and the variety of ways these needs may be made manifest and satisfied. It also confuses the subject's need for the object with the object's lack of separateness from the subject. In my opinion, current psychoanalytic theory, on the other hand, clearly provides for the existence of object needs derived from all phases of development before, during, and after separation of self and object.

Another major point of controversy centers on self psychology's reduction of neurosogenesis to a lack of parental empathy, which can hardly carry the heavy load of the complicated internal and external factors in a development spread out over many years. This oversimplification neglects biological factors in the child's equipment, differences in responsiveness, cognitive abilities, drive endowment, resilience, and tolerance for anxiety. Gross traumatization, physical and sexual abuse, accidents, and illnesses are not sufficiently considered either. More importantly, it does not adequately account for the child's contributions to the parent–child relationship, and ignores the child's drive-motivated fantasies and distortions of the parents' behavior. The child is seen as reactive to environmental failures and traumata, and any hostility is regarded as reactive rather than drive motivated. In his last book, Kohut (1984) attempts to correct this simplistic view by allowing for the possibility that a child may have a distorted perception of parental behavior. While this modifies the reductionistic environmentalism of stressing empathic failures, it does not explain the nature of the distortion of perception adequately. This is merely attributed to fragmentation of the self following traumatization by empathic failures, leading to a kind of perceptual immaturity. Distortion resulting from projection of hostile and sexual wishes and elaboration of fantasy is not considered.

The importance of empathy, which has become the central shibboleth of self psychology, derives from its dual function in that system as mode of observation and curative agent. Kohut (1977, p. 308) saw introspection and empathy as the essence of psychoanalysis and was willing to discard Freud's definition of the essence of psychoanalysis as transference and resistance. To view empathy as the provision of a selfobject use, a restorer of the self, and the means for structure building represents a departure from the centrality of the analysis of transference and resistance, in which empathy is a mode of data gathering to be used in connection with and subjected to the scrutiny of logic and cognition. The recommendation for "empathic immersion" can lead to a constraint on or, at least, a delay in objective evaluation of empathically perceived data. The high value given to empathy may subtly change the aim of therapy from understanding to nurturing and may encourage a perception of the analyst as a better parent than the originals. This fosters a nonconflictual growth model, with the analyst becoming, through validating, confirming responsiveness, a kind of judge. The goal of promoting the "fulfilling of the self's basic design" implies a form of "maturational morality" to which Kohut once objected in a comment about the fallacy of regarding maturational sequences as a movement toward an ideal maturity (Ornstein, 1978, p. 374).

In assessing the relationship between psychoanalysis and self psychology, the dialectic of conflict versus deficit is often stressed. I believe this deserves closer scrutiny since these two qualities are not on the same level of conceptualization. Conflict, as defined by psychoanalysis, is primarily intrapsychic, although as a result of projection it may be experienced as interpersonal and external. Deficit, on the other hand, is properly external, manifest, and behavioral. The adage that nature abhors a vacuum seems true in a psychological and developmental sense: while certain attitudes and actions may be missing in the mother's behavior toward her child, this does not necessarily mean that a gap or deficit is produced in the child's psychic structure. Rather, a malformation or developmental arrest occurs, and the child falls back on primitive defenses or qualities, which may then be elaborated by further compensatory structures and fantasy formations. Thus the deficit is in the interpersonal experience, and ultimately may result in some form of behavioral "deficit," again on the interpersonal, descriptive level. Even when the mother is not supplying certain specific functions or satisfactions, she is still doing "something." The child will internalize this and form a mental representation of the cold or unempathic mother, elaborated and distorted by his own drives and projections. Such a "deficit" in the mother's behavior may produce a different kind of reaction in the child than more empathic behavior by the mother, nevertheless, the child deals with the mother's behavior with his available resources, defenses, and identifications to form, not an "absence," but a "presence," not a lack of structure, but a structure, albeit distorted, by ideal standards.

The patient's experience and verbalization of a sense of deficit thus can be conceptualized as the expression of a fantasy (which is itself a structure) of something missing, of needs not adequately met, or of limitations. Clinically, such self-evaluations may prove to be reaction formations to disclaim and control dangerous impulses, or they may be more direct expressions of a sense of being crippled by personality malformations and fixations. Such a theory of deficits thus recommends that clinicians supply the experiences thought to have been lacking, so as to fill the postulated gap with new structure. This approach accepts the manifest at the expense of exploring additional dimensions and meanings in those patients capable of utilizing analysis. In those whose major psychopathology is based on development arrests, malformations, and primitive defenses, empathic interactions are thought to change the existing equilibrium by promoting identifications and enhancing available resources and adaptive structures, while diminishing the need for pathological, maladaptive personality structures. Many patients, however, exhibit both structural conflict and structural deformity, and require decisions about how best to accommodate the treatment to the needs of both areas of psychopathology. It is difficult to imagine how the analysis of the conflictual aspects can escape compromise when empathic interactions are employed to provide transmuting experiences.

While Kohut has stated, "It is not the interpretation that cures the patient" (1977, p. 31), and has also said, "The essential curative process in cases of self pathology is structure building via transmuting internalizations" (Ornstein, 1978, p. 928), other self psychologists advocate going beyond the supportive, "holding environment" of the empathic interaction by means of interpretation. There is a wide range of opinion among self psychologists concerning the curative effects of internalization of the empathic interaction as compared with interpretation and insight (see Goldberg, 1978)—although, when self psychologists refer to "interpretation," it is often in the broad sense of intervening, explaining, and identifying feelings and behavior, rather than in the classical sense of communicating warded off elements of drive and defense. Perhaps a better term for many of the interventions responding to empathic interactions would be "clarification," defined by Bibring (1954) as describing, connecting, and identifying perceptions, feelings, actions, attitudes, and repetitive behavior, which though vague, unverbalized, and unacknowledged, are, unlike repressed material, capable of being brought into coherent awareness without encountering unconscious resistance. This form of insight can help make objective and comprehensible what may have been subjectively vague and incoherent, and can be a significant means of mastery, of consolidation of diffuse self representations, and of more effective repression of disruptive conflict, especially when integrated by newly formed identifications with the analyst. (Parenthetically, the term "identification," appears infrequently in the literature of self psychology, perhaps because certain of its meanings have been preempted by "transmuting internalizations." In addition, since it is so closely linked to drive and object theory it may not have been found useful in self theory.)

As an example of the use of the term "interpretation," to mean the clarification of consciously held character attitudes and repetitive patterns, a vignette offered in a recent paper to illustrate the formulation of interpretations from the self psychological viewpoint may be instructive (Ornstein & Ornstein, 1980, pp. 208–210). A single woman who had lost her mother during latency came into analysis complaining of an inability to feel deeply, as if she had a "gaping hole" in her psyche. To fill this gap, she had been "searching for her dead mother," whom she had never mourned adequately. In the analysis she complained that the analyst missed indications of the presence of strong affects on several occasions. This was significant to her because she felt this meant that the analyst was unable to tolerate strong affects and she remembered this to be true of her father as well. At the time of her mother's death, she recalled, her father had not helped her mourn this loss.

While the patient was away on a business trip, someone brutally destroyed one of her pets. She was unable to cry, but was sad and agitated for days. She hoped to be able to break down and cry in the analytic sessions, but could not feel or express her loss in the analyst's presence. The analyst recalled that the patient had been devoted to pets and "could feel more for them than for people," having been quite upset when she had lost one of her favorite pets as a young child. Regarding this as a screen memory, most likely related to her mother's death, he made some effort to establish the connection. The patient responded by saying that she could not react to the recent loss of her pet because she felt that the analyst probably did not like animals and must be ridiculing her pain. The analyst reconsidered his focus and said that his attempt to connect her reaction to the loss of the pet with the childhood loss of her mother rightly created the feeling in her that he was bypassing or minimizing her current reactions (thus being like the unempathic father and justifying the patient's conviction that the analyst could not understand her pain and was ridiculing her). In the following sessions the analyst gave a "reconstructive interpretation" expressing a more complete genetic–dynamic understanding, not only about the meaning of the loss of her pet, but also about the patient's transference conviction that the analyst could not appreciate her feelings. The analyst could now say that this time it was important that someone understand exactly how she felt in order to validate her feelings and make them acceptable and real to her. In a subsequent session, when the analyst recognized and acknowledged that she was now feeling her sadness deeply, the patient burst into tears. She spoke once more of the loss of the pet in childhood, and added a new recollection: An aunt had known how the little girl felt and instead of ignoring her pain and ridiculing her, had comforted her affectionately. Thus, in spite of the patient's insistence that no one had understood her loss and grief, someone, in fact, had.

The authors conclude with several points. The patient's conviction that the analyst could not appreciate her feelings of loss was considered to be a transference repetition of the traumatizing failure of the father to tolerate and be responsive to the daughter's reaction to her mother's death. In keeping with the truism that all transferences are repetitions, but not all repetitions are transference, the assumption that this was transference in the specific, rather than broad sense must be questioned. The patient, said to have had an intensely ambivalent relationship with her father since the death of her mother during latency, had the persistent conscious image of her father as unable to tolerate strong affects or help her mourn the mother's death. This persistent view of her father, related to her intense ambivalence, appears to be a structuralized aspect of her characteristic way of relating, likely present with any important male, including the analyst. As such, it would better be conceptualized as a repetitive character defense (possibly serving a screen function) rather than a transference arising in the regression-fostering analytic situation as a result of the projection of dynamically active infantile object strivings across a weakened repressive barrier (Kohut, 1959, p. 472). At issue here is more than a semantic nicety. This example not only confirms the observation that many interventions described by self psychologists are clarifications of preconscious attitudes, repetitive patterns, memories, character defenses, and historical data rather than interpretations of warded off elements of still active infantile fantasy, but it also points to the danger that the self psychological approach may focus on the conscious, the manifest, the character defense at the expense of the unconscious, the latent, and the dynamically active infantile object strivings. It is, of course, necessary that current feelings, character defenses, and the like, be dealt with empathically and clarified in order to heighten self-awareness, to single out those ego-syntonic character defenses that have become resistances to the orderly analytic regression, and thus to mobilize new derivatives, especially in the form of transference.

To sharpen this distinction, I will approach the same material in a somewhat different way, in order to carry the analysis into dimensions not considered in the original report. In so doing I will draw conclusions from evidence in the report, but in the absence of more material and confirmatory responses this must of necessity remain somewhat speculative. For our purposes, however, my constructions need not be demonstrably valid to show what might be overlooked or underemphasized in the case report as presented.

The patient, while complaining of an inability to have deeply felt emotional responses, in paradoxically described as having an intensely ambivalent relationship with her father. At one pole of this ambivalent relationship she had always seen her father as unable to tolerate feelings and therefore unable to understand and help her mourn her mother's death. She apparently felt in general that no one had understood and appreciated her feelings, and in the analysis included the analyst in her conviction that a lack of understanding and even ridicule of her pain and loss was inevitable. Without minimizing the validity of her feeling, such a powerful conviction might arouse a suspicion of other sources of this persistent and insistent attitude. Was this solely a straight-line developmental effect of the father's failure to appreciate her pain and loss, or were other feelings and wishes for the father abolished by the common device of a reaction formation supported by exclusive focus on his failure to understand and help her mourn? I am suggesting that the latent pole of her intense ambivalence derives from her love for her father, possibly heightened by the loss of the mother, but likely overwhelmed by the guilt at the fantasied fulfillment of such wishes. In this construction her insistence on the painful conviction of not being understood or comforted would be at once her penance and her guarantee against the reexperiencing of dangerous sexual feelings for the father, and in the transference, for the analyst. A possible clue to the too absolute nature of her conviction is the revelation, after the analyst's clarifications and her abreactive crying, that someone (the aunt) had indeed understood and comforted her affectionately. This raises the distinct possibility that the father, too, might have offered more love and comfort than the patient could bear to remember. Thus her image of the cold, unfeeling father and the associated conviction that she could not be understood would have the structure of a screen memory. The "gaping hole" in her psyche, the inability to love or feel deeply would be her conscious metaphor to express the loss through repression of her forbidden love for her father, as well as the loss of her mother.

Conceptualized in this speculative way for purposes of contrast, it could be said that while the analyst demonstrated empathy and skill in clarifying with sensitivity the validity and meanings of the patient's current feelings as they related to her character resistances and memories, the defensive function of her conviction and the unconscious fantasies were not considered or explored. The assumption of a traumatic empathic failure on the part of the father thus acts as a reinforcement of the resistance against the emergency and analysis of the central transference and the underlying unconscious fantasies.

If, as seems evident from Kohut's last book (1984), self psychology is now to be expanded beyond application to narcissistic disorders to include neurotically structured psychopathology, it becomes important to question the effect of prolonged empathic immersion even if such supportive interactions are then to be analyzed (or clarified). The emphasis on empathic responses and confirmation of the patient's needs and grievances, even if this interaction is later clarified, can provide difficult resistances, and, in its concentrated attention on what *is* experienced, interfere with looking for what is *not* experienced because of repression and resistances. Thus the focus on empathic interactions may delay and deemphasize the analysis of resistance and object-related transference.

Efforts to extend the application of self theory and technique to psychoneurosis seem unfortunate as they becloud the potential contribution of self psychology to the range of therapeutic approaches. Clinical experience confirms the value of assessing qualitative and quantitative factors in psychopathology, personality organizations, and resources. Self theory implicitly accepts certain limits, for example, in advocating termination when "cohesion of the self" is considered to be achieved, without requiring a capacity for object love. Self psychology does itself a disservice when it neglects its limits and obscures the differences in capacity and potential between the neurotic patient who needs analysis of transference and resistance in structural conflict, and the vulnerable narcissistic patient who needs internalization of empathic and supportive interactions, with varying degrees of insight from analysis of those interactions, in order to develop a more stable personality organization.

Such considerations open anew the question, raised by Kohut and his followers, of the present and future place of self psychology in relation to psychoanalysis. Whether self psychology can remain in a complementary relationship with conflict psychology, that is, as a special area of psychoanalysis, or move beyond it as a new paradigm has yet to be resolved. Kohut's last reflections stressed incompatibilities in the basic view of man; he felt that the conceptual means were not available for integration at this time. Certainly, if adhered to strictly, the theoretical system of self psychology with its rejection of the centrality of drive, conflict, resistance, and transference would dictate a technical approach that stresses replacement and new experiences rather than analysis. Self psychology would move in the direction of the environmentalist–existentialist schools of thought. It is not enough to say that many who call themselves self psychologists actually practice differently, interpreting object-related transferences and resistances against sexual and aggressive drives. For that matter, there are surely many who consider themselves classical analysts who often provide empathic responses and experiences. The important task is to sharpen our awareness of the models we use and the way they influence our work with out patients.

For most clinicians the effect of self psychology will probably be a heightened attention to the patient's feelings and the analyst's countertransferences. Genetically, the emphasis on the significance of subtle child–parent interactions sustained over time may contribute to a balanced view of the role of experience and trauma in development. Refinements in the conceptualization of the transformations of narcissism and the descriptions of the various forms of the self experience at each stage of development can be useful clinically. They may also help counteract the common pejorative attitude toward narcissism as always primitive and pathological. In addition, for the analyst interested in the history and theory of psychoanalysis, self psychology will offer a sharp challenge to familiar and all too often unexamined assumptions, and serve as a reminder of the importance of assessing the value of new ideas from a historical perspective, as well as in light of the technical consequences of their application.

REFERENCES

Basch, M.F. (1980). *Doing Psychotherapy*. New York: Basic Books.
Bibring, E. (1954). Psychoanalysis and the dynamic psychotherapies. *Journal of the American Psychoanalytic Association*, 2:745–770.
Blum, H. (1982). Theories of the self and psychoanalytic concepts. *Journal of the American Psychoanalytic Association*, 30:959–978.
Eagle, M. (1984). *Recent Developments in Psychoanalysis*. New York: McGraw-Hill.
Freud, S. (1915). Instincts and their vicissitudes. *Standard Edition*, 14:117–140.
Glover, E. (1931). The therapeutic effect of inexact interpretation: A contribution to the theory of suggestion. *International Journal of Psycho-Analysis*, 12:397–411.

Goldberg, A. (1978). *The Psychology of the Self: A Casebook.* New York: International Universities Press.

Kernberg, O. (1967). Borderline personality organization. *Journal of the American Psychoanalytic Association*, 17:641–685.

Kohut, H. (1959). Introspection, empathy, and psychoanalysis: An examination of the relationship between mode of observation and theory. *Journal of the American Psychoanalytic Association*, 7:459–483.

Kohut, H. (1971). *The Analysis of the Self: A Systematic Approach to the Treatment of Narcissistic Personality Disorders.* New York: International Universities Press.

Kohut, H. (1977). *The Restoration of the Self.* New York: International Universities Press.

Kohut, H. (1980). Reflections on Advances in Self Psychology. In A. Goldberg, ed., *Advances in Self Psychology* (pp. 473–554). New York: International Universities Press.

Kohut, H. (1984). *How Does Analysis Cure?* A. Goldberg, ed., with P. Stepansky. Chicago & London: University of Chicago Press.

Ornstein, P., ed. (1978). *The Search for the Self: Selected Writings of Heinz Kohut: 1950–1978* (Vol. 1 & 2). New York: International Universities Press.

Ornstein, P.H., & Ornstein, A. (1980). Formulating interpretations in clinical psychoanalysis. *International Journal of Psycho-Analysis*, 61:203–211.

Rangell, L. (1982). The self and psychoanalytic concepts. *Journal of the American Psychoanalytic Association*, 30:863–891.

Singer, M. (in press). Fantasy or structural defect? The borderline dilemma as viewed from an analysis of an experience of non-humanness. *Journal of the American Psychoanalytic Association*.

Spruiell, N. (1981). The self and the ego. *Psychoanalytic Quarterly*, 50:319–344.

Turton, G. (1967). *My Lord of Canterbury.* Garden City, NY: Doubleday.

2

Can This Be Psychoanalysis?

MICHAEL FRANZ BASCH

I have entitled my chapter "Can This Be Psychoanalysis?" for it seems to me that this question is being asked by both friend and foe, by the sophisticated critic and by the uniformed blusterer—all that changes is the affective tone in which the question is put.

To make a very large subject manageable, I subdivided it into three parts: first, criticism based on fear or misunderstanding of self psychology, which can be safely disregarded; second, questions about the theoretical implications of self psychology that should be addressed seriously, and laid to rest; and third, critical questions that self psychologists should be asking themselves, the answers to which will determine whether or not psychoanalysis will finally be able to learn from history, and what the future holds for psychoanalysis as a science.

The most numerous of the criticisms directed against self psychology on the level of practice leave us at a loss to recognize any similarity between the perversions of psychoanalytic technique imputed to us and what we actually do. London (1985) has presented a collection of these misconceptions culled from the psychoanalytic literature. What is claimed, essentially, is that self psychology is a retreat from analysis to a form of psychotherapy, an evasion of resistance as opposed to its interpretation and working through. At the time of London's presentation I wrote a detailed "Critique of the Critics" (unpublished) and I will not now repeat that here, for I do not think we need to concern ourselves with this first group of critics. In the long run, such attempts to discredit Kohut and likeminded analysts will have no significant effect. The struggle within the establishment to keep analysis free of Kohut's influence has already been lost. I have no doubt that just as id psychology gave way to ego psychology, in 20 years or so the selfobject theory of motivation or "self psychology" will be synonymous with psychoanalysis.

My optimism may seem unrealistic, at best premature, at a time when most of us are only too aware of the atmosphere of hostility that often surrounds us, but it is based on the pragmatic consideration that the approach to patients that Kohut taught enables analysts to be effective with a much larger group of patients than was heretofore possible, as well as to analyze further and deeper the more classical patients for whom an oedipal conflict is central.

When, as happens with increasing frequency, graduate analysts who have had one or more so-called traditional analyses come to us for further work, they find it significantly different in terms of style and efficaciousness from what they have previously known. The experience is as convincing as anything can be that it is the application of Kohut's clinical principles that permits the analyst to live up to the standards of neutrality, abstinence, and nonintrusiveness that Freud advocated, and that the gratification of being understood, instead of hectored, enhances, rather than precludes, the in-depth exploration of one's character formation (Basch, 1983a).

Similarly, more and more young analysts come to us for supervision because what they have learned to do, namely to use on all their cases techniques at best suitable only for psychoneurotic patients, does not work. It is not unusual for these analysts to have the same dramatic experience that so many of us had when we first began to apply Kohut's insights, the experience of seeing patients who one feared were in a state of unremitting resistance, come alive and work productively in the analytic situation. Analysts whose patients have benefitted from supervision based on Kohut's insights will know from personal experience that accusations that Kohut and his students do not deal with aggression, do not know how to or choose not to analyze psychosexual conflicts, remain on the surface and do not plumb the depths, do not understand or do not work with unconscious fantasies, advocate cures based on love and on unanalytic attempts to gratify patient's wishes, and so on, reflect the anxiety of the critic and not Kohut's ideas or practice. Young analysts who have had firsthand acquaintance with the salutary power given to psychoanalysis by Kohut's discoveries will not, when they in turn attain their professional maturity and occupy teaching positions, sit idly by and permit their students and patients to be misled. When that day comes, what seems controversial now will be quite commonplace, and all the painful misunderstandings that create so many problems at the present time will be forgotten, or, if remembered, will seem pointless and quaint indeed.

Although the published criticisms of self psychology usually raise more questions about the critic's competence to engage in scientific debate than they do about the value or significance of Kohut's contributions to psychoanalysis, there are the rare but outstanding exceptions. One such is Curtis's review of *The Search for the Self* (Ornstein, 1978), published in the *Journal of the American Psychoanalytic Association* in 1983. In this scholarly essay, Curtis raises two basic questions that need to be, and I believe can be, answered satisfactorily by us. First, Curtis asks whether self psychology represents a new depth psychology "derived from but no longer part of psychoanalysis" (p. 272). Similarly, he writes that though Kohut has contributed a great deal that seems valuable or potentially valuable for psychoanalytic practice, "at present it is moot whether the already tenuous ties between psychoanalysis and the theoretical system of self psychology can be sustained in the face of the movement away from basic concepts which have served and continue to serve to identify psychoanalysis" (p. 285). I take these comments to mean that Curtis doubts that any psychology that does not subscribe to Freud's theory of instinctual motivation may call itself psychoanalysis.

The second important question that Curtis brings up in his essay is whether self psychology in its focus on empathic failure and empathic responsiveness has not sacrificed the exploration of the intrapsychic realm as it emerges in the psychoanalytic situation in the form of drive elaborated fantasies. Curtis asks whether Kohut did not substitute environmental reality in the form of interpersonal relationships for drive and conflict as both cause of and potential cure for psychological illnesses.

The answers to these questions are quite simple and straightforward; however, the documentation necessary to buttress those answers involves the entire history of psychoanalysis and can only be sketched here. I will answer Curtis's queries in the following way: first, the instinct theory of motivation, as put forward by Freud, was jettisoned some time ago, Kohut had nothing to do with that (Basch, 1984); second, Kohut's work reverses a trend toward the interpersonnal in psychoanalysis, a shift that has been masked to some extent by the retention of the terminology of drive theory in psychoanalytic literature and at psychoanalytic meetings, though the theory itself is no longer operative. I shall outline as succinctly as I can what happened to Freud's instinct theory, both on the theoretical and on the practical level.

Historical perspective corrects the not uncommon misunderstanding that psychoanalysis is somehow rigid and unchanging, clinging to Freud's ideas as if they were not only the first, but also the last to delineate the nature and practice of psychoanalysis. Our continued admiration of Freud and our devotion to his vision tends to obscure the great number of fundamental changes that have taken place under the umbrella provided by his seminal discoveries. Each generation of analysts has faced its particular clinical problems, found functional solutions, and then adjusted analytic theory to include these innovations. Periodically the clinical and attendant theoretical accommodations, whether codified or not, resulted in major reformulations of the underlying explanatory theory of psychoanalysis, what Freud called its metapsychology. So it was that Freud's change from the topographic to the structural theory legitimized, one might say, the mounting clinical evidence that "unconscious" was not a synonym for "disorganization," and that so-called secondary process or ego content could also be part of the dynamic system unconscious.

The next major evolutionary step to be taken let analysts account for the influence of chance and external reality, especially the impact of other people on development, in their clinical work. Through Freud began the movement in this direction in *The Ego and the Id* (1923) and in similarly oriented shorter papers, it came to fruition in the work of both Melanie Klein and Heinz Hartman. Melanie Klein formulated a theory that postulated instincts that were object directed from birth, rather than being blind forces. Though she was a staunch adherent of instinctual determinism, she inadvertently paved the way for what became an interpersonal view of the infant's relationship to the good and to the bad mother (Greenberg and Mitchell, 1983). Hartmann (1939) left the concept of undirected instinctual motivation essentially intact, but altered the vocabulary of the economic aspect of psychoanalytic metapsychology so that the ego's capacity for adaptation to external reality became a new force and, in practice, one on par with the instincts.

Each of these theoreticians opened the way to a clinical appreciation of the influence of external relationships on human motivation. Freud's explanatory theory was stretched until it appeared to accommodate an interpersonal dimension in psychoanalysis without giving up a deterministic theory of instinctual motivation. Appearance, however, were deceiving; psychoanalytic theory had changed radically, but the cavalier disregard for the niceties of theory formation and the careless use of words, which seems to be endemic to psychoanalysis, hid what had happened from view. There seems always to be this temptation to simplify our vocabulary, to speak in shorthand rather than to use those lengthier modified phrases that more accurately reflect the concept that the word was initially meant to convey. Probably in the early days of analysis it was not thought necessary to speak of instinctual objects because it was assumed that all analysts would know that when an analyst used the word "object" he meant an instinctual object, an intrapsychic representation. It was not long, however, before "object" came to mean "person," exactly the opposite of what Freud had originally intended that word to mean. As Greenberg and Mitchell demonstrate so convincingly in their book *Object Relations in Psychoanalytic Theory* (1983), psychoanalysis has changed from an intrapsychic to an interpersonal perspective, one in which a Sullivanian unconscious, where unconscious only means "unknown to the patient," has replaced Freud's dynamic view of unconscious forces governing mental life.

The theoretical shift toward an interpersonal perspective that I have outlined can be traced to clinical necessity. Even in Freud's time neurotics were not the only patients who applied for help from psychoanalysis. For many of these individuals, then as now, the aspects of intrapsychic life germane for their pathology were not in the form of unconscious symbolic fantasies around sexual and aggressive conflicts. Unfortunately, however, it was only the latter that were allowed for in Freud's instinctually based theory of development. If these patients were not dismissed as unanalyzable, attempts to help them steadily eroded the intrapsychic focus of analysis. From what Freud (1919, 1937) considered to be the need in every analysis for *Nacherziehung,* the belated upbringing of the patient by the analyst, to the parameters sanctioned by Kurt Eissler (1958), the analyst became more and more a person who, through benign interest, discipline, exhortation, advice, or other manipulation, helped the patient to face the reality of existence and adapt to it. The intrapsychic focus became a more interpersonal one; and when "object" became the equivalent of "person," "object relationships" came to mean what happens between people, rather than what happens on the level of mental representation (Greenberg & Mitchell, 1983). Or, it may be more accurate to say, the representational world came to be equated with a sort of mental stage on which the brain or mind replayed what was happening in the interpersonal world. It is true that analysts tried to keep faith with Freud's original concept by ultimately "analyzing" the interpersonal parameters deemed necessary for a particular patient. In practice this means forcing whatever analyst and patient are talking about into the language of oedipal fantasy, a reversal and perversion of what Freud's original discovery enabled us to do, namely, translating inchoate, unconscious wishes into everyday language.

Psychoanalysis, then, is not the firm, viable structure portrayed by our critics. It is not simply a matter of the explanatory theory of instincts, which has served for over 80 years as a base for the ever-deepening exploration of the human unconscious, now, for unknown and probably unsavory reasons, being attacked and undermined by self psychologists. The psychoanalytic establishment is rather, a ramshackle lean-to, built by verbal sleight of hand, that hides epistemological and clinical failures that must be faced if we are to be true to Freud's vision. In the face of all the evidence from clinicians and theorists within psychoanalysis, as well as that accumulated by developmental psychology and biology, demonstrating beyond reasonable doubt that the instinct theory, as Freud formulated it, and as other analysts have tried to amend it, is fatally flawed (Basch, 1984), we should be asking the psychoanalytic establishment why it continues to be taught in our institutes as the bedrock of psychoanalysis. Why does it continue to flourish in spite of the fact that, as I have already mentioned, adherence to that theory is essentially nominal, and no one now practices, if anyone ever did, what the theory actually mandates?[1]

We should ask those who insist on the validity and necessity of the instinct theory for psychoanalysis and who refuse to accept evidence to the contrary what evidence they need to persuade them that the instinct theory of motivation for human behavior cannot serve as an explanation for the clinical findings of psychoanalysis. If there is no answer to that question, if for our adversaries the instinct theory is a given, not subject to disproof, then, of course, we are dealing with a quasi-religious belief, not with a scientific hypothesis, and such a position speaks for itself.

If we do not accept that Freud's instinct theory is bedrock, what is basic for psychoanalytic theory and practice? Fundamental for Freud's contribution to science is, first, the idea that thought need not be con-

---

1. A partial explanation for this phenomenon may lie in the inexcusable lack of basic epistemologic sophistication among psychoanalytic candidates and teachers alike. Usually what one hears in defense of the instinct theory is the sort of question-begging rationalization advanced by Rangell (cited by Greenberg & Mitchell, 1983, p. 387): Rangell, in attempting to refute Fromm-Reichmann's contention that oedipal conflicts are rare, "claims that the 'deepest' data are discovered only by the use of a specific technique, and that the validity of the technique is proved by its ability to uncover these particular data! Moreover, both the utility of the technique and the 'depth' of the data are derivatives of a particular theoretical perspective!" Any argument in opposition can be dismissed, as Greenberg and Mitchell go on to say, "because the argument itself *proves* that the theorist has used an inadequate technical procedure." They conclude that Rangell's position is "tautological, unassailable, and theory bound." How can one have a discussion about theory when the basic rules for the formation and validation of scientific theories are not followed and probably not known by those concerned?

scious to be organized and effective, and, second, the concept that the manifest patterns of human behavior, verbal and otherwise, can be used to discover their nonconscious antecedents. In other words, it was not the instinct theory but Freud's discovery and conceptualization of the unconscious and of the transference that were and are fundamental for psychoanalysis. Kohut, through his formulation and systematization of the concept of the selfobject transference, permits us to take into account the external influences on character development while maintaining an intrapsychic perspective. His work has, therefore, enabled us to deal with nonneurotic patients as Freud taught us to deal with psychoneurotics, focusing on transference and resistance, and eliminating the need for nonanalytic maneuvers like *Nacherziehung,* introducing parameters, and so forth.

Prior to Kohut's work much of what patients had to tell us was lost because we were prepared only for the transference of secondarily repressed symbolic fantasy material. Kohut (1977, 1984) showed us that preverbal and/or nonverbal frustrations, overstimulations, or distortions of phase-appropriate needs are as open to Freud's method of investigation as are the developmentally more advanced unconscious wishes that give rise to the neuroses. Self psychology does not neglect unconscious aggressive and sexual fantasies when these are mobilized in the transference. The rejection of the instinct theory as an explanation does not imply a rejection of Freud's discovery of the vicissitudes and the importance of psychosexual development, of the oedipal phase, or the oedipal conflict, for none of these clinical phenomena require us to subscribe to an explanation based on drives as Freud envisioned their nature and operation. However, much of what is important developmentally occurs before evocative recall, essential for the formation of fantasy, is present. Piaget calls this the sensorimotor period (Basch, 1977). The permanently (because nonsymbolic) unconscious experiences of the first 18 months of life that form the basis of character can manifest themselves only in such forms as the nuances of affective responsiveness or lack of responsiveness, behavioral predispositions, or cognitive style. It is precisely such closed-off aspects of the dynamic unconscious that Kohut's selfobject concept both explains and opens to psychoanalytic intervention.

Furthermore, even when symbolic capacity makes fantasy possible, secondary repression is not the exclusive defense. Disavowal—a misunderstood and neglected major defense discovered and delineated by Freud late in his life (Basch, 1983b)—operates, as also does primal repression (Basch, 1977), by preventing fantasy formation; and these attempted protective measures that later can generate symptoms must be dealt with differently from the effects of the failure of secondary repression seen in the psychoneuroses. It is Kohut's emphasis on avoiding premature closure, that is, not automatically translating whatever the patient is experiencing into the language of sexual and aggressive symbolism, and, instead, maintaining an empathic stance, a readiness to experience what it is the patient is experiencing in the patient's terms before deciding what the meaning of that patient's associations or behavior might be, that potentially puts self psychologists in the position of returning to the endopsychic as opposed to the interpersonal realm.

Kohut achieved more than he realized. Given the current understanding of how the brain works we can say with Lashley (1958) that fundamentally all so-called mental processes are unconscious. Symbolic representation in words and images is only one way of replaying or making conscious some aspect of the end result of the brain's working over of stimuli (Basch, 1975). Disposition to action as indicated by the muscular and vascular components of affective communication, bodily attitudes, cognitive styles, what is heard and what is not heard, and the myriad other ways the patient has of responding or not responding, is equally indicative of the patient's characteristic attitudes and contains links to the developmental vicissitudes that gave rise to it. The mirror, idealizing, and alter ego selfobject transferences delineated by Kohut allow us to perceive the effects of a variety of defenses at various levels of development and prepare us to respond empathically to them. Curtis asks whether Kohut's work on the level of theory and apart from its practical contribution, is psychoanalysis. My answer, based on the study of the history of the field, is an unequivocal "yes." Not only is self psychology psychoanalysis, but it offers the possibility of bringing psychoanalysis to where it should have been, or could have been, had the imposition of the instinct theory not prevented Freud and other analytic pioneers from following the lead of the transference.

Self psychology has nothing to fear from its critics or from the present opposition to our work within the establishment. We should not ignore criticism, but on the other hand, it would be a mistake to expend too much effort refuting objections to self psychology that we have already dealt with in our publications or in public forums. We would do better to pay more attention to questions and problems that come up within our own ranks as we think about and apply Kohut's contributions. There are many such issues. Here I shall consider only a particularly important one of them, namely, the implications of the term "selfobject" for psychoanalytic theory. Others are taken up elsewhere (Basch, in press).

As I have said before, Kohut's work restores the intrapsychic perspective to psychoanalysis. Self psychology not only reestablishes the centrality of the unconscious, but expands the range of unconscious processes available to psychoanalytic investigation beyond the symbolically expressed fantasies prototypically associated with the oedipal phase of psychosexual development.

Freud created order where before there had been only confusion. He opened for scientific investigation and explanation an aspect of our existence that had previously been dealt with by mysticism and unproductive speculation when he discovered, that is, uncovered and isolated, the "unconscious" and "transference" processes and perfected the psychoanalytic method for their exploration. "Unconscious" and "transference" are bridging terms that refer both to what is observed and to the underlying processes that explain what is being observed. Specifically, they draw for an explanation on the information processing capacity of all living cells that seems to have been raised to its highest level of complexity in the human brain. On the level of neurophysiology and cybernetics, terms like "unconscious" and "transference" can be understood as referring to patterns of goal-oriented positive or deviation-enhancing, and negative or deviation-correcting feedback systems that form the programs governing adaptation. The psychoanalytic method enables us to study, in derivative form, patterns of expectation, that is, the hierarchy of feedback cycles that guide patients in their behavior, and why and how, insofar as patients have difficulties, these have become closed and circular rather than remaining open to potential alteration, modification, and growth.

In Freud's day, of course, neither neurophysiology nor cybernetics theory had been sufficiently developed, and he was forced to explain his observations in terms of a mechanistic instinct hypothesis that was based on the transformation of energy, not information. Kohut's concept of the selfobject, replacing the term "instinctual object," is the appropriate bridging term to complement Freud's "transference" and "unconscious." The concept "selfobject," on the clinical or practical level, lets us deal at all levels with the pathological outcome of faulty tension regulation, whether this manifests itself in the form of a developmental arrest, functional deficit, or dispositional conflict. Empathic immersion in the patient's experience, however that experience is expressed, permits us to attend to the vicissitudes undergone during various phases of development by both the affiliative tendencies, called "psychosexual" by Freud, and those toward mastery and competence, generally but incorrectly referred to in psychoanalysis as "aggression" (Stechler, 1985). The task Freud left unfinished is to link our clinical findings with the discoveries of developmental psychology as well as with pertinent neurophysiological information about what makes development possible, so as to formulate a viable metapsychology. The requisite knowledge to accomplish this task is now at hand, but there is some question as to whether we will be in a position to use this material appropriately. We must learn from rather than repeat our history. Already the ambiguous term "selfobject relationship," threatens to undermine Kohut's efforts to expand the intrapsychic realm of psychoanalysis and to transform it once again into an interpersonal form of therapy. We must guard against the kind of lexical distortion that has plagued our field. Unlike the physical scientists we cannot point to some material reality to prove our position. Words are all we have; we must respect them and guard their meaning zealously. "Selfobject" should refer to the endopsychic world, to the world of the unconscious glimpsed only indirectly through empathy and introspection, to psychic as opposed to either the environmental reality of the senses, or the subjective reality that constitutes our awareness. Just as "object" originally referred to the instinctual object, the instincts considered to be the fundamental motivation for all behavior, so the term "selfobject" should embody Kohut's concept that the self, a supraordinate, nonconscious organizing principle that governs character development, and draws on a multitude of experiences to establish and maintain its effective functioning. These experiences, by virtue of the use to which they are put, are called selfobjects. They should be distinguished from relationships, which are between people. To talk about relationships is to place ourselves in the interpersonal universe of discourse, which is not the concern of psychoanalysis per se. The realm of selfobject experiences refers to intrapsychic transactions between the self organization and the object as it is perceived in the light of past experience. We should, therefore, speak of self–selfobject experiences, not of selfobject relations or relationships, to indicate that we are dealing with endopsychic functions (see also, Goldberg, 1981).

"Transference" was originally used by Freud to describe both a process of exchange between the unconscious and the preconscious across the repression barrier, and the consequences of that process for dreaming and for the analytic relationship. In light of current communication and control theory (Basch, 1976), as well as what we now know about normal development (Basch, 1977; Lichtenberg, 1983; Stern, 1985) transference should be understood as a much broader process encompassing the repetition of established information processing patterns geared to maintaining the function of the self system and/or expanding its influence. The transferences in which we are particularly interested are those that are mobilized in order to sustain the cohesion, vitality, or organizing capacity of the self system—Kohut called these selfobject transferences. Atwood and Stolorow (1984), Schwaber (1979), and others have emphasized the intersubjective nature of the patient–analyst relationship, opposing it to the notion of a supposedly objective relationship of analyst to patient in which the former functions as an outside observer who interprets what the patient says. We now believe, as do most empirical scientists, that there is no observation without participation. What analysts do or do not do is perhaps the strongest influence on the patient's associations; the empathically attuned analyst will be alert to this and in appropriate fashion demonstrate to the patient how the analyst's behavior and attitude is affecting the analysis. Unfortunately, the intersubjective aspect of the clinical situation is often confused, not only by our critics but also by self psychologists, with an interpersonal explanation for what happens in the psychoanalytic situation. Intersubjectivity and transference are not mutually exclusive. On the contrary, the patterns of expectation transferred onto the analytic situation form the lens through which the patient perceives the analyst's activity or inactivity. Our empathic resonance with and acceptance of the patient's reactions to us should not alter our view of the transaction as being either a manifestation of the transference or the defense against the transference, both of which need to be understood in terms of the patient's past development (Basch, 1983c).

What happens to so-called object relationships in this schema? Since no endopsychic experience is possible without the participation of the supraordinate self organization, is there ever a reaction to an object as such? Stolorow (1984) suggests, and I agree, that we should speak of a self–selfobject experience when selfobject needs are in the foreground because the cohesion, vitality, and organization of the self system is in question. When the self is functioning adequately and is not endangered, then it can engage in self-object experiences, that is, experience others as independent centers of initiative in terms of love, anger, interest, or some other affect. Only the correct use of terminology, using words that actually describe the concept that is being enunciated, will save us from the sort of deterioration that set in once Freud's vocabulary was treated carelessly.

The issue that confronts us is not whether self psychology will survive, it will not only survive, it will prevail. Self psychology offers new hope not only to our patients but to psychoanalysis as a science. Whether the latter will be fulfilled is, for me, the most important question. The future of psychoanalysis may well depend on how well we prepare coming generations of analysts to understand both the history that led to Kohut's achievement and the implications of his work for bridging the gap that now exists between our field and the other sciences.

REFERENCES

Atwood, G., & Stolorow, R. (1984). *Structures of Subjectivity: Explorations in Psychoanalytic Phenomenology.* Hillsdale, NJ: Analytic Press.

Basch, M.F. (1975). Toward a theory that encompasses depression: A revision of existing causal hypotheses in psychoanalysis. In E.J. Anthony & T. Benedek, eds., *Depression and Human Existence* (pp. 485–534). Boston: Little, Brown.

Basch, M.F. (1976). Psychoanalysis and communication science. *The Annual of Psychoanalysis,* 4:385–421.

Basch, M.F. (1977). Developmental psychology and explanatory theory in psychoanalysis. *The Annual of Psychoanalysis,* 5:229–263.

Basch, M.F. (1983a). Affect and the analyst. *Psychoanalytic Inquiry,* 3:691–703.

Basch, M.F. (1983b).The perception of reality and the disavowal of meaning. *The Annual of Psychoanalysis,* 11:125–154.

Basch, M.F. (1983c). Empathic understanding: A review of the concept and some theoretical considerations. *Journal of the American Psychoanalytic Association,* 31:101–126.

Basch, M.F. (1984). Selfobjects and selfobject transference: Theoretical implications. In A. Goldberg & P.E. Stepansky, eds. *Kohut's Legacy: Contributions to self psychology* (pp. 21–41). Hillsdale, NJ: Analytic Press.

Basch, M.F. (in press). *How Does Analysis Cure?*: An appreciation. *Psychoanalytic Inquiry.*

Basch, M.F. (1985). Interpretation: Toward a developmental model. In A. Goldberg, ed., *Progress in Self Psychology* (Vol. 1, pp. 33–42). New York: Guilford Press.

Curits, H.C. (1983). Book review of Ornstein, P.H. ed. (1978). *The Search for the Self: Selected Writings of Heinz Kohut, 1950–1978.* New York: International Universities Press. *Journal of the American Psychoanalytic Association,* 31:272–285.

Eissler, K. R. (1958) Remarks on some variations in psycho-analytical technique. *International Journal of Psycho-Analysis,* 39:222–229.

Freud, S. (1919). Lines of advance in psycho-analytic therapy. *Standard Edition,* 17:157–168.

Freud, S. (1923). The ego and the id. *Standard Edition,* 19:3–66.

Freud, S. (1937). Analysis terminable and interminable. *Standard Edition,* 23:209–253.

Goldberg, A. (1981) Meaning and objects. In S. Tuttman, C. Kaye, & M. Zimmerman, eds., *Object and Self: A Developmental Approach* (pp. 129–148). New York: International Universities Press.

Greenberg, J.R., & Mitchell, S.A. (1983). *Object Relations in Psychoanalytic theory.* Cambridge, MA: Harvard University Press.

Hartmann, H. (1939). *Ego Psychology and the Problem of Adaptation.* New York: International University Press, 1958.

Kohut, H. (1977). *The Restoration of the Self.* New York: International Universities Press.

Kohut, H. (1984). *How Does Analysis Cure?* A Goldberg, ed., with P. Stepansky. Chicago & London: University of Chicago Press.

Lashley, K. (1958). Cerebral organization and behavior. In H.C. Solomon *et al.*, eds., *The Brain and Human Behavior.* (pp. 1–18). Baltimore: Williams & Wilkins.

Lichtenberg, J.D. (1983). *Psychoanalysis and Infant Research.* New York: The Analytic Press.

London, N. (1985). An appraisal of self psychology. *International Journal of Psycho-Analysis,* 66:95–107.

Schwaber, E. (1979). On the "self" within the matrix of analytic theory: Some clinical reflections and reconsiderations. *International Journal of Psycho-Analysis,* 60:467–479.

Stechler, G. (1985). The study of infants engenders systemic thinking. *Psychoanalytic Inquiry,* 5:531–541.

Stern, D.W. (1985). The *Interpersonel World of the Infant.* New York: Basic Books.

Stolorow, R.D. (1984). Varieties of selfobject experience. In P. Stepansky & A. Goldberg, eds., *Kohut's Legacy* (pp. 43–50). Hillsdale, NJ: Analytic Press.

3

Discussion

The Relationship between the Psychoanalytic Concepts of Conflict and Deficit

ELLIOTT MARKSON AND PETER G. THOMSON

INTRODUCTION

We are pleased to have this opportunity to respond to some of the issues raised by Basch and Curtis. As classically trained analysts we are aware of changes that have occurred in our thinking and our method, as we have familiarized ourselves with self psychology. It was not possible to appreciate the richness and complexity of self psychology without gradually reorienting ourselves toward a fuller participation within the inner experiences of our patients. Criticism of self psychology by those who have not shared in this altered orientation tends sometimes to be simplistic in nature. This is illustrated by Curtis's view of self psychologists as providing empathy to their patients in lieu of analysis.

Self psychological expositions however, can also be simplistic, notably when they neglect the effect of drives and unconscious imagery on development. While Basch appreciates the historical foundations of self psychology, he dismisses much of it and Curtis, who makes some very cogent criticisms of self psychology, nevertheless underestimates its complexity and potential.

In this chapter we examine some of the controversial issues provoked by recent events in the history of psychoanalysis. We will highlight a few of them, and illustrate our points with a case presentation.

We agree with Ornstein (1983) that one should not attempt to integrate the two psychoanalytic models at this time; to do so could result in a hybrid monster. We are inclined instead, like Curtis, to assess new ideas from a historical perspective. We find it more useful to view self psychology as one major step in the evolution of psychoanalytic thought.

Self psychology has its roots in what preceded it; it was not created *de novo*. It contains both implicitly and explicitly, a wide range of concepts and usages derived from traditional psychoanalysis. We need to examine the relationship between past and present more closely, as Bacal (1984) does in his perspective on object relations theory. We will adopt a similar position in dealing with some of the controversial issues that have arisen between these two theories.

Drives and Self Psychology

It is more profitable to clarify the relationship between the classical and the self psychological notions on drives, than to assert the primacy of one over the other. To view sexuality and aggression as merely "disintegration products" (Kohut, 1977) is unfortunate.

We agree with Basch that drive theory has been found wanting, but unlike him we would not discard the theory altogether. Sexuality, aggression, and their associated imagery, are powerful forces in human development. (We are speaking here of aggression in its broadest sense.) Self psychology has cast an important new perspective on drive theory, but in doing so it often underemphasizes the full significance of instinctual life.

The basic drive postulated by self psychology is one of a quite different order. It is a drive toward the evolution of the self and its full potential. This is similar to the concept of an innate drive toward the completion and mastery of development. We would suggest that the repetition compulsion is a manifestation of this developmental drive. Atwood and Stolorow (1984) have postulated the existence of a basic drive that is related to the drive toward the evolution of the self. This is a drive to maintain the organization of experience, and to retain an openness to new experience as well.

Self psychology conceives of aggression and sexuality as disintegration products in this way: when the process of psychic evolution and organization is thwarted, the classical drives are mobilized in order to salvage the integrity of the self. The drives are fire fighters. This view neglects the fundamental importance of sexuality and aggression in promoting the developmental process and in ensuring its continuity. Aggression and eroticism are basic forces in self evolution. Kohut (1983) does seem to acknowledge this briefly when he speaks of how "a strong, harmonious, cohesive self . . . is pushed toward others by sexual and aggressive drives" (p. 397).

Self psychology does not acknowledge sexuality as a significant force in human affairs, and as a fundamental source of pleasure. Not all erotic yearnings and fantasies are directed toward healing a damaged or threatened self organization. Self psychological theory would not be violated if sexuality was accorded its due.

The oedipal phase (which will be discussed in our case presentation), is probably not the paramount psychic organizer it was once considered to be. It is more likely, as self psychology asserts, that the Oedipus complex is an oedipal phase gone wrong, due to failure in selfobject responsiveness. Even so, self psychology case reports will likely reveal as Curtis has shown, that oedipal phase-appropriate eroticism and hostility are frequently unacknowledged.

Conflict and Deficit

The relationship between conflict and deficit is another controversial issue deserving consideration. This subject has been ably discussed by Ornstein (1983), and the lines have been drawn. On the one side are those who believe that structural conflict is the basis of most psychopathology. In this theory, unconscious drive-motivated fantasy, which has been shaped by perceptual distortions, is the pathogenic agent. On the other side are those who believe that structural deficits, resulting from environmental failure, constitute the basis of developmental disorders. Others, like Curtis, believe that both are operative in *some* cases.

We suggest that in *all* cases there is an intimate relationship between conflict, and deficits resulting from environmental failure. Development takes place within an intersubjective field (Stolorow, Brandchaft, & Atwood, 1983; Thomson, 1984). The intersubjective field comprises both the conscious and unconscious manifestations of the selfobject unit, as the members experience, react to, and influence one another. Both conflict and deficit are determined by operations within the intersubjective unit.

Developmental deficits occur when basic selfobject needs for safety, affirmation, and tension regulation are not adequately met. Most self psychologists would agree with Curtis that a deficit is not merely "Something missing." Deficits become hidden by defective structures consisting of defensive and compensatory mechanisms. These are the means employed by the child to contend with the continuing need state and the related affects, which are left in the wake of environmental failure. Traditional theory tends to regard deficits as inhibitions of ego functions, resulting from structural conflict. This certainly does occur, but we must still ask ourselves why the drives became conflicted, and why conflict resolution has not succeeded.

The close relationship between conflict and deficit is usually related to the outcome of cumulative traumata within the intersubjective field. A traumatic disruption within the self–selfobject unit, exposes the child to the continuing pressure of the developmental drive. This abiding need for selfobject nurturance exposes the child to the threat of retraumatization. This is the self psychological conflict par excellence.

This is not the only way in which conflict and deficit are related. When narcissistic trauma occurs, the injured but still vigorous self will make active attempts to effect a meliorative change in the selfobject. (This is a reflection of the tendency to mastery and competence referred to by Basch.) When these efforts are unsuccessful, aggression, rage, and the associated imagery are mobilized in order to restore a functional selfobject relationship. One outcome of this struggle is so-called structural conflict related to hate, aggression, and guilt. Rage may thus be regarded as an intermediary event between selfobject failure and structural conflict. Another outcome of this heightened drive state may be a threat to the integrity of the self structure. The "pathogenic fantasies" that are mobilized are based on a nucleus of historical reality, and are not simply perceptual distortions.

Under similar conditions of cumulative selfobject failure, erotic tendencies and the associated fantasies, may also be mobilized, and like the assertive tendencies can also result in structural conflict. In addition, ordinary phase-appropriate manifestations of aggression and sexuality can be traumatized by selfobject failure. The normal evolution of these drives and their associated affects of love and hate, depends upon proper selfobject responsiveness. When this fails, structural conflict ensues.

These are some of the ways in which conflict and deficit are related. There is no conflict of clinical dimension without underlying deficit. We believe as does Kohut (1983) that "selfobject failures . . . [are] . . . the ultimate cause of psychopathology" pp. 396–397). This is true whether we are speaking of structural conflict or of conflict involving the integrity of the self. Ultimately all conflict concerns self-esteem regulation, and the maintenance of self organization. Our case for example, demonstrates the presence of underlying deficit in a patient with typical hysterical conflicts.

The predisposition to illness will depend upon the capacity for conflict resolution, and the capacity for self maintenance. The fate of these capacities lies within the history of the intersubjective unit.

Our understanding of self psychology has led us to believe that there is no clear-cut distinction between neurotic and nonneurotic disorders. Conflict, defective structure, and underlying deficit are present in *all* cases. Curtis would agree that this is true in *some* cases only.

Ultimately, the distinction between different types of disorder may depend upon three basic criteria: (1) the degree to which self-esteem regulation is disturbed, (2) the degree to which self cohesion is impaired, and (3) the degree to which effective defensive and compensatory structures are present.

In clinical practice, careful attention must be paid to the narcissistic integrity of the patient in all cases, whether the predominant pathology involves structural conflict or narcissistic disturbance. The empathic position should inform all interventions. All interpretations should include some consideration of the selfobject dimension. A stable, good selfobject relationship within the analytic situation, facilitates access to the deeper reaches of the psyche. Curtis, however, appears to believe that the opposite is true.

Empathy

Empathy remains a very controversial issue. Curtis is concerned that a theory of deficit, with its emphasis on empathic failure, will lead to inspirational therapy. He is also concerned about empathists who collude with patient's resistances, and avoid the analysis of unconscious events, particularly in the sexual sphere. He sees self psychologists as "accepting" their patient's transferences instead of analyzing them.

Self psychology literature does provide some grounds for these fears, but we do not agree that an empathic posture inevitably leads to the errors he mentions. In fact, we believe the opposite to be the case. The mobilization of transference within an empathic ambience facilitates rather than hinders, the analysis of deeper strata. This ambience helps us to remobilize microevents within the intersubjective field, which led to disruptions in development. The empathic approach facilitates access to unconscious events, and to the sequelae associated with nuclear traumatic states.

The empathic position of the analyst is not a simple one, however. While it is primarily a way of understanding, it also provides the patient with a gratifying sense of having been understood. This form of gratification is essential if our work is to succeed. Optimal development is not enhanced by a consistent diet of frustration. As Basch points out, "the gratification of being understood . . . enhances, rather than precludes, the in-depth exploration of one's character formation" (p. 19).

Our "optimal responsiveness" (Bacal, 1983) does gratify the patient, and it is time for the apotheosis of frustration by analysts, to come to an end. We need to know much more about the position of gratification in the developmental and in the therapeutic processes. We need to know more about the healing power of empathy itself, even if this runs counter to the powerful emphasis on cognition in traditional psychoanalytic theory of the curative process. The "introduction of empathic and supportive interventions" that Curtis would allow for some patients, is probably necessary for all patients. Failure to do so can lead to a host of serious iatrogenic complications.

The primary aim of the empathic position is to promote understanding, so that arrested development may be resumed. Empathy provides a way to the depths; but it also provides a helping hand to the patient, along the way.

CASE REPORT

The case we have chosen is one of hysterical neurosis with an unresolved oedipal situation. This is the type of case Eissler (1953) regarded as the baseline for psychoanalytic therapy, the kind of case that many self psychologists would still consider to be suitable for the classical method.

Betty was a 27-year-old woman who sought analysis because she found herself compulsively falling in love with older men. Her positive sense of herself seemed to depend on being found attractive to these men with whom she became emotionally and sexually involved.

Betty spoke of her mother as a strong and dominant woman who was as proficient within the household as she was in community affairs. The patient had strongly identified with these qualities, but analysis revealed that this was a precocious development covering a fault or deficit. Memories emerged from the period following her sister's birth when the distraction of her mother's attention brought the experience of acute feelings of isolation, helplessness, and rage. She overcame these feelings by repression and reaction formation, transforming herself into Mother's good helper. This obsessional character defense won her much approval from mother. She described her mother's dominating character as "filling my childhood world." Thus the patient's need to protest and to assert her own "true self" received a severe setback at the age of 2, when her sister was born. There was a further significant factor emanating from the mother that, because of its cumulatively traumatic effect, produced a particular defect in her self-support structure. This factor, particularly pertinent to this presentation, was her mother's strongly prudish, antisexual attitude throughout the patient's childhood and adolescence.

The patient's father, had been emotionally remote from the children. She had no memory of receiving affection from him and felt his absence keenly.

During her teenage years her father began to drink excessively. One unfortunate event in her limited association with him stood out. When she was 9 or 10 he once came to her bed, and caressed her genitals. This was a traumatically overstimulating experience for her. It had its aftermath in the development of her acting-out symptom (which had a repetition compulsion quality). It also probably had a counterphobic element, in making her fearful of her sexual transference feelings in the analysis. The trauma in fact emerged at one point in analysis manifesting itself in somatic symptoms (shortness of breath, tachycardia) and in feelings of panic.

All the deficits that we mention emerged at various stages of the analysis, but we will focus on the contribution of these deficits to the quality of the erotic transference that developed. In classical terminology it could be said that the patient was, at this period, in the middle of a transference neurosis. One day after a good deal of anxiety and struggle with resistance she became conscious of her wish to "turn on" the analyst sexually. The analyst, aware of her guilt feelings, asked, "you feel its wrong to want to turn me on?" She replied, "it's just like wanting to turn on my father. Mother saw sex as wrong but sex with Father would be infinitely worse. And I see that you have become Father to me." She was also aware of how difficult it was to oppose her mother. (One reason for her reluctance to oppose her mother arose from her sense that behind her mother's dominating exterior there lay a state of vulnerability).

In the period immediately after this interchange, it became clear how much she needed to recognize that her wishes toward the analyst were innocent, as indeed they were, the innocent wishes of an oedipal girl. There can be no doubt here of a drive need, that is, a desire to experience sexual pleasure and to be found pleasurable. Even so, the selfobject components were probably more significant, namely, (1) the need for affirmation of her feminine identity (in her own words, "I want to feel pretty") and (2) the acceptance of her sexual strivings so that they need no longer feel dangerous and could be calmed and regulated, in a phase-appropriate way. We wish to emphasize that at earlier stages of the analysis she had no difficulty in expressing her affectionate feelings toward the analyst at a time when her erotic life was still inaccessible to the transference. Some case presentations by self psychologists give the impression that they regard only affectionate feelings as normally phase-appropriate for the young child. Following the period of analysis just described the patient became more able to integrate sexual and affectionate feelings.

We will now show in more microscopic fashion how the parental failures led to deficits, and so on to the unresolved oedipal conflict manifested in this patient's presenting symptom. We will also demonstrate how these failures contributed to the erotic transference. The particular deficit that originated at the time of her sister's birth had impaired her capacity to protest and to demand that her needs be heeded. One might say that she was unable to "turn on" her mother to her plight. Then at the oedipal stage this inability to protest robbed her of her capacity to confront her mother as rival. Such a capacity to oppose is part of the developmental line of aggression. The ability to confront the selfobject as antagonist all through development mobilizes the healthy aggression that promotes the cohesive strength of the self. As Wolf (1980) says, contradictory needs for an ally who is also an antagonist accounts for the inevitable ambivalence of the oedipal period. With regard to the erotic transference in this case, behind the manifest wish to turn on the analyst as father, one may assume the covert wish to turn him on as the mother from whom she longed for recognition as beloved rival.

Shortly after the "turning on" period, the patient arrived one day dressed in an old pair of jeans and sweater. She became aware in this session that she needed also to be free *not* to turn on the analyst. Here she asserted her claim on the selfobject to respond to her total self and not have to make him respond by eroticism alone. She wished not to have to feel beholden to the selfobject's own needs as had happened with the older men and with her father when he approached her sexually.

The various deficits arising from the selfobject failures of the mother and from the father respectively all contributed to the presenting oedipal symptom. The deficit in sexual expression arose from her father's absence as a heterosexual object in childhood and from her mother's prohibiting attitudes. The shock trauma of her father's sexual approach was also inhibiting to her sexual development. She sought through her sexual behavior to make good the deficits in sexual pleasure and freedom. She sought also to oppose, and to assert herself in such a way as might overcome her deficit in self-esteem and cohesive feminine self. This developmental drive was abortive, however, because the men she sought out had needs of their own that contradicted hers. Only in a therapeutic environment could her deficits be analyzed and understood.

We wish to reemphasize our opinion that the gratification of sexuality is a paramount source of pleasure in the individual quite apart from its other meanings. In this patient's sexual affairs she claimed this pleasure and defied her mother.

CONCLUSION

In conclusion we would like to list our views on the controversial questions that have been illustrated in the case. First, we believe that in all psychopathology, including psychoneurosis, structural conflicts have their origin in deficits in the supporting structures of the self. These deficits have arisen from the cumulative trauma of failures within the child–parent selfobject milieu. We differ from Curtis in his view that self psychology theory and technique ought not to be applied to the neuroses.

Second, we believe that by using the empathic–introspective technique the deficit will emerge within the self–selfobject unit of the analytic transference. The nature of the cumulative trauma then becomes revealed in those microinteractions that are repeated in the psychoanalytic situation.

Third, all transference, including the oedipal sexual transference of the neuroses, will have a selfobject dimension. Furthermore, this selfobject component is regularly its most significant part.

Fourth (and here we side with the critics of self psychology), we believe self psychology gives the impression, deliberately or not, that the erotic drive is never anything but a disintegration product or a means to restore the self. This seems a gross depreciation of the universality of sexuality in childhood and in mental life in general. Readers of self psychology case material often complain that it lacks the richness in psychosexual and psychoaggressive imagery seen in traditional case material. It seems that the concentration of self psychology on the environment needs some expansion to include in its theory a place for fantasy life. This should come from a greater emphasis on the kinds of fantasy that accompany selfobject needs and drive needs.

We see both sexual and aggressive drives as having an important function in promoting development and in urging their particular claims on the object. The patient's presenting symptom represented such a developmental drive to overcome internal states of deficit. This can also be seen as the self making active assertive claims to effect meliorative change in the object.

Fifth, we understand the process of recovery differently from Curtis. The already mentioned reconstruction of deficit in transference can only be achieved after painstaking and careful analytic work. Then and only then are analyst and analysand able to acknowledge, and together regulate the various self needs so that development can proceed in a more adaptive way within the empathic ambience. The effect of analysis has been to reopen the drive to development within the intersubjective unit of the psychoanalytic dialogue so that it may resume its efforts in a favorable milieu.

REFERENCES

Atwood, G., & Stolorow, R. (1984). *Structures of Subjectivity: Explorations in Psychoanalytic Phenomenology*. Hillsdale, NJ: Analytic Press.

Bacal, H. (1983). Optimal responsiveness and the therapeutic process. In A. Goldberg, ed., *Progress in Psychoanalysis*). Hillsdale, NJ: Analytic Press.

Bacal, H. (1984, October). *British object relations theorists and self psychology: Some critical reflections*. Paper presented at the 7th Annual Self Psychology Conference, Toronto.

Eissler, K.R. (1953). The effect of the structure of the ego on psychoanalytic technique. *Journal of the American Psychoanalytic Association*, 1:104–143.

Kohut, H. (1983.) Selected problems in self psychological theory. In J. Lichtenberg & S. Kaplan, eds., *Reflections on Self Psychology* (pp. 387–410). Hillsdale, NJ: Analytic Press.

Kohut, H. (1977). *The Restoration of the Self*. New York: International Universities Press.

Ornstein, P. (1983). Discussion of papers by A. Goldberg, R. Stolorow, and R. Wallerstein. In J. Lichtenberg & S. Kaplan, eds, *Reflections on Self Psychology*, (pp. 339–384). Hillsdale, NJ: Analytic Press.

Stolorow, R. D., Brandchaft, B., Atwood, G. (1983). Intersubjectivity in psychoanalytic treatment. With special consideration to archaic states. *Bulletin of the Menninger Clinic*, 47:117–128.

Thomson, P.G. (1984, February). *Analysis as an intersubjective field of communication*. Paper presented to the Toronto Psychoanalytic Society.

Wolf, E.S. (1980). On the developmental line of selfobject relations. In A. Goldberg, ed., *Advances in Self Psychology* (pp. 117–130). New York: International Universities Press.

4

Discussion

Beyond Dogma in Psychoanalysis

ROBERT D. STOLOROW

Faced with the task of discussing these two wide-ranging and thought-provoking chapters by Homer C. Curtis and Michael F. Basch, I have chosen to devote myself to a forceful and detailed rejoinder to Dr. Curtis's chapter, interspersed with occasional brief remarks that only allude to the many areas of agreement between my views and those of Dr. Basch.

Despite his advocacy of balance and comprehensiveness in psychoanalytic theory, many, if not most, of Curtis's objections to self psychology seem rooted in his uncritical adherence to the doctrine of instinctual drive. By repeatedly writing of "the drives" as if this phrase referred to demonstrated empirical facts whose existential reality no card-carrying Freudian psychoanalyst would ever call into question, he rests his case against self psychology on a singularly shaky scientific foundation. Paradoxically, it was never Kohut's intent to do away with drives and, indeed, traces of the drive concept can be found in both of his last two books (1977, 1984). However, thorough and systematic critiques of Freudian drive theory have been undertaken by numerous others (e.g., Gill, 1976; Holt, 1976; Klein, 1976; Kubie, 1975; Peterfreund, 1971; Rubinstein, 1967; Schafer, 1976) and, like Dr. Basch, I believe that the conclusions to be drawn from such studies are definitive. By listening to patients tell him about their experiences, Freud discovered—and it was a monumental discovery, still valid today—that symbolically encoded unconscious *meanings* play a central role in pathogenesis and in human psychological life generally. The theory of instinctual drive, by contrast, derived not from Freud's psychoanalytic work but from his attempt to graft his crucial clinical insights onto the Procrustean bed of 19th-century biology. It should by now be well known that the concept of mind as an energy disposal apparatus is completely at variance with current knowledge of the workings of the brain, an organ that, as Basch points out, functions principally to order and organize stimulation and process information (see also Basch, 1984). More importantly, if one accepts the proposition that the science of psychoanalysis is defined and demarcated by its observational mode of empathy and introspection (Kohut, 1959), then instinctual drives do not even fall within the conceptual domain of psychoanalytic inquiry, since I doubt that even the most gifted among us has ever been able to achieve empathic contact with such an entity. Thus, if there is a problem in this aspect of Kohut's theorizing, it is not that drives are diminished in importance by being reduced to disintegration products, but that remnants of the drive concept appear in his conceptualizations _at all_.

Basch raises the question of why it is that some analysts continue to cling to a theory that has been shown "beyond reasonable doubt [to be] fatally flawed" (p. 23). One important reason for this is that a mechanistic framework emphasizing instinctual determinism readily lends itself to analysts' self-protective and distancing efforts in the here and now of the analytic dialogue, by obscuring the profound impact of the analyst and his activities on the patient's psychological organization and on the analytic process (Brandchaft & Stolorow, 1984a; Stolorow, Brandchaft, & Atwood, 1983; Stolorow & Lachmann, 1984/1985). Most often when analysts present formulations about drives, if there are any empirical referents for such statements they consist of affect states or affect-laden fantasies. As both Basch and I have suggested on earlier occasions (Basch, 1984; Stolorow, 1984), what psychoanalysis needs is not a theory of drives but of affect and affective development, and it is precisely here that self psychology promises to make very important contributions (Socarides & Stolorow, 1984/1985).

I also join Basch in emphasizing that, although Curtis often couples the two as if they were synonymous, the theory of instinctual drive is _not_ equivalent to the concept of unconscious motivation, a cornerstone of _all_ psychoanalytic thought. Enduring motivations, conscious or unconscious, can be conceptualized as complex cognitive–affective structures that crystallize organically from a person's early formative experiences, with no assumptions about drive energies supplying their fuel. Nor is the importance of unconscious motivation diminished in the self psychological framework, although a person's _primary_ motivational strivings are indeed pictured quite differently from this perspective than from the viewpoint of Freudian drive theory. Primary selfobject needs may be quite unconscious to the individual, because they have been repressed, disavowed, or otherwise defended against out of a "dread to repeat" past traumata (A. Ornstein, 1974). Such defenses appear in treatment in the form of resistance to immersion in the selfobject transference experience (Kohut, 1971, 1984; Socarides & Stolorow, 1984/1985). Thus we see that, contrary to Curtis's concern, self psychology's emphasis on experience-near understanding does *not* preclude inquiry into what patients cannot permit themselves to experience consciously.

In view of my sharp reaction to Curtis's chapter so far, it may come as a surprise that I find myself to a significant extent in agreement with his criticism of the treatment in his first example of self psychologically guided therapy.[1] Specifically, it does seem possible to me that the patient may have temporarily renounced her sexual interests in direct response to the therapist's interpretation that her erotic transference feelings "were not those of a sexually excited woman, but of a child wishing to unite with a powerful parent." It is interesting to note that in this instance it is Curtis who enjoins against rejecting the patient's "actual experience" in the transference (which I applaud, even though I fear that he does so because the manifest content of her experience happened to be sexual in nature), while it was the treating therapist who chose to interpret an unconscious or latent meaning, probably prematurely. However, the therapist's technical error was not so much in offering a premature or "inexact" interpretation, but in apparently failing to analyze sufficiently the impact of his interpretation on the transference. Did the patient, for example, experience the interpretation as a rejection of her sexual feelings and therefore as a repetition of *oedipal* selfobject failure (Kohut, 1977)? And did she feel compelled to renounce her sexual interests, believing that this was necessary in order to maintain the vitally needed tie to the therapist? Alternatively, was the sexualization of the transference already a product of an unrecognized rupture in the bond, a rift that the patient first tried to mend with sexual fantasy and then, when this failed, by identification?

I will now take up eight important issues raised in Curtis's chapter.

1. Curtis charges that self psychological understandings are characterized by "imbalance," "reductionism," "simplicity," and "precon-

---

1. It should be noted, however, that the case was originally presented as an illustration of psychotherapeutic, rather than psychoanalytic technique (Basch, 1980). Whether or not this is a relevant distinction is a question that is open to debate.

ceptions." But what of the imbalance, reductionism, simplicity, and preconceptions that abound in a theory that finds the bedrock of human psychological life in a biologically preordained sequence of instinctually determined conflicts? The point is that *all* psychological theories are to some degree imbalanced and reductionistic, they *all* aim at ordering and therefore simplifying the staggering complexity of clinical data, and they *all* embody theoretical preconceptions and philosophical assumptions. These are not meaningful criteria for evaluating the superiority of one theory over another. The clinically valid criteria are whether theoretical frameworks enlarge or constrict our capacity to gain empathic access to patients' inner lives and whether they therefore enhance or diminish our therapeutic effectiveness.

2. Curtis characterizes the self psychological approach as an "effort to establish ideal empathic responses" that can "collude with a regressive defense" and "minimize the patient's autonomy," and that "overvalues the mother–analyst . . . at the expense of the patient's more mature needs and capacities," making the analyst and his "empathic successes or failures" responsible for the patient's feelings and self-esteem (p. 7). Needless to say, I do not regard this as an accurate characterization. The goal of a self psychological treatment is not to establish ideal empathic responses, but to analyze the vicissitudes of the analytic dialogue, including its inevitable derailments, from the perspective of the patient's own subjective organizing principles. The aim is not to collude with a regressive defense or to minimize the patient's autonomy, but to permit aborted developmental thrusts to become revitalized, an aim that *requires* that the analyst recognize and acknowledge the appearance of more mature needs and capacities and progressive strivings as these emerge in treatment as developmental achievements (Stolorow & Lachmann, 1980). The analyst is not in actuality made responsible for the patient's feelings and self-esteem because, as Basch stresses, a phrase such as "empathic failures" (when used precisely) is understood to refer not to things that the analyst does or fails to do, but to psychic reality— that is, to developmentally predetermined subjective experiences of the patient, revived and analyzed in the transference (Brandchaft & Stolorow, 1984b).

The self psychological approach does not, contrary to Curtis's belief, minimize the genuineness of patients' separateness. Indeed, it emphasizes that attuned responsiveness to the child's, or patient's, unique affective qualities and strivings for self-demarcation constitutes a critical selfobject function that *facilitates* the development of individualized selfhood, and stresses that it is the absence of such requisite responsiveness that solders the chains of masochistic enmeshment with others (see Atwood & Stolorow, 1984, Chap. 3; Brandchaft, 1984; Socarides & Stolorow, 1984/1985).

3. I agree with Curtis's criticism of the use of the term "self," to refer to a supraordinate psychic agency, motivator, or locus of experience. In my view, the "self" as a psychoanalytic construct should refer neither to mental content nor to an agency or existential agent, but to a psychological structure—a cognitive–affective schema through which self experience acquires cohesion and continuity and by virtue of which self experience assumes its characteristic shape and enduring organization (Atwood & Stolorow, 1984, Chap. 1; Stolorow, 1983). Self psychology is concerned with developmental transformations of these structures of experience. Contrary to Curtis's understanding, deficit, from this perspective, is not "external, manifest, and behavioral." Rather, deficits are weaknesses in the organization of subjective experience rooted in specific developmental arrests—weaknesses and arrests that are sometimes concretely symbolized by fantasy images of holes or gaps in oneself (Atwood & Stolorow, 1984, Chap. 4). The clinical implication of this viewpoint is not to supply what was missing, but to permit patients to establish in the transference a facilitating context in which the arrested development can resume.

4. I believe that Curtis is correct in noting that the concept of selfobject has sometimes been applied too broadly, as when it is extended to include virtually all needs for another person's care.[2] In an earlier work, Daphne Socarides and I (1984/1985) offered a refinement of the selfobject concept in which we suggested that selfobject functions pertain most fundamentally to the integration of *affect* into the organization of self experience, and that the need for selfobject ties pertains to the need for attuned responsiveness to affect states in all phases of development. Contrary to Curtis's claim, this emphasis on affect attunement and its derailments neither neglects the child's contributions to the developmental system nor leads to a simpleminded, reductionistic environmentalism. Instead it brings into bold relief the profoundly *intersubjective* nature of human psychological development, which is

---

2. Certain other issues raised in Curtis's critique of the selfobject concept—such as the interrelationships among the maturation of selfobject functions, the process of psychological structure formation, and the capacity to experience differentiated object relations—are discussed in detail in my chapter, "On Experiencing an Object: A Multidimensional Perspective" (see Chapter 20, this volume).

embedded throughout its course in the enormously complex, continuously shifting interplay between the differently organized subjective worlds of child and caregiver (Atwood & Stolorow, 1984, Chap. 3).

5. Contrary to Curtis's characterization, empathy, from a self psy-, chological perspective, is not the "provision of a selfobject use," "a departure from the centrality of the analysis of transference and resistance," or an arrogation of the analyst to the role of validating judge (p. 9). Empathy entails the attempt to understand a patient's expressions from within the perspective of his own subjective frame of reference (Kohut, 1959). The patient may *experience* the analyst's empathic understanding as a revival *in the transference* of an arrested, archaic selfobject tie—a merger, for example—provided that such a transference configuration is permitted to unfold. The resistances to, needs for, and subjectively experienced ruptures of such selfobject transference bonds provide the focus for systematic analytic inquiry. Once again contrary to Curtis's portrayal, analysis of transference, resistance, and conflict remains central in the self psychological approach, although the understanding of these phenomena is quite different from the classical one. It is such *analysis* that makes possible the "new" selfobject experiences with the analyst that worry Curtis but that patients seem to find extremely beneficial to their growth.

6. Curtis asserts that the therapeutic interventions offered by self psychologists are only clarifications and not truly interpretations. This, to my mind, is a glaring instance of argument by doctrine. As his commentary on the treatment of the patient with the "gaping hole" in her psyche clearly shows, whether or not an analyst's communications qualify as interpretations depends on whether or not they contain the content that is dictated by drive theory. Interventions that point out "warded off elements of drive and defense" are interpretations. Interventions that articulate other aspects of the patient's inner life are not and, by implication, such treatment should not be called psychoanalysis. I believe it is in the best interests of our science to eschew such parochialism and to conceive of our methods in general enough terms to include the therapeutic work of analysts of all theoretical persuasions. In the broadest sense, an interpretation is an act of illuminating meaning (Atwood & Stolorow, 1984, Chap. 1). All too often analysts use metaphorical terms like "latent," "deeper," and "underlying" to refer to those meanings that are favored by their theories, rather than those that are most salient in their patients' particular motivational hierarchies. The meanings we interpret should not be dictated by dogma but by our empathic –

introspective immersions in our patients' subjective worlds. Curtis falsely dichotomizes empathy and new experiences on the one hand and inter- pretation and insight on the other, as if they were antithetical. These are indissoluble aspects of the process that we call psychoanalysis.

7. Curtis has correctly observed a quality of indecision in Kohut's writings as to whether self psychology can remain in a complementary relationship with conflict theory, a topic that has long been of interest to me (Stolorow, 1983; Stolorow & Lachmann, 1980, 1981). It is my view that the wide gap that some analysts perceive to separate self psychology from conflict psychology is an artifact of the embeddedness of the classical conception of conflict in the doctrine of instinctual drive. When inner conflict is freed from the encumbering image of an energy disposal apparatus and is pictured solely as a subjective state of the person, the supposed antithesis between self psychology and conflict psychology vanishes. Our observational focus then shifts from the pre- sumed vicissitudes of drive to the subjective meaning-contexts in which conflict states crystallize. In a preliminary attempt to conceptualize con- flict along these lines (Stolorow, 1985), I proposed that conflict becomes structuralized developmentally when central affective qualities and mo- tivational strivings are perceived by a child to be inimical to the main- tenance of a bond vital to his well-being, and that conflict states emerge in analysis when this situation is replicated in the transference. From this perspective, the fruitless debate over self theory *versus* conflict theory is replaced by consistent empathic inquiry into the shifting figure– ground relationships among conflict states and arrested selfobject needs as these oscillate between the experiential foreground and background of the transference (Stolorow & Lachmann, 1984/1985). Empathic im- mersion is *not* antithetical to analysis of conflict and resistance. Failing to interpret these dimensions when they are most salient in the trans- ference is *not* empathy.

8. Curtis trivializes the clinical import of Kohut's contributions when he states that "for most clinicians the effect of self psychology will probably be a heightened attention to the patient's feelings and the analyst's countertransferences" (p. 16). For me, the most fundamental contributions of self psychology to clinical psychoanalysis are threefold: first, the unwavering application of the empathic–introspective stance; second, the shift in psychoanalytic inquiry from the motivational primacy of drive to the motivational primacy of self experience (conscious and unconscious); and third, the concepts of selfobject function and self- object transference. Once it is understood that the responsiveness of

48   *Theoretical Issues*

the surround, whether in childhood or in analysis, is experienced subjectively as a vital, functional component of a person's self organization,
one will never listen to analytic material in the same way.

REFERENCES

Atwood, G., & Stolorow, R. (1984). *Structures of Subjectivity: Explorations in Psycho-
    analytic Phenomenology.* Hillsdale, NJ: Analytic Press.
Basch, M. (1980). *Doing Psychotherapy.* New York: Basic Books.
Basch, M. (1984). Selfobjects and selfobject transference: Theoretical implications. In
    P. Stepansky & A. Goldberg, eds., *Kohut's Legacy* (pp. 21–41). Hillsdale, NJ:
    Analytic Press.
Brandchaft, B. (1984). *Ties that free; bonds that shackle: The selfobject transference in
    emergent selfhood.* Unpublished manuscript.
Brandchaft, B., & Stolorow, R. (1984a). The borderline concept: Pathological character
    or iatrogenic myth? In J. Lichtenberg, M. Bornstein, & D. Silver, eds., *Empathy II*
    (pp. 333–357). Hillsdale, NJ: Analytic Press.
Brandchaft, B., & Stolorow, R. (1984b). Reply to Gerald Adler. In J. Lichtenberg,
    M. Bornstein, & D. Silver, eds., *Empathy II* (pp. 367–369). Hillsdale, NJ: Analytic
    Press.
Gill, M. (1976). Metapsychology is not psychology. In M. Gill & P. Holzman, eds.,
    *Psychology versus Metapsychology: Psychoanalytic Essays in Memory of George S.
    Klein* (pp. 71–105). New York: International Universities Press.
Holt, R. (1976). Drive or wish? A reconsideration of the psychoanalytic theory of mo-
    tivation. In M. Gill & P. Holzman, eds., *Psychology versus Metapsychology: Psy-
    choanalytic Essays in Memory of George S. Klein* (pp. 158–197). New York: Inter-
    national Universities Press.
Klein, G. (1976). *Psychoanalytic Theory: An Exploration of Essentials.* New York: In-
    ternational Universities Press.
Kohut, H. (1959). Introspection, empathy, and psychoanalysis. In P. Ornstein, ed., *The
    Search for the Self: Selected Writings of Heinz Kohut, 1950–1978* (pp. 205–232) New
    York: International Universities Press, 1978.
Kohut, H. (1971). *The Analysis of the Self.* New York: International Universities Press.
Kohut, H. (1977). *The Restoration of the Self.* New York: International Universities Press.
Kohut, H. (1984). *How Does Analysis Cure?* A. Goldberg, ed., with P. Stepansky. Chicago
    & London: University of Chicago Press.
Kubie, L. (1975). The language tools of psychoanalysis. *International Review of Psycho-
    Analysis,* 2:11–24.
Ornstein, A. (1974). The dread to repeat and the new beginning. *The Annual of Psy-
    choanalysis,* 2:231–248.
Peterfreund, E. (1971). *Information, Systems and Psychoanalysis: An Evolutionary Bi-
    ological Approach to Psychoanalytic Theory.* New York: International Universities
    Press.
Rubinstein, B. (1967). Explanation and mere description: A metascientific examination
    of certain aspects of the psychoanalytic theory of motivation. In R. Holt, ed., *Motives
    and Thought: Psychoanalytic Essays in Honor of David Rapaport* (pp. 20–77). New
    York: International Universities Press.
Schafer, R. (1976). *A New Language for Psychoanalysis.* New Haven: Yale University
    Press.

Socarides, D., & Stolorow, R. (1984/1985). Affects and selfobjects. *The Annual of Psychoanalysis*, 12/13:105–119.

Stolorow, R. (1983). Self psychology—A structural psychology. In J. Lichtenberg & S. Kaplan, eds., *Reflections on Self Psychology* (pp. 287–296). Hillsdale, NJ: Analytic Press.

Stolorow, R. (1984). Varieties of selfobject experience. In P. Stepansky & A. Goldberg, eds., *Kohut's Legacy* (pp. 43–50). Hillsdale, NJ: Analytic Press.

Stolorow, R. (1985). Toward a pure psychology of inner conflict. In A. Goldberg, ed., *Progress in Self Psychology* (Vol. 1, pp. 193–201). New York: Guilford Press.

Stolorow, R., Brandchaft, B., & Atwood, G. (1983). Intersubjectivity in psychoanalytic treatment: With special reference to archaic states. *Bulletin of the Menninger Clinic*, 47:117–128.

Stolorow, R., & Lachmann, F. (1980). *Psychoanalysis of Developmental Arrests: Theory and Treatment*. New York: International Universities Press.

Stolorow, R., & Lachmann, F. (1981). Two psychoanalyses of one? *Psychoanalytic Review*, 68:307–319.

Stolorow, R., & Lachmann, F. (1984/1985). Transference: The future of an illusion. *The Annual of Psychoanalysis*, 12/13:19–37.

5

Rejoinder

HOMER C. CURTIS

In any dialogue in a forum such as we are using, it is necessary to highlight the major points of controversy, often slighting areas of agreement as well as points where we might build bridges. In responding to the previous chapters I have selected some of the issues that need further elaboration in order to improve future exchanges.

Dr. Basch, in his illuminating and thought-provoking chapter, refers to my review (Curtis, 1983) of *The Search for the Self* (Ornstein, 1978) in which I wonder whether the ties between psychoanalysis and self psychology can be sustained if the latter theory moves away from certain concepts long considered basic in psychoanalysis. Basch infers that I am referring here solely to Freud's theory of instinctual motivation. He also refers to my concern that self psychology's focus on empathic failure and responsiveness might sacrifice the exploration of intrapsychic drive elaborated fantasies. His answer to these questions is, first, that the "instinct theory of motivation, as put forward by Freud, was jettisoned some time ago" (p. 20) and, second, that far from moving away from the intrapsychic toward the environmental, Kohut reverses that very trend for which Melanie Klein and Heinz Hartmann are to blame (p. 20).

Depending on one's definition of drive motivation, it may or may not have been jettisoned. Certainly psychoanalysis, following Freud, has distinguished between drive (a not completely satisfactory translation of the German *Trieb*, which is a psychological concept with clinical referrents such as impulses toward goal-directed behavior, persistence and plasticity, discharge phenomena, compelling vis-à-tergo qualities, etc.) and instinct (in German *Instinkt*, referring to inherited, unchangeable patterns of behavior). In addition, psychoanalysis has refined its views of drive development to include such concepts as the organization of drives within the matrix of early affective experiences. Concepts of motivations other than the drives have been added to account for other forms of goal-directed behavior, but it is difficult to see how clinical theory can do without a drive concept. As pointed out by a number of critics, (e.g., Schafer, 1980; Stolorow, Chapter 4, this volume), even self psychology's concepts of the development of the self have drive-like qualities. Basch's preference for "affiliative tendencies" and "mastery" seems a kind of abstract, sanitized, disembodied version of those human impulses that in the child and patient often enough have primitive qualities of lust and rage.

While a concept of drive motivation seems essential for a theory attempting to explain clinical data and human development it is not the only means of defining psychoanalysis. It is to be subsumed under the more important concept of the dynamic unconscious with its organized fantasies influencing behavior. The concepts of transference and defense, as well as the views of neurosogenesis as being primarily derived from object-related experiences are basic to the definition of psychoanalysis. This does not deny the importance of preverbal influences, the frustrations and overstimulations of very early life. As Basch points out "the permanently (because nonsymbolic) unconscious experiences of the first 18 months of life that form the basis of character can manifest themselves only in . . . the nuances of affective responsiveness or lack of responsiveness, behavior predispositions, or cognitive style" (p. 24). In other words, these early experiences tend toward structuralization, influencing the mode of and capacity for dealing with the latter developmental tasks. But if these early experiences are revealed in deep, baseline character affective and cognitive styles without content, can they be analyzed the same as secondarily repressed material that has remained dynamically active and presses for verbal and object-related expression? The return of the secondarily repressed in the form of symptoms, transference, and the like, is what is analyzed (literally taken apart) and capable of being translated into verbal concepts. Affective predispositions, cognitive style, and remnants of early preobjectal needs, which Kohut (Ornstein, 1978, p. 220) differentiated from transference proper, can be observed, empathized with, described, clarified, and perhaps modified by experience, training, identification, and compensatory structuralization (transmuting internalization?), but not analyzed and interpreted the same as neurotic conflict.

In regard to the relationship of the intrapsychic and the interpersonal, I was struck by Basch's version of the history of the development of object relations and ego theory. Contrary to his reading of Melanie Klein, hers is not an object relations theory in the usual interpersonal sense of other British theorists. In her view, innate object-seeking fantasies are centered primarily on intrapsychic efforts to deal with a postulated death instinct (Bacal, 1984). Experience with reality and parents is not considered crucial in her theory and technique, leading Rapaport (1958) to call it an "id mythology." Thus it is unlikely that she could be blamed for leading psychoanalysis in an interpersonal direction. As for Hartmann's contribution to such a movement, it is easier to see how some aspects of his ego psychology could be used to support such an indictment, for example, his effort to expand the concepts of the ego's adaptive capacities. However, he repeatedly insisted that these views were to be integrated with existing conflict theory (Hartmann, 1958). Be that as it may, the question is, has psychoanalysis really strayed from its primary intrapsychic focus toward an interpersonal, environmentalist orientation? The answer I have given is a definite "no," and I cannot agree with Basch's claim that self psychology has come to the rescue with its selfobject concept. On the contrary, crucial aspects of self psychology emphasize the interpersonal: etiologically, the notion of lack of parental empathy; technically, the advocacy of providing empathic responses; therapeutically, the taking into the self of empathic interactions by transmuting internalizations, in order to build a more cohesive self. In addition, it is claimed that man needs selfobjects all of his life just as he needs oxygen. Thus the presence of another person is required for psychic well-being, not for object-related gratifications, but to maintain an ideally cohesive self.

Basch (personal communication, October, 1984) has called attention to the fact that the second case I present is taken from his book, *Doing Psychotherapy* (1980), and therefore is not to be considered an example of analysis conducted along self psychological lines. Indeed, it would appear to most analysts to fit in the category of psychotherapy with the limited goal of enabling the patient to attain a greater self-esteem and better adjustment through transference support and identification to a life of the intellect and professional achievement. However, Basch specifically contrasts the technique used with classical psychoanalysis, rather than with a self psychological form of psychoanalysis (p. 86). The therapy is presented as aiming at and achieving a resolution of resistance and transference, presumably the aim of psychoanalysis whether classical or self psychological. Since the author does not distinguish between psychotherapy and psychoanalysis as defined by self psychology, ambiguity remains, although the technique as presented seems compatible with Kohut's statements that the goal of analysis is cohesion of the self, without necessarily requiring a capacity for object love (Kohut, 1977). There are also many points of technical similarity between this case and several of those presented in *The Psychology of the Self: A Casebook* (Goldberg, 1978).

Of more basic importance is the question of the diagnostic evaluation. Apparently the narcissistic aspects of the patient's character were judged to be the direct-line effect of unempathic parenting, especially on the part of her father. The ambivalence and sexual conflict expressed by her vindictive teasing and rejection of men, as well as by the erotic transference, were bypassed in favor of the presumption of a selfobject disorder. The possibility that the patient's imperiousness, antagonism, and self-centeredness were narcissistic defenses to conceal conflicts in relations with men does not appear to have been considered. This led to the choice of a reparative internalization approach, whether called psychotherapy or psychoanalysis of a self psychological type.

Along with these disagreements, several areas of agreement should be noted. These include the centrality of the intrapsychic focus, although we differ in our interpretation of self psychology's contribution to this. We certainly agree on the importance of the traumatic influences in early preverbal life, but differ in our conceptions of the way these influences are represented psychically in the adult, and the extent to which they can be analyzed. I certainly agree with Basch's statement that aggressive and sexual fantasies should be analyzed, and also that the usual analytic technique should not be misapplied to nonneurotic patients. It is less clear whether he would agree with me that neurotics should not be treated by a technique developed for treatment of self disordered patients. This point becomes important in view of Kohut's (1984) statement that self psychology's theory and technique apply not only "to the analysis of analyzable self disorders but to the analysis of *all* analyzable disorders" (p. 110).

I find myself in agreement with much of Dr. Markson and Dr. Thomson's contributions. I appreciate their stress on empathy as a prerequisite for mutual awareness of inner experience and exploration; their warning that sexual and aggressive elements are not just "disintegration products" and may be slighted if dismissed as such; their observation that self psychology has drive concepts in the more abstract form of a drive for self-realization or a drive to retain the integrity of experience; and their reminder that we cannot take an *a priori* approach to our patients in the matter of deficit (I prefer malformation) or conflict, since both are always present. In regard to the last I am reminded of Freud's answer to Marie Bonaparte when she questioned him about the enthusiasm of some analysts for the concept of oral fixations. Freud's reply was,

> I am not surprised that the phrase "the eternal suckling" has somewhat impressed you. There is indeed something to it. Oral erotism is the first erotic manifestation, just as the nipple is the first sexual object; the libido is led along definite paths from these first positions into the new organizations. But the question that interests us is not the genetic one, but the dynamic one. (Quoted in Jones, 1957, p. 445)

In other words, while early developmental needs and problems are significant in their own right in forming basic character and influencing later stages, the clinical issue is to determine what the predominant dynamically active problems are, whether oedipal or preoedipal. In connection with preoedipal issues, question remains about the extent to which early developmental conflicts and problems are still dynamically active, or are transformed into malformations or compensatory structures that may be crucial psychopathologically, but are so fixed and calcified that they are not able to be mobilized into dynamically active analyzable material.

I am indebted to Dr. Stolorow for pointing out parts of my chapter that might benefit from some refinements of definition and usage. I am also reassured by the evidence that he has not limited himself to the theories and technical concepts of Kohut and is attempting to integrate self theory and conflict theory. Thus, even though my chapter emphasizes and highlights questions and controversies, I believe our differences may not be as great as they appeared at first.

Clearly, we can agree on the fundamental importance of unconscious motivation, while differing in our conceptualization of the nature of significant aspects thereof. For those peremptory, endlessly renewable, developmentally transformable and defensively modifiable strivings, experienced in numerous derivatives normally and symptomatically, I have preferred the term "drive," which carries the implication of genetic roots and an experientially modifiable motivational timetable related to defenses partly derived from interacting with the drives. As with those functions that serve defensive, executive, and adaptive purposes, the drives do not spring fullgrown but undergo development within the matrix of object-related experiences, becoming organized and refined as to aim and object. This conceptualization does not require the notion of a closed energy disposal system, but rather implies an open system allowing for experiential input, which contributes to the plasticity and possibility of countless derivatives.

Referring to Kohut's definition of psychoanalysis as that psychological field demarcated by the observational mode of empathy and introspection, Stolorow states that instinctual drives do not fall within the conceptual domain of psychoanalytic inquiry since he doubts that anyone has ever been able to achieve empathic contact with such an entity. Perhaps Stolorow is relying on a different, biological type of definition of drive rather than the psychological concept used by most analysts. Kohut referred to this in the following statement:

> much clarity is gained if we admit that the psychoanalytic term "drive" is derived from the introspective investigation of inner experience. Experiences may have the quality of drivenness (of wanting, wishing, or striving) to varying degrees. A drive, then, is an abstraction from innumerable inner experiences; it connotes a psychological quality that cannot be further analyzed by introspection; it is the common denominator of sexual and aggressive strivings. (Ornstein, 1978, p. 227)

Perhaps for dialectical reasons Stolorow has offered his definition of drives as being blind, impersonal, biologically programmed forces, pressing mechanically for tension reduction. He contrasts this with a concept of motivations as "complex cognitive–affective structures that crystallize organically from a person's early formative experiences" (p. 42). This definition has much in common with the conceptualization I have offered, but beyond the semantic question, I believe his definition does not sufficiently correspond to the clinical and experiential data nor to the simple, baseline fact of our connection with our bodies. By whatever name, this organized, distinctive, and unique inner motivation provides a basis for individuality and a safeguard against encroachment upon that individuality by external pressures.

In responding to my opinion that self psychology has simplified and reduced the complexities of human development as, for example, in the focus on failures of parental empathy, Stolorow points to the truism that all psychological theories are to some degree imbalanced and reductionistic. This does not sufficiently address the failure of self psychology to take into account additional pathogenic developmental influences besides those having to do with vicissitudes of empathy and the self experience. Such parsimony cannot be due simply to the relatively early stage of development of self psychology. It seems rather to reflect commitment to a theoretical program aiming to affirm its distinctive claim as a new paradigm.

Stolorow has misunderstood my point when he says, "The aim [of self psychology] is not to collude with a regressive defense or to minimize the patient's autonomy, but to permit aborted developmental thrusts to become revitalized" (p. 44). While such collusion is obviously not *aimed* at, there is the danger that the emphasis on and validating of the patient's sense of "deficit" as a result of lack of empathy encourages the patient's view of himself as victim, neglecting opportunities to gain access to his contribution to the developmental conflicts and malformations, as well as discouraging reliance on more mature capacities. While it is claimed that such responses are to be analyzed, at the very least the analytic work will be made more difficult by the resistances evoked by such an approach.

From the standpoint of maintaining ties with psychoanalysis, I am encouraged by Stolorow's agreement that the supraordinate, existential concept of the self is not useful. His view of the self as a structure, "a cognitive–affective scheme through which self experience acquires cohesion and continuity" (p. 45), links up with the concept of self representation as used by Jacobson, Hartmann, Sandler, and others. The developmental transformations of this self representation may be affected by a variety of internal and external influences, leading to deviations from what by various functional, interpersonal, and cultural standards may be considered ideal. Descriptive and metaphorical concepts such as "deficit" to designate these states tend to become concretized and need to be used judiciously, lest they influence us to accept the patient's subjective sense of something missing as literal rather than symbolic. Developmental arrests may indeed lead to impairment of certain functions, but this descriptive deficiency will coexist with malformations and compensatory structures derived from the same etiological factors causing the developmental arrest. Such deflections or tangents from expectable and potentially more efficient lines, from a broader perspective, can result not only in serious psychopathology but also in unique and valuable characteristics, and help account for the wide variation in human personality. Related to this seemingly limitless variety of end products of the interaction of experience and the psyche's wide range of capacities to adapt to trauma by forming different compensatory structures, is the question of the extent to which these structures can be given up or modified. It is not simply a matter of "permitting patients to establish in the transference a facilitating context in which the arrested development can resume" (p. 45), as described by Stolorow. The fixity of such structures, especially if they have been based on or acquired an imperative defensive or adaptive function, may preclude any resumption of a line of development that at an earlier time may have been more adaptive. In the case of ego-dystonic, dynamically active conflict, there is a greater possibility of a remobilization of the elements of a pathological compromise, with more adaptive solutions becoming possible (although even here we know from analysis how difficult this can be). In the case of fixed, developmental character malformations, such remobilization is much more difficult and therapeutic success may depend on formation of new and more adaptive compensatory structures and identifications rather than on resumption of an ideal development through a reparative experience in the transference. Such clinical difficulties make a theory of deficit and facilitating, reparative transference experience deceptively appealing.

Stolorow states, "analysis of transference, resistance, and conflict remains central in the self psychological approach, although the understanding of these phenomena is quite different from the classical one" (p. 46). While this means that he differs with Kohut, who came to the opinion that defenses and resistance are "less important today than they once were and should no longer be construed as centrally important to theory and practice" (1984, p. 115), and further implies that Stolorow wishes to maintain some connection with psychoanalysis as currently construed, he stresses a "quite different" understanding of these phenomena. Among other differences, he views the analysis of transference and resistance as a necessary *preliminary* to "make possible the 'new' selfobject experiences with the analyst" (p. 46), or as he stated earlier, "to establish in the transference a facilitating context in which the arrested development can resume." This is indeed a different concept of the analytic process and aim since analysis in these terms seems to be the means to the end of selfobject experiences with the analyst, presumably to foster transmuting internalizations. Kohut's view was that the "essential curative process is structure-building by means of transmuting internalizations" (Ornstein, 1978, p. 928), this process to be accomplished when,

> the analyst tries to be in empathic touch with the patient's life at all times, with the result that his failures are sufficiently small and of sufficiently short duration to allow the patient to respond to them via structure-building—just as should have happened in childhood. Friendliness is not cu-

rative in this sense—persistently pursued and, on the whole, successful empathic responses, however, are. (Ornstein, 1978, pp. 928–929).

This describes an essentially reparative process of multiple, small identifications whose success depends on empathic responses, thus a different conceptualization of the process of cure from the classical one of interpretation and resolution of conflict.

Rather than "arguing from doctrine" in the matter of understanding the nature of interventions used in the reports of self psychologically conducted therapies, I have pointed out significant characteristics of those interventions that seem to derive from self psychology's focus on empathy and experience-near considerations. It has been my contention that such a focus emphasizes the "here-and-now" interaction between the patient and analyst and neglects the exploration of the warded-off aspects underlying the experience with the analyst. In the example given in my chapter the interventions have been descriptive, observational, and clarifying, rather than explanatory of the dynamic unconscious motivations. As a way of sharpening this matter I have used a common definition of interpretation that differentiates it from the descriptive nature of clarification. More important than the definition is the principle involved, namely, the communication to the patient of the analyst's empathic and cognitive awareness of what the patient has been warding off by repression, denial, displacement, and so forth. The intention is to help the patient become sharply aware of affective and ideational elements that have been defensively avoided, rationalized, generalized, and displaced. The use of "broad reconstructions of total feeling states of childhood" (Ornstein, 1978, p. 883) as advocated by Kohut is a related manifestation of a tendency to stay with the global, generalized, vague, and rationalized, rather than proceeding to the specific, affect-laden details of warded-off motivations and fantasies. Such broad generalizations seem to follow naturally on the reduction of pathogenesis to empathic deprivation, rather than the more complex etiological possibilities usually considered, which demand interpretive attention to details of defensive derivatives and compromise. Obviously, analysis must proceed from the general to the specific, from the known to the unknown, from the descriptive to the explanatory; to remain at a manifest or intermediate level of experience and clarification may indeed be therapeutic, but puts at risk the greater structural change possible with analysis and resolution of conflict.

I have appreciated this exchange of viewpoints and consider that our dialogue has helped to delineate the controversies raised by the emergence of self psychology. I cannot predict the course or outcome of this controversy but I am encouraged that there can be an enrichment of psychoanalysis by the findings and formulations of those working in the special area of self psychology. There remains much to be done in the evolving theory and practice of psychoanalysis and it is to the credit of self psychology that it is exerting a catalytic effect on our continuing self-examination.

REFERENCES

Bacal, H. (1984). *British object relations theorists and self psychology: Some critical reflections*. Paper presented at the 7th Annual Self Psychology Conference, Toronto.
Basch, M.F. (1980). *Doing Psychotherapy*. New York: Basic Books.
Curtis, H.C. (1983). Book review of Ornstein, P. H., ed. (1978). *The Search for the Self: Selected Writings of Heinz Kohut: 1950–1978*. New York: International Universities Press. *Journal of the American Psychoanalytic Association*, 31, 272–285.
Goldberg, A. (1978). *The Psychology of the Self: A Casebook*. New York: International Universities Press.
Hartmann, H. (1958). *Ego Psychology and the Problem of Adaptation*. New York: International Universities Press.
Jones, E. (1957). *The Life and Work of Sigmund Freud* (Vol. 3). New York: Basic Books.
Kohut, H. (1977). *The Restoration of the Self*. New York: International Universities Press.
Kohut, H. (1984). *How Does Analysis Cure?* A. Goldberg, ed., with P. Stepansky. Chicago & London: University of Chicago Press.
Ornstein, P.H. (1978). *The Search for the Self: Selected Writings of Heinz Kohut: 1950–1978* (Vols. 1 & 2) New York: International Universities Press.
Rapaport, D. (1958). An historical survey of psychoanalytic ego psychology. *Bulletin of the Philadelphia Association for Psychoanalysis*, 8, 105–120.
Schafer, R. (1980). Action language and the psychology of the self. *Annual of Psychoanalysis*, 8:83–92.

SECTION TWO

CLINICAL PROBLEMS

6

How Does Self Psychology Differ in Practice?

ROBERT S. WALLERSTEIN

In two previous conferences devoted to self psychology—one in New York in December 1979, at the fall meeting of the American Psychoanalytic Association (Wallerstein, 1981) and one in Boston in November 1980, under the auspices of the Boston Psychoanalytic Society and Institute (Wallerstein, 1983a)—I presented in the first a clinical, and in the second a theoretical critique of the self psychology approach from within what I called the perspective of "classical" psychoanalytic psychology. The explicit point of reference for the first panel was Heinz Kohut's case of the two analyses of Mr. Z (Kohut, 1979) but the more overarching framework was the progressive unfolding of Kohut's conceptualizing in his two landmark books, *The Analysis of the Self* (1971), the expression of the psychology of the self in the narrower sense—as contents of the agencies of the mental apparatus, that is, as mental representations within the id, ego, and superego—and then *The Restoration of the Self* (1977), the statement of the psychology of the self in the broader sense, as a supraordinate constellation, with the drives and defenses subsumed as constituents of this self. This is what came to be called the bipolar self, in which, with maturation, normally self-assertive ambitions crystallize as one pole and attained ideals and values as the other—the two poles being connected by a tension arc of talents and skills.

We now have available for critical discussion and response, what has turned out to be Kohut's last and posthumous book, *How Does Analysis Cure?* (1984), which is a proper capstone to the clinical and theoretical edifice that he, together with his many colleagues and collaborators, has fashioned. In this manuscript, happily edited for publication by Arnold Goldberg with the collaboration of Paul Stepansky, Heinz Kohut has pressed his thinking to many of its logical conclusions and from within that vantage point has elaborated for us self psychology's effort at a comprehensively unified theory of normal growth and development, of personality functioning and psychopathology (i.e., its dysfunctions), and of therapy, cure, and psychic health or "normality." Certainly, he has provided us with ample basis to address meaningfully the central question posed to this panel "Do Self Psychologists Treat Patients Differently?" Depending on the answer that one emerges with to this question—and as you can expect, it will most probably be a qualified and debatable answer—we can next assess where we currently variously stand on the place of the whole corpus of the self psychology development in relation to the central body of established classical psychoanalytic psychology.

At the two preceding self psychology conferences in which I participated, I developed my own viewpoints on self psychology (Wallerstein, 1981, 1983a) within a dialectical interplay between the writings of Kohut and his followers on the one hand and that of the various commentators upon and critics of self psychology on the other; unlike that, this chapter will be built essentially upon an interpretation just of Kohut's text in his third and last book. I will do this by first presenting my understanding of Kohut's finally crystallized concepts of normal development, of life goals and normal mental health, of analyzability and of the theory of psychoanalytic technique according to self psychology, all this to be then compared and contrasted with his statements on the theory of psychopathology and then of treatment and cure according to what Kohut calls "traditional analysis." This will lead to my assessment of the similarity and difference in what self psychologists actually *do* as compared with so-called "traditional analysts" and the basis in theory of discerned differences in practice. I trust that it is almost superfluous to add the caveat that my overview of Kohut's work can only be highly condensed and presumes in the audience shared interest in, and basic familiarity with, the major tenets of self psychology. Also, I will stick as much as possible to Kohut's own words through quotation.

First then, for Kohut's view of the human psychological developmental process. His most tersely comprehensive statement on this is the following:

> Self psychology holds that self–selfobject relationships form the *essence* of
> psychological life from birth to death, that a move from dependence (sym-

biosis) to independence (autonomy) in the psychological sphere is no more possible, let alone desirable, than a corresponding move from a life dependent on oxygen to a life independent of it in the biological sphere. The developments that characterize normal psychological life must, in our view, be seen in the *changing nature* of the relationship between the self and its selfobjects [from archaic embeddedness to mature tie], but not in the self's relinquishment of selfobjects. (p. 47, italics added).[1]

That is, we live our lives within a "responsive selfobject milieu without which human life cannot be sustained" (p. 21).

Properly unfolded within a milieu provided by responsive enough parental selfobjects, normal development culminates in the consolidation of a fully coherent self, a condition of psychological health which Kohut defines "in terms of structural completeness . . . achieved . . . when an energic continuum in the center of the personality has been established and the unfolding of a productive life has thus become a realizable possibility" (p. 7). This "energic continuum from one pole [of the bipolar self] to the other . . . [Kohut] considers the dynamic–structural essence of mental health" (p. 43). When established it enables the individual to live "a meaningful life through the ability to realize the program of his nuclear self via the instrumentalities of work and love" (p. 43). Or, in another place, maintaining the nuclear self "preserves the potential to fulfill its nuclear program and realize his specific psychologic destiny" (p. 132). All this is made a little less nebulous when at the very end of the book Kohut talks of the "ultimate fruition via creative–productive action of a person's central life program as shaped by his particular ambitions, talents and ideals" (p. 205). It is this that is declared to be "the clinical significance of normality . . . functioning that is in accordance with structural design" (p. 190); and of these "structural preconditions of a good life" (p. 44) as Kohut calls them, he adds his firm "conviction that traditional analysis cannot even approximate the meaningful message that self psychology can give us here" (p. 44). Though all of these conceptualizations indeed suffer from an undue and excessive vagueness,[2] it is at least clear that by structure

---

1. Unless otherwise specifically noted, all quotations are from *How Does Analysis Cure?* (Kohut, 1984).

2. In a sympathetic and at the same time thoughtful critique of self psychology theory discussed among *Recent Developments in Psychoanalysis*, Eagle, in his new book (1984) takes Kohut to task for this vagueness and lack of specifiability of much of his theoretical terminology. As example, this one from a discussion of Kohut's central explanatory construct on the mechanism of the curative process in analysis, Eagle says, "One difficulty which Kohut also shares with other psychoanalytic writers is an unnecessary degree of vagueness, even obfuscation, in description of the process mediating change in therapy . . . one of the key theoretical concepts Kohut appeals to account for therapeutic change—

Kohut is "referring neither to the structures of a mental apparatus nor to the structures of any of the constituents of a mental apparatus but to the structure of the self" (p. 99). This "structure of the self" is nothing more than "an uninterrupted tension arc from basic ambitions, via basic talents and skills, toward basic ideals. This tension arc is the dynamic essence of the complete, nondefective self; it is a conceptualization of the structure whose establishment makes possible a creative–productive fulfilling life" (pp. 4–5).

Given this overall conception of healthy development and normality, how does Kohut conceptualize the treatment and curative process in those who have experienced pathogenic development, who suffer the varieties of disorders of the self (a spectrum that I will specify in Kohut's most current terms further on) that cause them to seek out analytic treatment? It is indeed the nature of this treatment and cure process that is the declared core of this entire book. To begin with, "Self psychology does not find the essence of the curative process in the cognitive sphere per se" (p. 64). I will return to this later in reference to Kohut's statements about the "truth and knowledge morality" declared to characterize classical or traditional analysis. Here I want only to say that Kohut means that though an increased scope of consciousness is the usual outcome of successful analysis, it "does not always occur, and it is not essential" (p. 64); that is, "self psychology does not see the *essence* of the curative process as lying primarily in the expansion of the domain of the ego" (p. 64, italics added).

Rather, the treatment and cure process as conceptualized within the framework of self psychology resides in the following characterization of the analytic work:

> every analyst cannot avoid erring many times in his understanding of the analysand and in the explanations he offers to him. . . . In all such instances

---

"transmuting internalizations"—both in and outside of therapy. . . . When one attempts to ascertain what Kohut means, specifically, by 'transmuting internalization,' one reads, for example, that this involves the creation of internal psychic structures through the withdrawal of cathexes from object images. But what are psychic structures? And what does it mean to withdraw cathexes from object images? Unless one's responses to these questions are reasonably clear and with empirical content and reference, the explanation of "transmuting internalizations" remains as vague as the term itself. Unfortunately, I believe one has to conclude that at this point, this key concept, employed by Kohut to describe and explain therapeutic change, has at best only approximate or perhaps only apparent meaning" (p. 70). This same charge of excessive vagueness can be levelled even more pointedly of course at such phrases as "energic continuum," "to realize the program of the nuclear self," "to fulfill one's psychological destiny," or "to function in accord with one's structural design."

. . . no harm ensues if the analyst recognizes the patient's retreats and responds to them with appropriate interpretations. Such errors constitute optimal failures. . . . Each optimal failure will be followed by an increase in the patient's resilience vis-à-vis empathy failures both inside and outside the analytic situation; that is, after each, optimal new self structures will be acquired and existing ones will be firmed. (p. 69)

It is this activity that "opens a path of empathy between self and self-object, specifically, the establishment of empathic intuneness between self and selfobject on mature adult levels. . . . [I]t supplants the bondage that formerly tied the archaic self to the archaic selfobject" (p. 66). In this way optimal failures or "optimal frustrations" or "nontraumatic frustrations" lead through what are called "countless repetitions" finally to an "empathic resonance" (all on p. 70), or a "mature selfobject resonance" (p. 219) that emanates from the selfobjects of adult life (p. 70), from the "human surroundings and other humanness-sustaining aspects of present day reality" (p. 76) and enables the subject to be "sustained [well enough] most of the time" (p. 70).

To summarize all this, Kohut writes,

a successful analysis is one in which the analysand's formerly archaic needs for the responses of archaic selfobjects are superseded by the experience of the availability of empathic resonance, the major constituent of the sense of security in adult life. Increased ability to verbalize, broadened insight, greater autonomy of ego functions, and increased control over impulsiveness may accompany these gains, but they are not the essence of cure. A treatment will be successful because . . . an analysand was able to reactivate, in a selfobject transference, the needs of a self that had been thwarted in childhood. In the analytic situation, these reactivated needs were kept alive and exposed, time and again, to the vicissitudes of optimal frustrations until the patient ultimately acquired the reliable ability to sustain his self with the aid of selfobject resources available in his adult surroundings. According to self psychology, then, the essence of the psychoanalytic cure resides in a patient's newly acquired ability to identify and seek out appropriate selfobjects . . . as they present themselves in his realistic surroundings and to be sustained by them. (p. 77)

There is little to be added to this summary description. Later on (pp. 99, 101), Kohut reminds us that this process of structure formation is what he has designated "transmuting internalization." He also reassures us that optimal *frustration* is *not* "optimal *gratification* because, through the analyst's more or less accurate understanding, an empathic bond is established . . . between analyst and patient that substitutes for the de facto fulfillment of the patient's need" (p. 103). And mostly—and this leads directly to the issue of exactly how these curative changes are accomplished—optimal frustration is provided "via optimally frustrating correct interpretations" (p. 153).

Clearly, such interpretive work must be directed toward patients deemed analyzable and Kohut repeats in the very first pages of this newest book his general (though not completely rigid) interdiction of analysis for those diagnosed as borderline as well as, of course, for the overtly psychotic. But within the range of what he calls narcissistic personality disturbances, his criteria for analyzability are generous. He says,

> In order to be capable of cure by psychoanalysis, the analysand must be able to engage the analyst as selfobject by mobilizing the sets of inner experience that we call selfobject transferences. . . . [T]he analyzable patient who suffers from a conflict neurosis or a narcissistic personality or behavior disorder is an individual whose self—or, to be more exact, a remnant of whose self—is still, potentially at least, in search of appropriately responsive selfobjects. . . . [He] must be able to mobilize in the psychoanalytic situation the maturation-directed needs for structure building via transmuting internalization of the revived selfobjects of childhood. (pp. 70–71)

This is then stated less technically and more clearly at a further point in the context of a case vignette portraying a patient who as a child had "still managed to keep a significant remnant of his nuclear self alive, thus remaining at least potentially capable of responding with renewed structure-building to new opportunities for further growth. Expressed in technical terms, he remained potentially analyzable. Expressed in everyday human terms, he never quite gave up hope" (p. 131).

In carrying out these analyses and creating the best possible conditions for psychic functioning in the terms stated by self psychology (i.e., creatively fulfilling one's "nuclear program"), the self psychologists have never wavered in their insistence that the chief vehicle for doing so has been the same unalloyed interpretive process that has always characterized psychoanalysis centrally. Yet these declarations of the continuing centrality of the psychoanalytic interpretive process have been at the same time those most attacked by the various critics of self psychology—and those most disbelieved (but more of that controversy at a later point). The insistence on self psychology's adherence to interpretation as the still central technique in psychoanalytic work was highlighted (as if to respond to or to anticipate attack on this very point) in *The Psychology of the Self: A Casebook*, edited by Arnold Goldberg (1978), which was a set of descriptions at some length of six patients treated according to the tenets of self psychology under Kohut's influence and/or his direct supervision. There in the introductory section Goldberg states, "The activity of a psychoanalyst is *interpretation.* Analyses of narcissistic personality disorders are no different in this respect from those of the more familiar neurotic syndromes" (1978, p. 9). And this is amplified in the concluding section of the book as follows.

> The principles determining the use of the interpretive process in narcissistic personality disorders are no different from those involved in the oedipal neuroses. The analyst listens with even-hovering attention, which is his counterpart of the analysand's free associations. By virtue of his own analysis, training, and experience, the analyst is acutely sensitive to his inner experiences and thus becomes consciously aware of mental states evoked in him through empathic contact with the analysand. Such empathically derived data then become the raw material for processing into the hypotheses that are tested by interpretations. (1978, p. 446)

Lest this be in any way misunderstood, Goldberg goes on to add, "this is the essence of the analytic treatment: interpretation without gratification per se. . . . [A]n analytic ambience gratifies neither narcissism nor sexuality, but is equivalent to the average expectable emotional environment that facilitates the analytic process. . . . The analyst does not actively soothe; he interprets the analysand's yearning to be soothed" (1978, p. 447). He goes on with more examples. To complete this exposition of interpretive rigour, Goldberg further adds, "Broadly speaking, no interpretation is complete without the reconstruction and inclusion of the genetic context which was precursor to the contemporaneous dynamic. This supports and buffers the transference interpretations" (1978, p. 448).

Kohut, in turn, in his latest book tries to be equally unequivocal on this same point, specifically reiterated in very similar words at four different places in the book (pp. 75, 81, 107, 208). One will capture the tone of them all, "self psychology relies on the same tools as traditional analysis (interpretation followed by working through in an atmosphere of abstinence)" (p. 75). Where then is the interpretive difference, if it does exist? Clearly, it is declared to be not in the *process* but in the *content* of interpretation. Here of course the focus is unswervingly on the selfobject transferences, "since . . . the renewed search of the damaged self for the development-enhancing responses of an appropriately empathic selfobject always occupies center stage in the analysand's experiences during the analysis, it follows that the analyst's pivotal communications to the analysand are those that focus on the psychic configurations to which we refer as selfobject transferences" (p. 192). These are stated in this book to be threefold in nature (an expanded classification from Kohut's earlier grouping),

> (1) those in which the damaged pole of ambitions attempts to elicit the confirming–approving responses of the selfobject (mirror transference); (2) those in which the damaged pole of ideals searches for a selfobject that will accept its idealization (idealizing transference); and (3) those in which the damaged intermediate area of talents and skills seeks a selfobject that will make itself available for the reassuring experience of essential alikeness (twinship or alter ego transference). (pp. 192–193)

Therapeutic resolution of such damage to the self or the happenstances of more or less healthy development in the first place can lead to

> variations within the spectrum of normality or maturity. Certain people are predominantly creative and self-expressive, and their creative selves are sustained by the actually occurring, or at least confidently expected, approval of the selfobject milieu in which they live. Others are predominantly sustained by feeling uplifted by ideals . . . Finally, there are still other people who derive the sustenance that maintains their selves mainly from feeling surrounded by alter egos. (p. 203)

This all adds up, of course, to what a good analysis will have achieved. In Kohut's close to final words in his book,

> A good analysis will have explained to the patient how the shortcomings of the selfobject milieu brought about the deficits in his self structure and how, in consequence of the absence of the joy that results when the self feels welcomed and supported by its selfobjects, the drives become isolated as a depressive self attempted to maintain itself through joyless pleasure seeking. And a good analysis will have explained to the patient, furthermore, that the anxious clinging to the archaic selfobject and its functions was not due to a childish reluctance to give up old gratifications; instead, it was a welcome indicator that the striving to complete the development of the self had never been totally given up. And finally, a good analysis will have explained to the patient how the stalemated development of the self led to the emergence of the persisting—and, again, in essence welcome—demands, often deeply buried in the personality, that the selfobject ultimately respond adequately so that development may proceed to completion. (p. 209)

The fullest achievement of this desired state depends ultimately of course upon the analyst's capacity, to wit, "each time the analyst's interpretations are wrong, inaccurate, or otherwise faulty, there is the anxious question of whether the selfobject analyst, often in contrast to the parental selfobject of childhood, will be able to recognize his mistake and thus transform a potential trauma into a development-enhancing structure-building optimal frustration" (p. 207).

Along the way to creating this self psychological perspective on the nature of the analytic treatment and cure, Kohut makes a number of derivative or ancillary points. Some of them are somewhat surprising in the context of earlier writings from within self psychology, like the assertion that the empathy of the psychoanalytic self psychologist does not differ in essence from the kind of empathy employed by analysts before the advent of self psychology (p. 172), though it is claimed that self psychology "has supplied analysis with new theories which broaden and deepen the field of empathic perception" (p. 175).[3] Less unexpected are the claims that self psychologists "behave in a (comparatively speaking) less reserved manner than the majority of analysts" (p. 81); that their "expanded *scope* of empathy" conduces to the "generally calmer and friendlier atmosphere of self psychological treatment" (p. 82); that the self psychologist's interpretations have "a certain accepting coloration" (p. 90). The expectable counterpart of this stance is that "confrontations should be used sparingly" (p. 173) since it "is not the task of the analyst to educate the patient via confrontations but, via the consistent interpretation of the selfobject transferences, to cure the defect in his self" (p. 173). However, again, lest there be misunderstandings, Kohut does take the trouble to add, "Clearly, it is not enough for the analyst to be 'nice' to his patients, to be 'understanding,' warmhearted, endowed with the human touch" (p. 95). Here as elsewhere, the slogan, "Love is Not Enough," is pertinent. Nonetheless, to some extent the concept of "sustaining empathic resonance" does awaken memories of Franz Alexander's "corrective emotional experience" and to the extent that such comparison has real substance, Kohut responds in two places in his text (pp. 78, 153) with the identical phrase: "so be it"—but again he hastens to avow that in fact he is really talking about "optimally frustrating correct interpretations" (p. 153).[4]

At this point, in order to try to make as clear as possible whether, and, if so how, this entire structure of psychoanalytic endeavor *à la* self

---

3. For a contrary view that at least some leading self psychology theories have indeed radically redefined empathy—and along with it psychoanalysis—and equated them both into self psychology theory, see my theoretical critique (Wallerstein, 1983a, pp. 585–587).

4. On this issue, I agree with the self psychologists that Kohut's approach is to be distinguished from the superficially somewhat similar Alexandrian conception of the "corrective emotional experience" and that the attribution of compelling similarity has been unfairly leveled at Kohut's work by a number of its critics (See Wallerstein, 1981, p. 385).

psychology differs significantly from classical or (in Kohut's phrase)"traditional" analysis, I will turn, albeit more briefly, to Kohut's statements about the nature of classical analysis together with his explicit or implicit assertions about what the self psychological psychoanalyst does *not* do.

First, whether most analysts will agree with this way of formulating the classical Freudian position (and Freud's own position) or not, is Kohut's overall view that traditional analysis is embedded in a constraining and not so subtly detrimental "truth mortality" (p. 54). For Freud (and presumably for classical analysts since Freud), to quote Kohut, "To have knowledge withheld from him was experienced as an intolerable narcissistic injury" (p. 54). This is so because knowledge is juxtaposed with mastery and with the ego, the functional seat of mastery (p. 55), and in terms of the therapy conceptualized through the theory, the claim is "traditionally accepted . . . that the acquisition of verbalizable knowledge (often referred to as insight) constitutes the essence of the psychoanalytic cure—'the talking cure' " (p. 56). Kohut insists that in speaking this way "I am not demeaning knowledge and truth values" (p. 58), just removing them from their "disproportionately exalted position—alone at the pinnacle of his [Freud's] value hierarchy" (p. 58) and "emphasizing . . . that other important values exist—values that may at times occupy a rank as high or even higher than those concerning the facing of truth and the search for knowledge" (p. 58).

Accurate as this characterization of the essential core of classical psychoanalysis may or may not be, it is never made clear throughout Kohut's text how it is more—or less—moralistic to espouse Freud's search for truth and knowledge as the central treatment and health value, than it is to espouse Kohut's search for his analysand's untrammeled fulfillment of his nuclear program in terms of his ambitions, his values and ideals, and the intermediate tension arc of talents and skills that connects these twin poles of the self. Nonetheless, Kohut strongly asserts that the derived technical prescriptions of *classical* analysis lead to a moralistically tinged "confrontation posture" (p. 72), with reliance on "inappropriate and incorrect confrontation . . . [rather than on] appropriate and correct understanding" (p. 74); that classical analysis is "steeped in a morality-tinged theory about the therapeutic centrality of truth-facing that is interwoven with a comparably morality-tinged scientific model about the need to make the unconscious conscious" (p. 141); that "interpretation can only be truly analytic . . . if it is given without the hidden moral and educational pressure that is *unavoidable* as long as the traditional emphasis on drive primacy, the infant's helplessness, and

the pejorative connotation of the concept of narcissism are retained"
(p. 210, italics added); and that finally, even if the formulations of ego
psychology could be stripped of their moralizing, that they would anyway
be insufficient since "they do not allow us to formulate in a satisfactory
way those crucial attributes of the psyche as it moves toward health:
the capacity for self-soothing, the sense of the continuity of the self in
time, and the crucial role of the selfobject in providing the opportunity
for the acquisition of these attributes" (p. 65). In the light of all the
foregoing, it will come as no surprise that self psychology accords insight
a far lesser place in the curative scheme of things than does classical
analysis. Kohut says,

> the self psychologically informed analyst holds that with regard to *all forms*
> of analyzable psychopathology the basic therapeutic unit of the psycho-
> analytic cure does not rest on the expansion of cognition. (It does not rest,
> for example, on the analysand's becoming aware of the difference between
> his fantasy and reality, especially with reference to transference distortions
> involving projected drives.) Rather, it is the accretion of psychic structure
> via an optimal frustration of the analysand's needs or wishes that is provided
> for the analysand in the form of correct interpretations that constitutes the
> essence of the cure. (p. 108, italics added)

This is a cure affected with or without concomitant insight, it should be
added.

Within the framework of this conceptualization of the essential
ingredients of classical analysis, and with his own downplaying of the
centrality of conflict resolution via interpretation and working through
leading to insight as the standard hallmarks of the proper psychoanalytic
process, the various other perspectives that Kohut advances through
this book all fall into place. The centrality of the Oedipus complex as
the organizing nodal point of character formation —or deformation—
is gone. Rather than an Oedipus complex and its attendant anxieties
with which we all have to come to terms individually, we have only an
oedipal phase which the "healthy child of healthy parents enters . . .
joyfully . . . [since] this achievement elicits a glow of empathic joy and
pride from the side of the oedipal-phase selfobjects" (p. 14). It is this
kind of oedipal phase that is declared to be ubiquitous or rather normative and it is castration anxiety derived from the neurotic Oedipus
complex that "should be considered pathological" (p. 14).[5] Such path-

---

5. Kohut distinguishes (1) the oedipal stage, a 'joyfully experienced step of normal
development', (2) the Oedipus complex, a set of 'pathologically altered experiences of
the child', (3) the oedipal period, a 'time limited phase in the life of the child', consisting
of 'normal or pathological experiences', and (4) the oedipal phase, 'to stress the devel-
opmental-maturational regularity of this period' (all on p. 214).

ological formation of an Oedipus complex "arises in response to the defective empathy of the child's parents, that is, in response to the flaws in a selfobject matrix that does not sustain the child" (p. 16), which leads then to "the disintegration of the healthy oedipal self, character-ized by affectionate and assertive attitudes . . . [with the taking over by] the fragmented oedipal self, characterized by sexual and destructive fantasies and impulses" (p. 16).

Along with the Oedipus complex, drives in general then become secondary pathogenic phenomena, for example, "my views concerning . . . the *secondary* nature of phenomena (lust and destructiveness) that are traditionally considered primary" (p. 12, italics added). The analysis of conflict also becomes less important: "Thus, although self psychology does not disregard psychic conflict and analyzes it when it presents itself in the transference, it does so only as a preliminary step on the way to what it considers the essential task of therapeutic analysis: the explo-ration, in its dynamic and genetic dimensions, of the flaws in the struc-ture of the self via the analysis of the selfobject transferences" (p. 41). From this, it follows concomitantly that defenses and resistances are equally diminished in import. They are, after all, only "mechanisms . . . that are intrinsic to a drive-psychological/ego-psychological orientation . . . [and] are necessarily restricted in their explanatory power by the confining influence of the moralistic framework provided by the 'pleas-ure principle' . . . and the 'reality principle' " (p. 114). They are thus "less important today than they once were and should no longer be construed as centrally important to theory and practice. They are, to be sure, still important for the beginning student who undertakes his first analyses under supervision" (p. 115).[6] Somewhat further on, Kohut

---

6. This same condescending tone emerges at a number of other places in Kohut's book as well. For example, in another place when talking of resistance and defence in the context of a case vignette, Kohut says, "Occasionally, rarely, he [the self psychologist] might for a moment pay attention to the details of a mental mechanism that may be discernible—like a master pianist who will for a moment think of finger positions and the like. But on the whole, this is not the self psychologist's interest any longer. Like the pianist who devotes all his attention to the conception of the work he performs and to the artistic message it transmits, so also the experienced self psychologically informed analyst: the details recede as he scrutinizes the gradual strengthening of his patient's self and the selfobject factors that enhance or hinder his development" (p. 143). And this tone enlarges to encompass a wide transcendent imperialism by analogy when at another place (of theoretical exposition) Kohut declares, "The relationship between traditional analysis and analytic self psychology may thus be seen to parallel the relationship between the physics of Newton (who explored the macrocosm) and the physics of Planck (who explored the atomic and subatomic particles that form the microstructures)" (pp. 41–42).

talks of the "so-called defense-resistances [that] are neither defenses nor resistances" (p. 141), and then still further on declares that the "resistances" (now put in quotation marks) are properly interpreted by the "self psychologically informed analyst as healthy psychic activities, in all their ramifications, because they safeguard the analysand's self for future growth" (p. 148). Within this context it becomes no surprise, albeit startling in its flatfootedness, that "the conflicts evoked by this type of aggression [object-directed aggressiveness] (e.g., guilt or an unstable equilibrium between currents of fondness and anger) are *not constitutive of psychopathology*, however severe they might be, but part and parcel of *normal* human experience. The role of narcissistic rage, however, is keenly appreciated by the self psychologically informed psychoanalyst" (p. 138, italics added).

All of this leads ineluctably to Kohut's final placement of the phenomena of the classical psychoneuroses heretofore explained essentially in terms of the classical conflict psychology paradigm of so-called "traditional analysis," their placement in a subordinate relationship to the phenomena of the narcissistic disorders around which Kohut and his followers have erected the theories of self psychology as a psychology of deficit and its repair rather than of conflict and its resolution.[7] Throughout this last book by Kohut, it becomes increasingly clear that the self psychological understanding and technical approach has long been felt to have transcended its origins as a special theory and technique fashioned specifically for the treatment of the narcissistic disorders while leaving the field of the traditional psychoneuroses to the understandings of classical ego psychology as was the original wont of the self psychology writings. For example

> Self psychology is now attempting to demonstrate . . . that all forms of psychopathology are based either on defects in the structure of the self, on distortions of the self, or on weakness of the self. It is trying to show, furthermore, that all these flaws in the self are due to disturbances of self-selfobject relationships in childhood. Stated in the obverse, by way of highlighting the contrast between self psychological and traditional theory, self psychology holds that pathogenic conflicts in the object–instinctual realm—that is, pathogenic conflicts in the realm of object love and object

---

7. For an extended discussion of this fundamental issue of the meaning of this distinction postulated by Kohut between classical psychoanalysis as a psychology of conflict and self psychology as a psychology of defect or deficiency, and of the profoundly divisive impact that this (to me) fundamentally flawed conceptualization of the nature of the psychoanalytic enterprise has upon our science, see Wallerstein, 1981, pp. 388–390, and Wallerstein, 1983a, pp. 561–575, especially pp. 568–575.

hate and in particular the set of conflicts called the Oedipus complex—
are not the *primary* cause of psychopathology but its result. (p. 53)

The so-called transference neuroses thereby become "analyzable *self*
disturbances in the wider sense" (p. 80, italics added) and it follows
that "the specific therapeutic approach of self psychology should also
be employed in the analysis of these disorders . . . [since] the oedipal
neuroses are to be conceptualized as specific disturbances of the self,
that is, as arising in consequence of flaws in the selfobject functions of
the surroundings of the child during the oedipal stage of development"
(p. 91).

Put most boldly (and baldly) in summary, Kohut states,

> [I want to] underline . . . the fact that . . . the theory of therapeutic care
> that I am presenting (1) does not apply only to the analysis of analyzable
> self disorders (in the narrow sense) but to the analysis of *all* analyzable
> disorders and (2) does not apply only to analyses that are conducted by
> self psychologically informed psychoanalysts but to all analyses, past and
> present, in which transferences were interpreted and worked through. (p. 110)

So much for my now detailed ordering (or reordering) and expli-
cating the logic of Kohut's argument in this final book of his, the self
psychological statement of how analysis is said to cure. Does it indeed
compel major distinguishable differences in how self psychologists think
clinically and what they do clinically as compared with the analyses
carried on in accord with the theory and technique of classical analysis?
Clearly, I have constructed my own exposition explicitly to highlight
differences, with all of the explicit and implicit implications that those
differences have for clinical practice, for actual clinical therapeutic doing.
Yet my own main thesis here is that the various critics of self psychology,
whether sympathetic or otherwise, have for the most part focused the
main thrust of their critical argument improperly on an inessential, and
perhaps a not even very significant, set of differences, while leaving
undeveloped the real issue of the place of the self psychological clinical
approach as a theoretical variant—and a real *variant*—of standard, or
classical, psychoanalytic theory and technique.

What do I mean by the issue of a misplaced (and largely incorrect)
emphasis in so many of the critical assessments of the kind of departure
of self psychological analytic work from that characterizing mainstream
or classical analysis? As an excellent case example (but it is only one
of many), I will take Frederic Levine's (1979) elegant disquisition on
the clinical application of self psychology based upon the close reading
of the six cases in Goldberg's *Casebook* (1978). Levine outlined five

major criticisms that had been variously made of the clinical implications of Kohut's views: (1) that self psychological treatment depends upon the overlooking of conflict, or its suppression by encouraging patients to intellectualize, or through other ego-supportive tactics; (2) that it lends spurious confirmation to patients' neurotic fantasies of defect or weakness by accepting as valid statements of reality their feelings of deficit and fears of loss of control; (3) that mirroring and idealizing transferences are gratified rather than analyzed; (4) that certain conflicts and fantasies around aggressive impulses are especially overlooked and unanalyzed; and (5) that certain mental contents like dreams and fantasies are too often dealt with at a manifest and literal level. Overall this is declared to add up to a psychotherapeutic rather than a psychoanalytic treatment, albeit a psychoanalytically oriented psychotherapy (Levine, 1979, p. 4). Through the subsequent pages of his article, Levine documents significant instances of each of these psychoanalytic failings culled from the Casebook reports. And he concludes that the charges against self psychology are substantially supported, that though "a number of these patients achieved very impressive gains in treatment" (Levine, p. 17) that these are psychotherapeutic rather than psychoanalytic results, that the "progress was not usually seen in qualitative modifications of inner processes, but typically in gradual, quantitative shifts in adaptive functioning and defense effectiveness" (Levine, p. 17)— though he fails to specify how he could possibly have arrived at this finely differentiated judgment. In any case, Levine ends by declaring that "Such [psychotherapeutic] methods perform important functions when appropriate, but they are not comparable to or interchangeable with psychoanalysis" (p. 17).

My own position on this issue differs quite fundamentally. For the purposes of this critique of Kohut's third book within the context of this chapter, I have looked again through the Goldberg *Casebook* (1978), as well as Kohut's (1979) case of the two analyses of Mr. Z—about which I had previously written at length (Wallerstein, 1981)—and have also studied a long clinical article by Paul Tolpin (1983) spelling out in considerable process-note detail the vicissitudes of an idealizing transference over at least a 2½ year analytic span. In one sense my reaction to all of this is on all fours with Levine's: enough clinical interchange is given in these various case accounts so that examples can indeed be found, and at times seemingly egregious examples, of each and every kind of supportive psychotherapeutic activity that Levine—and others before him—have adumbrated.

However, that to me is not the real crux of the matter. Mainstream psychoanalysis, including the effort at even the purest kind of classical analysis can equally be faulted (if that is the correct word) in exactly the same way, and perhaps often enough to a similar extent. Here I speak not specifically from my own cumulative experience, professional observation, and professional exchange with colleagues, but in a more general and more solidly documented way from the work and experience of The Psychotherapy Research Project of The Menninger Foundation. This project comprised an intensive and comprehensive study, over a total 30-year span, of the treatment careers and the subsequent follow-up life careers of a cohort of 42 patients, half in psychoanalysis proper and half in intensive and equally long-term psychoanalytic psychotherapy, and has been written up in final overall clinical accounting in my book, *Forty-Two Lives in Treatment* (Wallerstein, 1986). In a summary paper abstracting the principal conclusions of that book (Wallerstein, 1983b), I recapitulate the detailed clinical documentation from the Menninger project that the postulated distinctive therapeutic modalities of psychoanalysis and of analytically informed and guided expressive and supportive psychotherapies hardly exist in anywhere near ideal or pure form in the real world of actual clinical practice; that real psychoanalytic treatments in actual practice are inextricably intermingled blends of more-or-less expressive–interpretive and more-or-less supportive–stabilizing elements; and that almost all treatments (including even presumably pure psychoanalyses) carry more supportive elements than originally intended, and these supportive elements account for substantially more of the changes achieved than had been originally anticipated. Put another way, I am saying that the same kind of fine psychoanalytic scrutiny that Levine has directed towards the case reports of Goldberg's *Casebook,* would probably yield an equally significant harvest of discerned psychotherapeutic activities, were it directed toward any comparably detailed case material assembled from more classical or traditional psychoanalytic sources. Whether there would be distinguishable differences in amount or kind of supportive therapeutic interventions in the one sample as compared with the other, as well there may be, I think is nonetheless still a largely unexplored empirical question, not an *ex cathedra* or *a priori* judgment that can be made today with any certainty.

Given this position on the status of self psychological analytic work qua analysis as analysis, which is admittedly not the prevailing view in critical psychoanalytic circles, what do *I* then see as the significant difference in what self psychology professes and actually does and how do I then place it within the psychoanalytic scheme of things? Here I can again take my point of departure from within Kohut's own text, material from which I will use to highlight my own sharply different conclusions as to how and where self psychology ought best fit in relation to the total psychoanalytic corpus. I start here with Kohut's account (pp. 92ff) of an interchange with a Kleinian colleague from Latin America who told him how she had responded interpretively to a patient's silent withdrawal from the analytic work in the hour immediately after notification of the planned cancellation of a session in the near future. The interpretation had followed the presumed standard Kleinian format, that the patient's basic perception of the analyst had been abruptly altered by the announcement, that the analyst had shifted from being a good, warm, feeding breast to becoming a bad, cold, withholding one, and that the patient had responded with sadistic rage against the analyst qua bad breast, a rage that was defended against through a general inhibition, with a particular inhibition of oral activity, of "biting words."

Kohut, in his account, expressed surprise that this (to him) "far-fetched interpretation" (p. 92), albeit given in a "warmly understanding tone of voice" (p. 92) nonetheless elicited a very favourable response from the patient. He went on to say that the analyst could equally have couched an interpretation within classical ego psychological, conflict–drive–defence terms (the cancellation experienced as an abandonment by the oedipal mother locking the child–patient out of the parental bedroom), or, for that matter, within self psychological terms (the loss of a self sustaining selfobject leaving the patient feeling empty and not fully alive). Since the amount of clinical context afforded Kohut here was insufficient to decide which interpretation would be closest to the mark in this instance, he settled for calling all three, examples of "wild analysis." The lesson that Kohut drew from the favourable response however was that though the (Kleinian) *content* of the interpretation may have been wrong, off the mark, it was nonetheless a therapeutically effective "inexact interpretation" in Glover's (1931) sense, since it was "in its essence more right than wrong" (p. 97) since the analyst was conveying (indeed in any one of the three alternative interpretive forms presented, could have been conveying) her understanding that the patient was sorely troubled over the announced cancellation and was understandably reacting unhappily to it. One should however add here that despite the tone at this point of an evenhanded receptivity to any of the three proffered alternative interpretive routes, depending on the explication of the missing clinical context, it is only fair to say that the entire balance of Kohut's whole book, as demonstrated in my numerous quotations from it in this chapter, is bent to the service of his thesis that self psychology, from its central focus on the vicissitudes of the establishment of the coherent and cohesive self, provides by far the best supraordinate and overarching framework within which *this* clinical encounter as well as the total psychoanalytic process can and should be best conceptualized, including even those occasions when such "secondary phenomena" as oedipal anxiety or secondary "disintegration products" like fragmented drive or defence manifestations do come to the interpretive fore.

That is, Kohut has self-consciously followed a path that can now be clearly traced across his three books in the development of self psychology as a separate "movement" or "school" within psychoanalysis, just as Kleinian analysis is, the kind of "separate kingdom" that Segal (1981, p. 470) so much decried; a new theory and a new metapsychology for psychoanalytic work, in all the ramifications of the psychology of the self in the broader sense, a psychology founded on concepts of deficit and repair of deficit, rather than on conflict and its resolution, and including all the theoretical ramifications in the conception of the bipolar self and the special and separate new psychology of Tragic Man. This is a perspective on self psychology that I have already noted and documented at considerable length in my earlier paper of theoretical critique (Wallerstein, 1983a). I will only add here that this third book definitively completes that self chosen task of separate theoretical creation.

Seen in this way, what self psychology does that is different in its practice is to carry the psychoanalytic interpretive task within a clearly very different (self psychological) theoretical perspective, again just as Kleinian analysis interprets within its clearly differing theoretical perspective. And for the rest of us, that is, for the mainstream of classical psychoanalysis, our task is to come to terms with the self psychology variant school as another way to try to do proper and good psychoanalytic work within our overall disciplinary and scientific framework, to live with it, and to learn from its special clinical emphases and clinical insights—its highlighting of the mirroring, idealizing, and alter ego transferences and the specific countertransferences that they characteristically evoke—just as we have to come to terms with, to live with, and to learn from, our Kleinian colleagues.

I cannot end, however, without pointing out that another developmental path has all along been available to self psychology, one that I can only wish it had followed. It is simply the alternative route that I have described in detail in both my prior papers on self psychology (Wallerstein, 1981, 1983a) as the path of both/and, rather than Kohut's—and self psychology's—either/or. To quote from the most concisely pertinent section of my 1983 theoretical critique,

> Let us grant that Kohut's central clinical contribution may well be in seeing so many aspects of the psychopathology of pregenital development, not as regressive defences against the emergence of oedipal transferences *alone*, but also as recreations of deficient and impoverished childhood constellations within mirroring and idealizing selfobject transferences. Granted all this, it is the qualifying word "alone," that is to me the crux of this particular issue. For in the flow and flux of analytic material we are always in the world of "both/and." We deal constantly, and in turn, both with the oedipal, where there is a coherent self, and the preoedipal, where there may not yet be; with defensive regressions and with developmental arrests; with defensive transferences and defensive resistances and with recreations of earlier traumatic and traumatized states. (1983a, p. 564).

What I said there was of course not new; it was simply the application once again of the psychoanalytic principle of overdetermination, and in Waelder's (1936) terms, of multiple function.

This same argument about the unnecessary and, even more, the therapeutically deleterious consequences created by self psychology's positing a theoretical dichotomy between developmental and structural defects on the one hand and dynamic conflict on the other has been put equally sharply by Morris Eagle (1984) in his current very comprehensive book critically evaluating in a thoughtful and balanced way the recent decades of theoretical development in psychoanalysis, prominent as one among them, the growth of self psychology as both a clinical emphasis and a theory formation. To quote Eagle, "structural defects and dynamic conflict are [but] *different aspects* of and entail different perspectives on a *continuing* set of complex phenomena" (p. 128, italics added). And, "for Freud, neurosis is not simply a dynamic conflict between fully intact structures . . . but is, from one vantage point, *also a developmental failure.* . . . Part and parcel of early traumas which presumably led to developmental impairments and structural defects are conflict-laden wishes, longings, and other *affective reactions*" (p. 129). And again, "The fact is that we have intense reactions (e.g., rage) to experiences of trauma and deprivation and that we are most conflicted in the areas in which we are deprived. . . . It is precisely the person deprived of love who is most conflicted about giving and receiving love" (p. 130). Which leads to the technical therapeutic prescription,

> whatever the level of one's constitutional or historically endowed degree of ego strength or self-cohesiveness, unresolved conflict and accompanying anxiety weaken the personality, and the resolution of conflict and decreases in anxiety strengthen the personality. . . . I strongly suspect that for all patients help in the recognition and resolution of conflicts is a primary means of promoting increased feelings of intactness and self-cohesiveness." (p. 135)

Had this path, that I and Eagle and others have indicated, been accepted by self psychology, we might today be in a different position, not only of enrichment of the clinical capabilities of classical psychoanalysis through the heightened awareness of the archaically anchored mirroring and idealizing and alter ego transferences (and their counterpart countertransferences) with their graduated transmutation into more mature form variants in response to appropriately empathic interpretation, which indeed I trust has been the response of psychoanalysis to the clinical insights of Kohut and his coworkers—but along with it the real integration of these clinical insights from the self psychological perspective as a potent addition and emphasis *within* the ever-growing mainstream of classical psychoanalysis, not outside it. In that case we would have grown together and what the mainstream psychoanalysts and the self psychology informed analysts do—and how they conceptualize it—would hardly be different at all, a matter perhaps of some emphasis rather than significant substance. As Rangell (1981) put it: "The 'Two Analyses of Mr. Z' reported by Kohut (1979) would have [I would modify that to should have] comprised one total classical analysis" (p. 133). I trust that I have by now given my own best answer to the question posed implicitly in the title of this chapter. How does, or rather, how *should* self psychology differ in practice?

REFERENCES

Eagle, M. (1984). *Recent Developments in Psychoanalysis: A Critical Evaluation.* New York: McGraw Hill.

Glover, E. (1931). The therapeutic effect of inexact interpretation: A contribution to the theory of suggestion. *International Journal of Psychoanalysis,* 12:397–411.

Goldberg, A., ed. (1978). *The Psychology of the Self: A Casebook.* New York: International Universities Press.

Kohut, H. (1971). *The Analysis of the Self: A Systematic Approach to the Psychoanalytic*

Treatment of Narcissistic Personality Disorders. New York: International Universities Press.

Kohut, H. (1977). *The Restoration of the Self.* New York: International Universities Press.

Kohut, H. (1979). The two analyses of Mr. A. *International Journal of Psychoanalysis,* 60:3–27.

Kohut, H. (1984). How Does Analysis Cure? A. Goldberg, ed., with P. Stepansky. Chicago & London: University of Chicago Press.

Levine, F.J. (1979). On the clinical application of Kohut's psychology of the self: Comments on some recently published case studies. *Journal of the Philadelphia Association for Psychoanalysis,* 6: 1–19.

Rangell, L. (1981). From insight to change. *Journal of the American Psychoanalytic Association,* 29:119–141.

Segel, N.P. (1981). Narcissism and adaptation to indignity. *International Journal of Psychoanalysis,* 62:465–476.

Tolpin, P.H. (1983). A change in the self: The development and transformation of an idealizing transference. *International Journal of Psychoanalysis,* 64:461–483.

Waelder, R. (1936). The principle of multiple function: Observations on overdetermination. *Psychoanalytic Quarterly,* 5:45–62.

Wallerstein, R.S. (1981). The bipolar self: Discussion of alternative perspectives. *Journal of the American Psychoanalytic Association,* 29:377–394.

Wallerstein, R.S. (1983a). Self psychology and "classical" psychoanalytic psychology: The nature of their relationship. Psychoanalysis and Contemporary Thought, 6:553–595. Also in A. Goldberg, ed., *The Future of Psychoanalysis* (pp. 19–63). New York: International Universities Press.

Wallerstein, R.S. (1983b, Oct.). Psychoanalysis and psychotherapy: Relative roles reconsidered. Presented as a plenary address at the Boston Psychoanalytic Society and Institute, Boston.

Wallerstein, R.S. (1986). *Forty-Two Lives in Treatment: A Study of Psychoanalysis and Psychotherapy.* New York: Guilford Press.

7

Discrepancies between Analysand and Analyst in Experiencing the Analysis

ERNEST S. WOLF

I

It has been stated by contemporary philosophical authorities that there can be no single absolute reality. Indeed, philosophers tell us that the worlds around us and inside of us that we perceive as real are constructions, a kind of invention within the limits set by our individual constitution, by our societal role, and by our past experiences. The same disturbing view has also been repeated by some of our most perceptive modern poets. T. S. Eliot (1930, p. 60) said, "what is actual is actual only for one time / and only for one place" ("Ash Wednesday"). The so-called reality of our inner mental life, especially the whole world of unconscious thinking, feeling, and fantasizing that psychoanalysis claims to have discovered is thought by many to be the product of our overheated imaginations. Moreover, in the psychoanalytic situation we have the experience quite often that the reality that we as psychoanalysts perceive so clearly, seems utterly strange, if not insane, to some of our patients and vice versa. Are we then justified in holding any strong opinion or firm beliefs if there is no correct and true reality in which to anchor our perceptions? To find oneself adrift in a world where nothing is reliably true and nothing can be proved to be false is an unsettling experience at best. We are told that reality is something that we construct as part of the process of trying to know the world inside us and around us. As psychoanalysts we must make a choice, indeed, we must continuously choose, among the innumerable and constantly changing realities that we are able to construct from the analytic data. Whose reality and which kind of reality are we experiencing, constructing, and addressing in the analytic situation?

Michels (1985) outlined three views of reality that traditionally have governed psychoanalytic constructions. All three recognize that we can say nothing about reality per se, whether outer or inner, except that through the *act of knowing* it we create a version of reality that appears to us as real at that moment. To this creation we bring the distortions introduced by the very nature of our perceptual apparatus, the distortions introduced by our wishes, fears, and conflicts whether they are conscious or unconscious, and, I would add, the distortions introduced by deficits in structure that impair optimal functioning of our creative processes.

In harmony with Kant, whom Freud studied with his teacher, the philosopher Brentano, Freud learned to view reality as being outside the experience of knowing it, that is, in essence as unknowable. We can postulate a reality outside of us that codetermines our experience but is not part of it. There is an external material world from which we derive something with which we create perceptions that give us a sense of an external reality. There is also a deep inner reality from which we derive something with which we create wishes that give us a sense of an inner reality. The fusion of these two realities of perceptions and wishes creates an image of subjective experience that we usually call psychic reality. According to Michels (1985) psychoanalysis has viewed this psychic reality from three perspectives: (1) by focusing on the external reality component and attempting to correct so-called distortions, or (2) by focusing on the inner sources of wishes, fantasies and so forth, and freeing them from repressions, disavowals, and other constraints, or (3) by focusing on the psychic reality itself, that is, on the infinite variety of subjective inner experiences.

Along with Michels (1985), I prefer the latter approach. We define a psychoanalytic reality that we construct via psychoanalytic theories and psychoanalytic methods with the aim of helping patients reconstruct their personal subjective reality. Our views of reality, like our theories, are neither true nor false, but either more or less useful. The variety of psychoanalytic theories are not to be taken as definitive statements about man or his mind, according to Michels, but as guidelines for constructing a psychoanalytic reality. What makes a theory psychoanalytic? A useful criterion is whether it guides us—and our analysands—to new insights and understanding within our chosen field of observation. Of course, with Kohut (1959), we would define and restrict the field we call psychoanalysis by the method we use to obtain data, that is, the field where we can obtain data by introspection and empathy.

These considerations about psychoanalytic reality give us an appropriate framework for considering the clinical problems that as analysts we face in the daily task of helping our analysands construct a version of reality. How do we go about constructing such a psychoanalytic reality when we engage in the psychoanalytic process with our analysands? What are the methods for arriving at this psychoanalytic reality? What are the criteria we use to select an appropriate reality for ourselves as well as our analysands as we are confronted with innumerable possible reality constructions? And, most important, how do we manage to communicate with our analyands whose reality may be and usually is quite different from ours?

The construction of an appropriate analytic reality, in my view, must be in harmony not only with the analyst's perceptions of his own inner and outer realities but must also be a version of reality that includes in its process of knowing the subjectivities of others, and especially, of course, that of the analysand. In other words, the psychoanalytic reality we construct must contain aspects of the reality experience of each of the two participants. Arnold Goldberg (1984) has proposed that analyst and analysand negotiate a shared reality. How do analyst and analysand negotiate such a shared reality?

II

The concept of an ostensive insight was introduced into psychoanalysis by the philosopher Jerome Richfield 30 years ago, but has rarely been made reference to in discussions of psychoanalytic reality. Richfield (1954) pointed out that we need to differentiate knowledge by *acquaintance* from knowledge by *description*. Knowledge by acquaintance is knowledge obtained without logical dependence upon any inferential process or other knowledge of facts. For example, I have knowledge of both morphine and alcohol. I know that one is a bitter, white crystalline narcotic base; the other, I know to be a colorless, volatile, inflammable liquid that is intoxicating. Beyond this my knowledge of the two substances is no longer comparable. Of alcohol I have actually experienced the effects: I have knowledge by direct acquaintance. This is specific knowledge that no amount of discourse on the effects of alcohol could produce. I have no such direct cognitive experience of the effects of morphine and what I know about it is known to me only by analogy and inference. Richfield introduced the term "ostensive" for knowledge acquired by direct acquaintance with events that have occurred to a person.

Richfield's distinction between ostensive and descriptive knowledge is of great importance because it helps us to clarify some crucial clinical issues. By definition psychoanalysis deals with the data of inner experience that we call psychic reality and our access to these data via introspection and empathy clearly marks our knowledge of psychic reality as an ostensive process, that is, a process of knowing data by direct acquaintance. To be sure, when we are theorizing we can describe and talk about psychic reality as if it were something out there in the world; but the clinical meaning of the data of psychoanalysis can only be grasped ostensively by direct experience. In fact, that is what we mean by posing introspection and empathy as defining and delimiting the field of psychoanalysis. Therefore, I would suggest that the new analytic reality constructed during a psychoanalysis by an analysand with the help of the analyst can be different from the version of reality that he brought into the analysis only to the extent that it was constructed out of *ostensive* knowledge acquired during analysis. *Descriptive* knowledge provided by the analyst will be effective only if it leads the analysand to experience something new, in other words, if it leads to direct acquaintance with subjectivities that become part of the process of constructing the new version of reality. Mutative insights—a concept introduced many years ago by James Strachey (1934)— consequently must be not merely descriptive insights, they must be ostensive insights. This means, for example, that interpretations made by the analyst will have little mutative power to effect changes in the analysand if these interpretations merely describe something that is going on, that is, if they do nothing more than convey information to the analysand. In order to have the power to effect changes the interpretation must lead to an ostensive experience that is new and that usually comes as a surprise to the analysand, and, perhaps, also to the analyst. Quite obviously, if the interpretation concerns a person who is emotionally very important, who also happens to be present in the room at the time, and who is himself making the interpretation, then there is much greater likelihood of a direct experience than if the interpretation concerns somebody far away in time and space, such as a deceased and well-mourned relative.

Considerations of this kind give some support to the contentions of those, like Merton Gill (1982), who stress the primacy of transference interpretations over extratransference interpretations. However, it would be a mistake to conclude that transference interpretations are always superior to extratransference interpretations. The decisive question is not whether the interpretation is intraanalytic or extraanalytic, or about the transference or displaced from the transference, but whether an interpretation leads to new knowledge by direct acquaintance, that is, is experienced as ostensive, rather than being descriptively about something. Thus in many analyses, and often for a long time, defenses against the transference and defenses against being aware of the transference make transference interpretations quite useless because they are experienced as descriptive and not ostensive. Early in the analysis, therefore, extratransference interpretations concerning immediate and highly charged extraanalytic relationships are likely to be experienced as more ostensive and direct, and therefore are likely to be more effective until resistance to awareness of the transference has diminished enough to make transference interpretations optimally profitable. Indeed, one could define the task of the analyst in the analytic situation as bringing about new ostensive knowledge through the skillful use of interpretations. Though this sounds at first very much like the time-honored prescription of insight through interpretation, I think I have made it clear that mere information is not enough but a lived experience is required.

I am not advocating a return to Alexander's (1961) "corrective emotional experience" either. Actually, the experience of an ostensive truth in a present relationship is something totally different from experiencing a role played by the analyst, as advocated by Alexander. Alexander (1961) hoped the patient would experience the analyst as different from the way he experienced his parents in childhood and toward this end Alexander would purposefully try to be different than he understood the patient's parents to have been. Alexander attempted to play an emotional role that would be different from the emotional role of the parent and thereby become a corrective emotional experience. In contrast, the ostensive, direct experiences that I am suggesting as a necessary part of mutative interpretations are effective not because the analyst is so different from the parent but because these ostensive experiences lead to new constructions of reality *in spite* of the fact that the analyst is experienced momentarily as being just as frustrating, distant, and nonunderstanding as the parent was. Such new reality constructions are indeed most useful because the ostensive experience with the analyst is so very much like the archaic experience with the parent. In this new situation, however, the self of the analysand is stronger than in childhood and more capable of constructing a new reality in harmony with his own self structure instead of being forced to accept the parent's reality as his own. The analyst is different from the parent of childhood in his empathic understanding of the analysand's legitimate and inevitable need to experience the analyst's minor and even trivial empathic failures as excruciating and often humiliating traumas. Thus, the major significant difference between the traumatic archaic experience with the caretakers of early childhood and the therapeutic quality of the here-and-now experience with the analyst is the latter's acceptance of the analysand and of his experience as a legitimate experience among many possible legitimate experiences. To accept the analysand's experience as legitimate does not require that the analyst have the same experience. Nor does it require of the analyst that he approve or agree with the analysand in his thoughts, fantasies, wishes, or plans. All that it requires of the analyst is that he recognize, understand, and accept the patient's experience of the patient's reality as a given without having to accept the patient's reality as his own reality. On the contrary, as I will discuss below, the discrepancy between the analyst's and the analysand's experiences are the proper material for the interpretive work that accepts and explains both experiences as legitimately occurring. The calamity of childhood trauma that rejects the child's experience as "bad" results in the substitution of what Winnicott (1950) called a "false self" for the child's own "true self."

To summarize, the analyst's reality is experienced by the analysand often as just as strange and frightening as the child experienced the parent's reality. However, in childhood this *difference* in what is real cannot be accepted or even negotiated—neither by the child nor by the parent—though somebody's view had to prevail. Usually this means that the parent's experience of reality is right and the child's is wrong, with traumatic consequences for both. In the analytic situation, optimally, no such right and wrong exist, and any number of realities can be constructed, coexist, and be accepted by both.

III

How do new psychic realities come into being in psychoanalysis? I believe the most frequent and the most effective opening for constructing a new analytic reality occurs when a discrepancy exists between the analyst's experience of the analytic situation and that of the analysand. Inevitably, analyst and analysand interact with each other; and inevitably, they experience this interaction differently. Much as the analyst might attempt to understand correctly the patient's experience of an intervention—let us say an interpretation—the analyst, even the most unbiased analyst informed by empathy and guided by the most appropriate theory, will, sooner or later, misunderstand the patient's experience and misconceive the patient's mental processes. Clearly, one may guess at or infer another's version of reality but one cannot know it. Analogously, the patient will inevitably misunderstand the analyst, misjudge the analyst's experience of the patient, misconstrue the analyst's intentions, and misread the analyst's real misunderstandings into an exaggerated half-truth–half-fiction to fit the patient's previously learned experience. Misunderstanding is inevitable because two people perceive the same situation with differing points of view from different vantage points with different affective reactions and therefore have a different experience of what is going on. It is not a question of who is right and who is wrong. They both are. It is the discrepancy in subjectivities that matters and must be analyzed, that is, must be understood by both. One may hope, perhaps, that the analyst's experience is less determined "by a concealed repetition of earlier experiences and relationships" (Sandler, 1976, p. 39)—after all, he has been analyzed—and more by the mutual goals of the here-and-now situation than that of the analysand. Even so, there is little room for either participant in the analytic situation to claim superiority for his experience over that of the other. Since the purpose of the analysis is to analyze the analysand one has to *start* with analyzing the patient's experience of the analyst and of the analytic situation, that is, the analytic ambience as experienced by the analysand. Therefore, in clinical practice, it becomes incumbent upon the analyst first to accept and confirm the patient's experience as legitimately occurring before proceeding to understand it and to subject it (and the patient) to a dissecting kind of scrutiny. To start by questioning another's experience per se, for example, to suggest he is "really feeling or thinking something else," is to question another's sanity or honesty. When this is done, albeit inadvertently and with the best of intentions, by the authority represented by the analyst, the effect is often devastating on the analysand and the analysis. Such obvious technical errors occur more often than we usually care to admit and can be largely prevented by incorporating in our clinical theories the fact that our conceptualizations describe the relationship between two distinctly different experiences, that is, two distinctly different versions of reality.

Most discussions of psychoanalytic treatment focus attention only on what is going on within the patient, on the patient's psychodynamics. References to the "actual situation" acknowledge that the patient has perceptions that are not transference of genetic material, that is, not necessarily caused by the archaic psychodynamics of early childhood though transferences may, of course, influence the way the present actuality is experienced. While it is certainly correct to talk about the "actual situation" and to discuss the interaction between patient and analyst as resulting in a new experience for the patient, many discussions of the analytic process do not mention that the analyst also is experiencing something, indeed, something that is markedly different from the patient's experience. This discrepancy between the analyst's and the analysand's experiences can easily become the major pivot around which the analysis may either be derailed or moved forward. Our tradition of logical positivism makes us hesitate to leave the safe ground of being the objective observer of interactions and interrelationships. We fear we will contaminate the purity of our scientific observations by personal bias and by the unconscious projection of our unresolved conflicts if we allow ourselves to become involved as participants rather than just commenting observers. We know, of course, that we are active participants in the analytic relationship, whether we like it or not, and we might even admit, if pressed to it, that we participate in accord with our personality and that our experience of this participation is affective as well as cognitive. In much analytic writing one gets no real whiff or taste of this affective participation, no allusions to our participating subjectivity but only the image of the objectively observing scientist. Beyond the formal acknowledgment of their importance we usually hear little about the nature of the experiences of either analyst or analysand. Thus what is experienced by both participants in this uniquely evocative analytic situation, which determines to a large extent the course of the analytic endeavor, remains a peripheral issue rather than becoming the center of our attention in elucidating transference and countertransference possibilities. The intersubjective aspects of the interactions have not yet become scientifically respectable data and one often hears these aspects of the work of an analyst referred to as the art of doing analysis for which tact is required.

In a different context I have described some of the common interactive reactions of analyst and analysand to each other:

> . . . it seems clear that the selfobject transferences consist of more than the reactivation of archaic forms of the persisting needs for selfobjects. Amalgamated with the reactivated archaic needs are the expectable age-appropriate selfobject needs of the analysand . . . that may easily be mistaken for resistances. Second, the analytic situation facilitates regression,

and, as a result, the more archaic forms of needs for selfobjects become very prominent. . . . Third, analysts often become aware introspectively of an equally nonspecific reaction to the patient's initial reluctance. The analyst's reaction is derived from his healthy narcissistic involvement in his analytic work and from a misperception of the analysand as "resisting the analysis.". . .

The analyst, just like the analysand, enters the analytic situation with certain needs for selfobjects. To be sure, it is expected that the analyst's own analysis has allowed him to work through the more archaic forms of his needs. . . . Still, after all is said and done, there always remain unfulfilled longings to be mirrored and unfulfilled strivings to merge. . . . Selfobject countertransferences, therefore, are an indispensable part of psychoanalytic treatment since they provide the major channel for those empathically collected data which make the formulation of psychoanalytic hypotheses possible. (Wolf, 1979, pp. 585–586)

Stolorow, Brandchaft, and Atwood have summarized

. . . that psychoanalytic treatment seeks to illuminate phenomena that emerge within a specific psychological field constituted by the intersection of two subjectivities—that of the patient and that of the analyst. In this conceptualization, psychoanalysis is not seen as a science of the intrapsychic, focused on events presumed to occur within one isolated "mental apparatus." Nor is it conceived as a science of the interpersonal, investigating the "behavioral facts" of the therapeutic interaction as seen from a point of observation outside the field under study. Rather, *intersubjective*, focused on the interplay between the differently organized subjective worlds of the observer and the observed. The observational stance is always within, rather than outside, the intersubjective field or "contextual unit" (Schwaber, 1979) being observed, a fact that guarantees the centrality of introspection and empathy as the method of observation (Kohut, 1959).

In a properly conducted analysis, it seems to me, the discrepancies in subjective experience between analyst and analysand are bound to become the foci of the working through process. An examination of the discrepancies will reveal how much the influence of the past has contributed to the particular interpretation of the present actual relationship between analyst and analysand. They will recognize that not only the analysand's interpretation of the here and now is influenced by past experiences giving it an often idiosyncratic meaning, the transference; the same is true for the analyst's subjectivity and, therefore, for his interpretation. Therefore, he should avoid interventions that imply either participant is distorting or is having inappropriate or incorrect experiences since they are inappropriate only from the other's point of view. In this way the analyst creates an analytic ambience in which the discrepancies of their differing subjectivities can become discernible, understandable, and explainable, in other words, analyzable. Ideally, by focusing on the discrepancies, the investigation will begin to involve the analysand as a partner, not necessarily equally skilled in the mutual analytic endeavor, but equally respected for his essential contributions to the analytic process. Understanding the discrepancies between the two versions of reality as inevitable differences in meaning derived from their different pasts allows both participants to accept each other's interpretations, not unconditionally, but as appropriate within their individually different contexts. The analyst's empathic perceptions of the patient's experience will then eventually be matched by the patient's increasing empathy for the analytic task performed by the analyst. The newly constructed analytic reality will then have three constituents: (1) the analysand's reality, mainly private but to some extent accessible to the analyst by empathy; (2) the analyst's reality, mainly private, but to some extent accessible to the analysand by empathy; and (3) the shared mutual reality of the understood and explained discrepancy between the two. This shared mutual reality, as it expands, guarantees an aspect of here-and-now actuality and thus acts as a preventive against either participant going off into the wild blue yonder of solipsism.

Appropriate mutual acceptance of all these three constituents is equivalent to empathy at the highest level and strengthens the self cohesion of both. With their newly gained strength the selves of both may be able to accept even their own shortcomings and be willing to analyze them. By gaining the strength really to see what they have been looking at, both participants benefit from new perceptions that become part of the construction of a new reality for each, the analytic reality.

In the words of a Polish poet who is otherwise unknown to me: "All our separate fictions add up to joint reality" (Stanislaw Lec, 1962).

REFERENCES

Alexander, F. (1961). *The Scope of Psychoanalysis*. New York: Basic Books.
Eliot, T.S. (1930). Ash Wednesday. *The Complete Poems and Plays*. New York: Harcourt, Brace and World, 1971.
Gill, M. (1982). *Analysis of Transference*. New York: International Universities Press.
Goldberg, A. (1984). The tension between realism and relativism in psychoanalysis. *Psychoanalysis and Contemporary Thought*, 7:367–386.
Kohut, H. (1959). Introspection, empathy and psychoanalysis. In P. Ornstein, ed., *The Search for the Self: Selected Writings of Heinz Kohut. 1950–1978*. New York: International Universities Press, 1978.

Lec, S. (1962). Unkempt thoughts (Jacek Galazka, translator). In *International Thesaurus of Quotations*. New York: Crowell, 1970.

Michels,R. (1985). Panel report: Perspective on the nature of psychic reality. *Journal of the American Psychoanalytic Association*, 33:645–646.

Richfield, J. (1954). An analysis of the concept of insight. *Psychoanalytic Quarterly*, 23:390–408.

Sandler, J. (1976). Dreams, unconscious fantasies, and 'identity of perception.' *International Review of Psychoanalysis*, 3:33–42.

Stolorow, R., Brandchaft, B., & Atwood, G. (1983). Intersubjectivity in psychoanalytic treatment, with special reference to archaic states. *Bulletin of the Menninger Clinic*, 47:117–128.

Strachey, J. (1934). The nature of the therapeutic action of psychoanalysis. *International Journal of Psychoanalysis*, 50:275–292, 1969.

Winnicott, D.W. (1958). *Collected Papers*. New York: Basic Books.

Wolf, E.S. (1979). Transference and countertransference in the analysis of disorders of the self. *Contemporary Psychoanalysis*, 15:577–594.

8

Discussion

What Makes for Effective Analysis?

PAUL H. TOLPIN

The contribution to psychoanalysis of the authors of the two previous chapters can be broadly summarized by the question "What makes for effective analysis?" Both Wallerstein and Wolf implicitly address that question from different vantage points. I will demonstrate this by briefly summarizing and then discussing them.

The main point Dr. Wolf makes in his clinically oriented chapter is as follows: Progress in psychoanalytic treatment is achieved through the reconciliation of the discrepant realities of the patient and the analyst as these develop in the interactions of the analytic situation. These discrepant realities arise from the particular psychological experiences of the two participants. Relevant to this is the notion of ostensive knowledge—that is, knowledge or insight obtained through firsthand emotional experience. Opposed to it is descriptive knowledge or insight that derives from secondary (intellectual) sources. The latter is more experience-distant cognition; the former is experience-near, gut knowledge. The two points, discrepant reality and ostensive insight, are connected by way of the question of what leads to an optimally effective working through process in treatment. The indepth, empathic *ostensive* grasp of each other's (analyst and patient) conveyed realities optimally leads to the understanding and eventual resolution of the patient's core disturbances. Wolf emphasizes two points: (1) that the discrepancies are recognized, made public, as it were, and accepted; and (2) that as they are dealt with a mutually agreed upon psychoanalytic reality evolves that leads to working through and eventually to termination.

In contrast to Wolf's clinical–technical interest, Dr. Wallerstein takes up large-scale theoretical issues that, while they have important

practical clinical implications, are directed more at questions of classification and basic psychoanalytic assumptions. Wallerstein asks whether
Kohut's self psychology does or does not fit into what he designates
"mainstream psychoanalysis." His conclusion is that self psychology
does not. He says that it has been set up as a separate school outside
of "mainstream psychoanalysis," which is, as I understand him, an updated, expanded, and revised neotraditional psychoanalysis. Further,
Wallerstein believes that, so far as his theory was concerned, Kohut had
the choice of a conceptual developmental pathway to take: He could
have chosen (1) to keep it within "mainstream psychoanalysis" or (2)
to set it up as a school different from traditional analysis, that is, as a
psychology founded on, and I quote from Wallerstein, "concepts of
deficit and repair of deficit rather than on conflict and its resolution"
(p. 80). Unexpectedly (and indirectly), the issues of discrepant realities
and psychoanalytic reality emerge in this disagreement between Wallerstein and Kohut, but I shall return to that at the end of my discussion.

In his chapter, Wolf focuses on one particular way of attempting
to deal with the problem of the discrepancies in psychological reality
that surface in treatment in the interactions between analyst and patient.
For a variety of reasons that Wolf describes, at certain moments the
analyst understands the patient—what he has said, dreamt, done— in
one way, and the patient understands or partly understands himself in
another. In relevant ways the same holds for patient in relation to the
analyst. The discordance that results requires resolution. A kind of
negotiation of the disagreement or misunderstanding of the differing
realities occurs, and from this psychological mismatching is constructed
what Wolf calls a psychoanalytic reality. By combining, in various degrees, the reality of both patient and analyst, the discrepancies are, it
is hoped, resolved into the new reality. That resolution and that new
reality are psychologically crucial as far as the specific positive therapeutic effect of treatment is concerned, both because of the crucial
clarification of the meaning of the content of the discrepancy and the
powerful, self-firming, growth-promoting transferential effect that in-
depth, ostensive understanding can have for the patient in relation to
the selfobject–analyst. The resolution of the discrepancy is both cognitive and deeply affective. Repetition and working through of such
discrepancies occur again and again in the course of treatment.

An example of Wolf's discrepant experiences can be found in Kohut's analysis of Miss F (Kohut, 1971). Miss F was the patient who
objected that one of Kohut's interpretations added an idea of his own

to her description and personal understanding of an event she had related. The idea he added, though possibly true, was, nevertheless, at that moment not *her* idea. Kohut meant to call her attention to the existence of an aspect of the father transference—his reality at the moment—about which she had said nothing. For Miss F, this was utterly derailing. Kohut was not at all calling attention to the possibly enlightening notion of an erotic father transference; for Miss F, he was simply calling attention to himself, to his thoughts and his interests. The patient recognized this as exactly what her self-centered, hypochondriacal mother had done when Miss F came home from school and eagerly told her of some wonderful, everyday, but for her, remarkable event. Instead of the sense of involvement with her mother that Miss F expected, her mother's eyes glazed over and gazed inward as she interpolated some comments about *her*self, *her* thoughts, *her* feelings, *her* aches and pains. She focused on herself, not on her daughter; she ignored her daughter's story, her desire for attention, her wish to be the center of her mother's life in some way for the moment. When Kohut at last understood the meaning of the patient's shrill denial of his extension of her associations, he realized that he had to focus on Miss F's reality, on *her* understanding of his remarks, rather than *his* reality, *his* understanding of the meaning of his remarks. Consequently, the impasse of descrepant realities was able to be resolved.

I have used the case of Miss F here for several reasons. The first is simply to provide a clinical vignette to illustrate Wolf's idea about the resolution of discrepant realities between patient and analyst and to demonstrate how that can lead to salutary progress in the therapeutic endeavor. As far as Wolf's thesis is concerned, I find it a quite useful idea that organizes the day-to-day empathic, intersubjective work of the analyst and patient within the framework of a novel operational concept, and I applaud and endorse its technical direction and particularly its clinical spirit, which strongly argues against an authoritarian or adversarial stance. I would also like to underscore what I feel is a particularly important point for analysts to keep in mind: In the negotiations, I believe it is the analyst who has to be far the more flexible of the two—just as Kohut was with Miss F, though not alway as dramatically so. The analyst's empathy depends on his total immersion in the "truth" of the patient's reality so that he can really understand the patient in depth from the patient's ostensive knowledge of his own world, however sketchy or inarticulate he may be. The burden of effort then lies initially with the analyst—to abandon or modify his prejudices that both at more abstract theoretical and more experience-linked clinical–theoretical levels may interfere with his ostensive insights into the patient's reality. In other words, it is up to the analyst to keep saying "What does this all *really* mean for the patient?"

I have used the case of Miss F to illustrate a further point that adds another dimension to the analytic work and is outside the range of the reconciliation of discrepant realities and the consequent construction of psychoanalytic reality that Wolf addresses. With Kohut and Miss F, the hidden reality of Miss F's mother's pathology and the affective meaning of that reality would never have come to light had it not been for a series of fortuitous circumstances. Among these were the patient's determined insistence, and the analyst's intellectual flexibility, his ability to examine clinical data with a relatively naive, phenomenological set, and his ability to resonate empathically with the empirical data. The last point includes what I assume to have been present in Kohut—a unique sensitivity to Miss F's particular sense of loss because of some broadly cognate experiences of his own to which he had the ability to gain access. Such potentials probably exist to some extent in all of us if we can overcome our inattention, our indifference, or our defenses against them, and make use of our self-observing capacities. At any rate, from all this Kohut developed initially a not very fancy, experience-near, low-level theory about the patient, which he verbalized to her as a tentative reality that was new to both of them. The method Kohut used with Miss F is one we should all use with our patients—the discovery of realities in the patient that he or she will probable never arrive at and will never discover without the analyst's sensitively in-tune help. Such realities, which are barely formed and are certainly unformulated in the patient's mind as well as in the analyst's, must be crystallized by the analyst's attention to the inchoate data the patient presents him. It is even more of a challenge when the patient's realities are quite different from the analyst's experiences with himself or other patients, but the analyst must stretch beyond those to recognize them and give them what Shakespeare calls "a local habitation and a name," to make them available for analytic work. These nascent discoveries can then be subject to the specific kind of working through process and to the psychoanalytic reality that Wolf has spoken about in his chapter. Actually, this discovery of new realities is some of the analyst's most exciting work.

In summary, to conclude this discussion of Wolf's chapter, there seems to be a continuum of reality discovery ranging from the recognition and understanding of a patient's everyday, small-scale experiences to the larger discovery of realities of larger scale, overarching theories that we use as our guidelines to the working of the mind.

Wallerstein's chapter is filled with so many interesting and challenging ideas that space does not permit me to go into them in detail. My discussion, then, will focus on a few major points.

In his summarizing and searching chapter, Dr. Wallerstein restates the position on self psychology he has held for a number of years. I think the essentials of his position, which derive from a number of complex interlocking issues and from several sources—theoretical, clinical, personal, practical, and perhaps, even political—can be reduced to two core statements.

The first: Wallerstein believes that Kohut was wrong in having arrived at the conclusion that the "vicissitudes of the establishment of a coherent and cohesive self provides . . . the best supraordinate . . . framework within which [the psychoanalytic] clinical encounter as well as the total psychoanalytic process can and should best be conceptualized. . . ."

The second: Wallerstein believes that Kohut should not have "self consciously" followed a "self chosen path of separate theoretical creation" but should have placed his findings within the framework of classically derived or as he calls it "mainstream psychoanalysis." Had he done that his ideas would have enriched and expanded the "mainstream" with the important insights of deficit or preoedipal psychology and would not have endangered their integration and assimilation into the traditional fold. Self psychology and mainstream psychoanalysis "would then have grown together" and the two groups "would hardly be different at all [except as] a matter perhaps of some emphasis rather than significant substance" (p. 82).

I will discuss these two points in reverse order. First, the issue of "the self-chosen path of separate theoretical creation."

Wallerstein's distress about "separateness" is clearly a heartfelt one, and I believe I understand something about his position. If I read him correctly, even if only from the manifest content, I believe Wallerstein's intent is to preserve the best of whatever creative ideas have emerged from the intellectual ferment begun by Freud and continued by innumerable contributors (whether orthodox or heterodox) to psychoanalytic theory and practice. He wants to see them integrated into a revised and updated theoretical establishment of somewhat altered shape and proportions but, and this is crucial, still maintained as a unity with the basic propositions and assumptions of Freud—particularly regarding the primary developmental and pathogenetic role of drives and their vicissitudes—as their backbone. I think we can all appreciate his efforts in that direction. Many of us have struggled with the same issue. Kohut had similar tendencies, at least initially, as *The Analysis of the Self* (1971) demonstrates, and in later years he periodically wondered aloud whether he was a Pied Piper leading the children of Hamlin down a dangerous road out of town. But what about the development of new theories?

As far as large-scale theory formation is concerned, Arnold Goldberg, in his 1984/1985 paper, "Translations Between Psychoanalytic Theories," described the several possibilities open to the fate of new ideas or clusters of ideas in psychoanalysis. The first is the unitary approach in which all new ideas are integrated or translated into old ones that are guided by basic tenets. Another, opposite, is the radical approach that insists that translation is not possible between theories. The middle, compromise, or integrationist position would allow for a family of connected and similar theories that overlap in some areas and remain separate in others. Divergents would be brought "back into the family by way of translation" from one cluster of ideas that make up a theory to another (Goldberg, 1984/1985, p. 123). There are advantages and disadvantages in each, and there are complex logical and personal reasons for choosing one over the other.

I think it is clear that in the course of Kohut's continuing development as a psychoanalyst he found that the conceptualizations of his psychoanalytic forebears were inadequate to the task of understanding a whole group of patients to whose particular pathology he had become increasingly sensitive—surely, because he was particularly able to, just as Freud could be sensitive to his own and his patients' sexual and aggressive complexes. That Kohut began to explicate his understanding of these narcissistic personality disorders, as he called them in *The Analysis of the Self*, within the framework of traditional theory and traditional language is testimony to the enduring influence of his bond to the fundamental insights of his predecessors. Perhaps, as others have done, he could have somehow continued to integrate his discoveries into the preexisting framework, woven them more adroitly into the traditional fabric without letting the new threads show too much. Much could have been absorbed, translated from "one cluster of ideas that make up a theory" to another. (This has been and is being done now with a great deal of his work.) Certainly, if in his continuing revision of classical drive theory he had stopped his work before he reversed figure and ground and placed the self and selfobject experiences in a position supraordinate to drives and their vicissitudes, he could more readily have accomplished this. (He would also have had better press and an easier life within the neotraditional establishment.) Others, notably some of the object relations theorists, have managed that with more or less logical sense and with more or less success. Nevertheless, Kohut was unable to do that; why he could not must remain, in part at least, an unanswered question. Wallerstein implies that some kind of conscious personal motivation caused him to set up self psychology in what Wallerstein calls a new "movement or school in psychoanalysis." The reasons for Wallerstein's judgment are not stated and one can only speculate about what he means or, if he is correct, what Kohut's motivations might have been. At any rate, whatever they are, such personal factors must contribute to each discoverer's impassioned pursuit of ideas, and perhaps finally the personal issues become irrelevant—particularly if the discoveries lead to the creation of a useful end product.

Possible or presumed conscious motivations aside, I think there is something more organic in the development of Kohut's self psychology (albeit that some constructions within it are less useful than others and perhaps do not necessarily follow as closely or arise as clearly from the basic propositions). Once Kohut had developed and accepted as highly persuasive and clinically useful both the concept of the selfobject in its various clinical forms and the allied constructions regarding the formation of the cohesive self, a series of related ideas emerged; a conceptual mechanism was tripped that led him to correlated ideas at various levels of abstraction, and the new model unfolded. As I indicated earlier, it diverged with traditional theory in a significant way: Selfobject experiences and self were seen to be the primary organizers of psychological development. A basic assumption was arrived at that contravened a basic assumption of the traditional past.

Of course the inductive method I have suggested to explain the unfolding of Kohut's ideas is too simplistic. Was there some preexisting embryonic notion about all this before his conclusions became clear? Was he unconsciously influenced by the object relations theorists? Were they all influenced by some other sources? Whatever the case, I believe *Kohut* had no choice about his conclusions. For him they explained data that had not been explained before and they resolved a number of inadequacies and inconsistencies in standard theory, which had become increasingly unacceptable and unhelpful in his work with patients.

Wallerstein's concern is the problem of the centrality of the self–selfobject concept. As said earlier, it seems to me that the crux of the disagreement between Wallerstein and Kohut is the latter's repositioning of the traditional drive–conflict–structural model of the mind within the supraordinate framework of the vicissitudes of the development of the self in relation to its selfobjects. Following this view, then, the traditional drives, though they are understood to arise from their own biopsychological matrix and to have a semiautonomous developmental line, are seen for the most part as constituents of the self and as expressing the needs of the self in a unique form with uniquely felt qualities. These qualities have a powerful psychological valence and vividly color the relations of the self with it selfobjects. Even so, they still are channeled by an overriding urge for a selfobject connection.

To understand human development and pathology in this way, Kohut, like Freud before him, followed his personal experience of the psychological universe. Kohut began with his comprehension, as with Miss F, of the young child's need for an environment adequately responsive to his or her phase appropriate developmental needs, that is, for the in-tune, optimal responsiveness of his caretakers. For Kohut there is clearly an innate, drive-like, peremptory requirement for experiences with objects, more specifically selfobjects, for responses from human caretakers who guide psychological development; and it is the adequacy or inadequacy of these self–selfobject experiences that crucially organize and shape the infant, the child, and the adult in health and in disease.

Wallerstein does not accept the overriding dominance of the requirement for self–selfobject experiences as the primary force in human psychology. While he does agree that Kohut has added an important clinical dimension to the understanding of pregenital development in terms of deficiencies in caretaking or the effects of traumatic experiences, he does not follow Kohut's contention that the guiding force in human development is the need for connections to objects (or to selfobjects, in Kohut's terminology), which is not limited to preoedipal development. As I said earlier, this is a basic assumption. Accepting it is like learning that the earth is not flat but round and discovering the profound consequences of that discovery. Once this assumption is accepted, the roles of sex and aggression fall into place with a different accent: they are understood uniquely to shape and intensify self experiences and self–selfobject experiences; they can sometimes seem to substitute for them; they can be used defensively to stabilize the disintegrating self; they can effect all of these at once; and the oedipal phase and its pathological variants are shaped by the need for phase-specific selfobject experiences as well.

Given this orienting baseline perhaps Wallerstein's criticism of Kohut's emphasis on deficient and/or impoverished childhood constellations can be seen in a somewhat different light. Kohut does not emphasize only massive deficiencies, although the development of self psychology originated in the study of some types of such disorders. He more recently emphasized more subtle qualities of self–selfobject experiences in his discussion of a relatively healthy oedipal phase in *How Does Analysis Cure?* (1984).

Some of the specific clinical quarrels can also be seen in a different light and perhaps resolved, given the orienting baseline. I return briefly to a few of Wallerstein's specific criticisms. Wallerstein states that analysts deal constantly with both the oedipal and preoedipal depending on the degree of the coherence of the self at different moments in treatment. The implications of this are that day-to-day fluctuations in self coherence call for the use of a different orienting framework to understand the essential pathology to which we regularly address ourselves for extended periods of time. I believe, however, that it is unlikely that shifts in manifest content are best understood by switching back and forth from one basic orientation to another, as Wallerstein seems to advocate. In my experience such shifts, unless they are linked to or grounded in the general organizational framework of the patient's understood pathology, tend to be confusing to, vitiating and derailing of the analytic effort. Instead, the manifest content shift can be better understood as the varying use of a varied mixture of defensive or characteristic expressive patterns that cover or convey the primary constellation of the dominant underlying disturbance. We must consistently keep that in mind as part of our broad understanding of the patient. Understanding what is primary and what is secondary, what is manifest and what is latent content and meaning is part and parcel of our everyday work. The following is an example of how this is done: A male patient who feels deeply injured by each vacation interruption in the treatment sessions often dreams of torrid sexual encounters with women starting a few weeks before the interruption is to begin. Within a few days, however, he becomes increasingly phobic in a very specific way and then coldly critical and angry at the analyst for some perceived failure of interest on his part. The interruption has in the meantime been put out of his mind. Unquestionably, he feels sexually aroused in his dreams and he is enraged at his perception of coldness on the part of the analyst. He also becomes fearful about walking across the bridge that spans the river on the way to the analyst's office. More recently, when there have been interruptions he has had homosexually tinged feelings in relation to an older man he knows. Does this change in the sexual orientation of his fantasies require a shift in understanding or in theoretical framework with respect to his core problems concerning certain chronic experiences in relation to his mother and father? I do not believe so; rather, it requires an awareness of the variety of reactions to the loss of a previously experienced, self-enhancing transference connection to his analyst. At the same time it also requires an understanding of why certain methods of self-stabilization are used, the recognition of recurrent defense patterns, the reasons for the particular kind of concealed rage that is a regular part of his reactions, the explication of that rage, and so on. It does not require a radical shift in one's theoretical conviction (arrived at after considerable empathic immersion into the patient's mind) about the origins of the patient's essential pathology.

Wallerstein (pp. 81–82) quotes Eagle who states that "structural defects and dynamic conflict are [but] different aspects of and entail different perspectives on a continuing set of complex phenomena" and that "we are most conflicted . . . [where] we are deprived [and] it is the person deprived of love who is most conflicted about giving and receiving love." These broad, somewhat aphoristic statements have some immediate clinical–theoretical appeal, but I believe it is more apparent than real. To some extent they depend on definitions for clarification, for example, the term "conflict," as defined by Wallerstein and Eagle, is broader and more colloquial than is usually understood in the drive–conflict–structural model and embraces to an extent some of the "conflicts" that would be considered part and parcel of self–selfobject psychology. The statement that those deprived of love are most conflicted about giving or receiving love is too broad to be clinically useful (and there are those deprived of love who give and feel more than their share in relation to others whose responses to them they require). At any rate, I believe that such statements detached from their individual clinical base are difficult to rely on as guidelines to analytic work.

To conclude, I return to a central point emphasized in Wolf's chapter, the discrepant psychological realities of the patient and the analyst and how in the course of treatment a negotiated psychoanalytic reality may be reached. Is there some comparable method of resolving the discrepancies in the two theoretical realities I have just discussed? What is or is not mainstream psychoanalysis must be defined by what is at present the most broadly encompassing set of conceptualizations about human psychology that is available to us. It cannot be defined simply by what is the most familiar, the most dominant, or the most entrenched.

The only way to resolve this discrepancy is to deal with it as one does with our patients—in a clinical setting or with clinical material. I can envision clinical workshops dedicated to that effort attended by open-minded partisans of both realities attempting to resolve their discrepancies in the context of a clinical dialogue where ostensive insights can be better reached. Perhaps then we can reach a consensus on what makes for effective analysis as Wallerstein and Wolf have attempted to do in their chapters. I believe that is not too vain a hope—even today.

REFERENCES

Goldberg, A. (1984/1985). Translations between psychoanalytic theories. *Annual of Psychoanalysis*, 12 & 13:121–135.

Kohut, H. (1971). *The Analysis of the Self: A Systematic Approach to the Psychoanalytic Treatment of Narcissistic Personality Disorders.* New York: International Universities Press.

Kohut, H. (1984). *How Does Analysis Cure?* A. Goldberg, ed., with P. Stepansky. Chicago & London: University of Chicago Press.

9

Discussion

To Negotiate or Not Negotiate Controversies

JOSHUA LEVY

Dr. Wallerstein's and Dr. Wolf's chapters raise questions about controversies in the practice of psychoanalysis and lead me to ask: As analysts, what is our attitude toward and capacity for negotiating controversies? In discussing this question I confine my comments to the material provided by the two chapters.

In a well-documented, comprehensive, and systematic manner, Wallerstein highlights essential differences between self psychology and what he regards as the main stream of psychoanalysis. From this chapter as well as his other published papers (1981, 1983), Wallerstein emerges as a balanced critic of self psychology, as well as a defender of self psychology against unwarranted and unfounded criticisms. These qualities suggest the statesman who is deeply aware of the dynamics of divisive and cohesive forces in the psychoanalytic community, and who works energetically to keep the divisive forces from getting out of hand. In respect to the conflictual theoretical systems, Wallerstein is urging us to adopt an attitude of both/and, which is in accord with well-established psychoanalytic principles (Waelder, 1930). My first question is what would have been Kohut's position to Wallerstein's proposition of both/and? To suggest an answer, let us go back to the exchange between Kohut and his Latin American colleague, as it is presented in Kohut's (1984) book *How Does Analysis Cure?* Though as a clinical vignette, it is an unsatisfactory one, it nevertheless focuses sharply on the controversies. Both Wallerstein and Kohut utilized it to identify and assert basic differences among systems of interpretation.

In the initial phase of his discussion, Kohut is sympathetic to the three different systems, which led Wallerstein to write: "despite [Kohut's] tone . . . of an evenhanded receptivity to any of these proffered alternative interpretative routes . . . the balance of Kohut's whole book . . . is bent to the service of his thesis . . ." (pp. 79–80). Further on in his text, however, Kohut's assertions are nothing but evenhanded. He tells us that his purpose in providing the vignette is to state that the psychotherapeutic act is comprised of two separate but interdependent steps: (1) understanding, and (2) explanation. He emphasizes that in fact all three alternative interpretations—Kleinian, Freudian, and Kohutian—could be correct in conveying an understanding to the patient. All three systems of interpretation seem to convey the message of an analyst transmitting correct emphatic perception. He goes on to stress that this message

> indicates that being nice, friendly, understanding, warmhearted, and in possession of the human touch cures neither the classical neuroses nor the analyzable disturbances of the self—at least not in the sense in which psychoanalysis, in general, and psychoanalytic self psychology, in particular, define the therapeutic goals for treatment. (p. 95)

The crucial difference between the systems becomes apparent when we move to the second stage of the therapeutic act, explanation. If the patient of the Latin American colleague suffered from analyzable narcissistic personality disorder, Kohut states, "The Freudian and the Kleinian interventions would have been equally erroneous in their explanatory dimensions (i.e., the interpretative aspect), but the Freudian intervention . . . would have been farther off the mark because in essence it would have been concerned with the conflicts and emotions of a firmly cohesive self and not with the devastating experience of a crumbling or seriously weakened self" (p. 98). This differentiation between the level of emphatic perception and correct interpretation is crucial for Kohut and he comes back to it on many other occasions (e.g., 1977; see also Ornstein & Ornstein, 1985). He proposes that different points of view as to what constitutes the essence of psychopathology do provide optimal therapeutic responses. However, Kohut states unequivocally that only self psychology's viewpoint, which concentrates on the working through of selfobject transferences and their reconstructions, leads to cure. Having taken this position in the controversy, how would Kohut have answered Wallerstein's question, "How does self psychology differ in practice?" He would probably be sympathetic to adopting a both/and approach regarding the first stage of the psychotherapeutic act. However, it seems to me, he would have rejected this approach regarding the second and crucial stage of the psychotherapeutic act, because, in his opinion, self psychology is different from the other two systems by its being superior in its therapeutic effectiveness in the majority of our present-day patient population.

I wonder how Dr. Wolf would respond to the both/and approach? It is noteworthy to quote from Wolf's recent article, "Empathy and Countertransference" (1983).

> As a physician, a scientist, and a responsible human being, I cannot ethically ignore the vistas opened up by self psychology, but this does not mean that classical psychoanalytic theory is wrong. Rather, classical theory is merely another way of looking at and organizing data and for some patients it is the most useful and effective way for doing so. (p. 316)

In contrast with Kohut, does Wolf suggest a more conciliatory approach to both/and?

In the aforementioned clinical vignette and on other occasions, Kohut is convinced of the determining effect and the high correlation between the content of interpretation and the cure by psychoanalysis. I would suggest that this position of confidence of a charismatic leader is, no doubt, a significant factor in his therapeutic effectiveness. Nevertheless, this is a far cry from systematic examination and testing of hypothesis with acceptable scientific–clinical rigor. Many of us have had the humbling experience of realizing that clinical material from analytic sessions that sounded so confirming of our hypotheses, became far less so when examined critically away from our patients. At present, we are insufficiently committed to the kind of research that would prove or disprove Kohut's claims, though Wallerstein, who has extensive experience in psychoanalytic and psychotherapeutic research, be able to comment further on this point.

In studying Wallerstein's chapter I found, on page 81, the following comment about: "[the] therapeutically deleterious consequences created by self psychology's positing a theoretical dichotomy between the developmental and structural defects on the one hand and dynamic conflict on the other. . . ." These are rather strong and sharp words that definitely implies that self psychology is clinically harmful if applied in the treatment of certain patients. Wallerstein requires clinical material to substantiate this assertion.

Dr. Wolf adds another significant contribution to comprehending the analytic situation in depth with his chapter in this volume. In other papers he has discussed the analytic ambience (1976), transference and countertransference (1979), and empathy and countertransference (1983). We know that there are different perceptions of the psychic reality of the analytic situation from the one Wolf presents. The opposite view would emphasize the discrepancy between the patient and the analyst in perceiving and interpreting the totality of the analytic situation as being due to the basic differences in their mental organizations. The patient's is infantile and organized around primary process, while the analyst's is mature and rational and organized around the secondary process. Wolf's desire to turn the discrepancy between the analyst's reality and the patient's reality into a shared, mutual reality, would be considered from this point of view as violating the essence of the analytic relationship, which, by nature and definition, is tilted (to use Greenacre's [1954] phrase). Discrepancy has to be accepted for the effective conduct of the analysis. An adherent of that persepctive might wonder whether Wolf's orientation would lead, at times, to having two analysts in the same consulting room. In order to minimize misunderstandings, Wolf's approach needs further clarification as to how, in fact, a shared reality is negotiated.

Wolf's outlook is closer to those who regard the analyst's interventions as potentially, if not actually, related to and influenced by the analyst's infantile conflicts. The possibility that analysts, just like their patients, are relating in the analytic situation via transferences, is to be kept in mind. This view of the analytic situation reminds us that the analytic instrument is vulnerable to regression when specific stresses either in or outside the analytic situation reactivate various developmental issues and conflicts. The innovative aspect of Wolf's approach is his hypothesis that the discrepancy, due in part to the analyst's potential vulnerability, can be turned into analytic benefits. Thus, he goes a step further toward not only recognizing potential countertransference interferences, but also converting analyst's transferences, if processed properly by both patient and analyst, into a shared analytic reality that is "equivalent to empathy at the highest level and strengthens the self cohesion of both." This is only one example of Wolf's many elegant and constructive statements. However, presently, he gives us no clinical material to evaluate how his approach is translated into actual analytic interactions. Questions that still need to be addressed include, What is the nature of the interactions that facilitate negotiating shared analytic reality? Does Wolf's approach result in the analyst's communicating inner experiences of discrepancy that are better, some may argue, if processed privately? Does it result in an overemphasis on the reeducational aspects of analysis?

Coming back to the question of psychoanalysts' attitude toward and capability for negotiating controversies, let us, for the moment, change Wolf's title from "Discrepancies between Analysand and Analyst in Experiencing the Analysis," to read, "Discrepancies between Self Psychology and Classical Analysis in Experiencing the Analysis." Would Wolf's recommended steps for reaching shared, mutual reality be applicable to the controversies and move us closer to Wallerstein's both/ and goal? Clearly, Wolf regards misunderstandings as inevitable and is committed to turning them, through negotiations, into a mutually acceptable reality; he warns us against solipsistic fantasies and calls tolerance of discrepancies. Could Wolf's message be that the discrepancies not only in the analytic situation, but also among different theoretical orientation are the clinical data for strengthening and invigorating the self?

Many questions about controversies in psychoanalysis have been raised and the divergencies have been specified, not for the first time. Yet, the significant task of how to negotiate differences among the diverse systems of interpretation has hardly been touched on. While it should become a major topic of future discussion, this will require sufficient agreement on what constitutes clinical evidence in the complex communications between patient and analyst, which is, of course, another source of controversy.

REFERENCES

Greenacre, P. (1954). The role of transference: Practical considerations in relationship to psychoanalytic therapy. In *Emotional Growth* (Vol. 2, pp. 627–690). New York: International Universities Press, 1971.

Kohut, H. (1977). *The Restoration of the Self*. New York: International Universities Press.

Kohut, H. (1984). *How Does Analysis Cure?* A. Goldberg, ed., with P. Stepansky. Chicago & London: University of Chicago Press.

Ornstein, P.H., & Ornstein, A. (1985). Clinical understanding and explaining: The empathic vantage point. In A. Goldberg, ed., *Progress in Self Psychology* (Vol. 1, pp. 43–61). New York: Guilford Press.

Waelder, R. (1930). The principle of multiple function: Observations on over-determination. *Psychoanalytic Quarterly*, 5:45–62.

Wallerstein, R. (1981). The bipolar self: Discussion of alternative perspectives. *Journal of the American Psychoanalytic Association*, 29:337–399.

Wallerstein, R. (1983). Self psychology and "classical" psychoanalytic psychology: The nature of their relationship. In A. Goldberg, ed., *The Future of Psychoanalysis* (pp. 19–63). New York: International Universities Press.

Wolf, E. (1976). Ambience and abstinence. *Annual of Psychoanalysis*, 4:101–115.

Wolf, E. (1979). Transference and countertransference in the analysis of disorders of the self. *Contemporary Psychoanalysis 15* (3):577–594.

Wolf, E. (1983). Empathy and countertransference. In A. Goldberg, ed., *The future of psychoanalysis* (pp. 309–326). New York: International Universities Press.

DEVELOPMENT

10

The Self and Its Selfobjects: A Different Baby

MARIAN TOLPIN

From the beginning of life, the self is an amalgam of "givens" and "experience," and its vitality and intactness correspond to the degree to which these two dimensions of selfhood complement one another in growth-promoting ways. As examples of the optimally dovetailing relationship between givens and the experience of parental selfobject functions, we might consider how the baby's maturing visual capabilities— the ability of his eyes to converge and focus on a midline object about 8 inches away—are complemented by the tendency of parents, siblings, friends, and relatives to position themselves precisely where the baby can best focus on them. Mothers, in particular, unconsciously match their "multiple functions" with their babies' maturing perceptual capabilities (Papoušek & Papoušek, 1977; Stern, 1977). Similarly, the species-characteristic tendency of mothers, fathers, and others to move through the baby's visual field at a speed commensurate with the latter's ability to follow moving objects testifies to the way in which a selfobject function dovetails with an inborn capacity.

The integral interdependency of self and selfobject function suggests the profound difficulty of conceptualizing givens and experience in discrete, static terms. Just as the infant's inborn givens can be realized only through an environment of complementary selfobject functions, so the parents' provision of these functions represents a given of sorts. To wit, the parents' ability and readiness to sustain the infant's self development by providing selfobject functions are, themselves, basic and ordinarily nonconscious aspects of their own self organizations. It is revealing, in this connection, that when mothers were asked to explain their selfobject functions they, the babies and the investigators alike became upset (Brooks-Gunn & Lewis, 1979; Stern, 1977).

The far-reaching interdependency of givens and experience transcends our inability to differentiate between these notions at the outset of life. It has an historical dimension encompassing the entire life cycle as well. The infant's original givens and experience change as they are shaped and reshaped by newly emerging givens and ongoing experiences. The self that bears the imprint of emergent givens and successive layers of experience will, in turn, determine the impact and meaning of givens that have yet to emerge and experiences that have yet to be undergone. We may say, in the idiom of self psychology, that the changes wrought on the self at any point in time—whether via inborn givens or the experience of selfobjects—will necessarily influence the further vicissitudes of self and selfobjects.[1] The child whose mirroring, idealizing, or alterego needs are not adequately met by one parent, for example, may emerge from his disappointment with new resources with which to turn to other parent, to siblings, or to friends. It is from the vantage point of this modified, frequently augmented self that he tries to extract selfobject sustenance from these significant "others." This capacity of the self to evolve structurally out of selfobject disappointments as well as successes opens up far more developmental possibilities for the traumatized child than were previously imagined. By the same token, via the lens of self psychology, we can envision varieties of early pathogenic experience that were previously unexplored.

The idea that the self, a product of earlier givens and previous selfobject experiences, continues to be shaped by emergent givens and new self–selfobject encounters, suggests that the self is, throughout the life cycle, a self in transition, a changing self. From a developmental standpoint, we may profitably focus on certain transitional junctures as pivotal steps that take the self—and its selfobjects—from one developmental phase to another. I refer to the junctures at which new givens

---

1. The possibilities for change in the self depend on a series of interacting factors that amount to a new and greatly enlarged complemental series (Freud, 1905). This series includes: (1) the species-specific perceptual, cognitive, and affective–motivational processes as these emerge from infancy through adolescence; (2) the individual's genetic make-up, including the ways in which this make-up influences earlier and later givens and past and present selfobjective experiences; (3) transmuting internalizations of the selfobject functions that enable the givens to "work right"; (4) age-characteristic symbolic transformations of the self; (5) verbal and cognitive capacities that foster more effective self-assertion and increased control of both self and selfobject; and (6) age-characteristic compensatory and defensive measures that strengthen and protect the self.

It should be noted that Piaget's (1969) concepts of assimilation and accommodation are also related to the interactive, cogwheeling relationship between givens and experience that I am emphasizing, but the processes involved in filling in the nuclear self are beyond the area of his investigations.

and new experiences with selfobjects optimally issue in phase-characteristic transmuting internalizations of selfobject functions, with a corresponding consolidation of the self. Under less favorable circumstances, these junctures may lead to the establishment of compensatory channels or the recourse to defensive measures mobilized by selfobject failures. When the selfobject failures are particularly severe and unremitting, defensive measures are inadequate and the way is paved for actual self deficits.

From the preceding, it follows that the self of infancy is less a completed composition than an outline or, more accurately still, a range of outlines. Individual givens (e.g., genetic inheritance) and individual self–selfobject experiences interactively account for this range of possible outlines for a person, even as they enter into the matter of which outline or outlines will consolidate and be filled in to constitute the self of later childhood and adolescence. Even in this latter respect, however, we may not speak of earlier givens and experiences as "determining" the structure of a particular self in advance. At most, these givens and experiences account for the selection of a path to selfhood at a particular point in time. They cannot tell us which alternative outlines of self development have been definitively obliterated, and which potentially exist susceptible to the shaping influence of givens yet to emerge and later experiences. This open-ended quality of self development is reinforced by yet another tendency of the self. The self is not only shaped and changed by its own givens and its ongoing experiences with selfobjects, but is capable of changing itself and its selfobjects, thereby creating new opportunities for change on behalf of further development.

In the examples to follow, I wish to show the intermeshing of givens and experience that form the infant self. I also want to show how the self can promote change by taking initiative to actively influence its selfobjects, and that this assertive capacity is, itself, inborn.

THE BABY'S SELF: GIVENS AND EXPERIENCE IN EARLY LIFE

The Self in Action: The Hungry Baby

The assertiveness of the hungry baby exemplifies an aspect of the phase-characteristic infant self in action. The baby's driven hunger is part of that self, as is the baby's independent initiative to reach for and grasp the nipple, and to work at nursing. Also, the angry protests and imperious insistence that greet thwarting of the need to assuage hunger are part of the normal infant self.

However, here we are faced with the problem that delineation of the baby's needs and the psychological functions provided by the mothering person is a complex phenomenological and theoretical issue. The baby's need for food is biological, and insofar as the mother meets these requirements she is a physiological caretaker. From a classical psychoanalytic perspective, the baby's primary psychological need is for satisfaction of an "oral drive" through discharge on the object of the drive. Insofar as the mother served this function she is conceptualized as an "object" or "part object" of a drive seeking satisfaction. However, from the perspective of self psychology there is never a time in normal development when an isolated oral drive strives for discharge on an isolated drive object. The normal drive experience is not limited to zonal erotism. Erotism, zonal pleasure, and oral satisfaction are always amalgamated to, always a part of, the healthy self and its normal psycho–physiological functioning, and drive satisfaction is normally experienced as self enhancing and cohesion promoting. As long as the mother carries out the many functions that surround successful feeding she performs selfobject functions. For instance, picking the baby up, talking to him, soothing and holding him in such a way that he stops screaming and calms down enough to be able to nurse are selfobject functions. (See in this connection Kohut's (1971) speculations on the relationship between the mother as the unempathic carrier of the infant and later susceptibility to motion sickness. Carrying is an example of selfobject function.)

In certain respects the many psychological functions we designate as selfobject functions were recognized and investigated prior to the development of self psychology. For example, Spitz's (1950) pioneering work on infants' failure to thrive when care was not attuned to basic psychological needs gave rise to the conceptualization of the mother as "auxiliary ego," and thus ego psychology expanded the earlier view of the "oral phase" and "oral satisfaction." That is to say, normal infantile development required psychoanalysis to go beyond views based on the vicissitudes of drives seeking discharge. However, in spite of the advance of ego psychology, continuing adherence to earlier psychoanalytic views on the primary role of drives in the infantile "psychic apparatus" made for retention of the outlook that earliest infantile mental experience centers around an "oral drive organization." Self psychology, on the other hand, considers the infants' endopsychic experience of self and selfobject functions (all of those calming, strengthening, and confirming experiences necessary for the maintenance and restoration of self-cohesion) to be psychologically the most central issue in early mental organization, and considers the normal drive one that always belongs to the superordinate self experience. (A drive manifestation in isolation is evidence that the self as a coherent organization is threatened or overcome by enfeeblement and fragmentation.)

My point is that the hungry baby's strivings and affective outbursts can be seen from the vantage point of any psychoanalytic theory of early development. What we owe expressly to Kohut's self psychology is the ability to see that it is not the drives alone but the baby's biological and psychological givens and his experiences with parental selfobject functions that form the smallest units of development that constitute the infantile self.

The constellation of sensations, affects, and initiatives that compose the baby's experience of hunger and nursing—including his anger and frustration—is not pathogenic. The experiences of the hungry baby do not fuel archaically destructive attacks on inner objects and/or part objects; nor do they mobilize archaic defense mechanisms that split the baby's inner world of self and objects. On the contrary, primary "oral" tendencies—including, once more, the baby's angry imperiousness and voracious drivenness—normally engender the responsiveness of reasonably attuned adults able to reverberate with these "oral" dimensions of the baby's experience of self. Pathogenic defenses are instituted only when parents cannot so reverberate, and instead repeatedly thwart the strivings and initiatives of a growing self. Thus, self pathology takes root only when phase-appropriate selfobject functions "really" fail to complement the givens of the early self, including the anger and imperiousness that are, at this stage of life, integral to self assertion and continuing initiative.

The Self at Play: Connecting for the Fun of it

At three weeks, a healthy baby boy began to have fussy periods. At such times, he did not need to be burped or changed, and he would not quiet down when his mother held him in his favorite calming position. On one such occasion, the young housekeeper placed him on his back in the basket that served as his bassinet. Drawing the two handles of the basket together, she tied onto them a plastic rattle in the shape of a jointed clown with a schematized clown face. The clown rattle, fortuitously, occupied the center of the baby's visual field, about 8 inches from his eyes, that is, the very point at which babies' eyes focus and coverage. The fussy baby instantly became an animated baby, energized from head to toe. At first, he was transfixed by what he saw; but he immediately proceeded from this state of rapt attention to one of invigorated delight. He kicked, squealed, and gurgled with pleasurable excitement, making noises that resembled the sounds of adults chortling with laughter. In this instance, the housekeeper had intuitively realized what the mother had not: that the infant's fussy time was his play time.

This is not the place to trace the psychical thread of joy, delight, and laughter that begins with such a given in conjunction with experience. We should at least note, however, that this baby's transformation on "greeting" the schematized configuration of a human face is the sign of an inborn given. In fact, the ingrained pleasure in connecting for the fun of it, together with the selfobject functions of "real" human beings who understand and affectively respond to this pleasure, is of crucial importance in early development. This primary tendency must be consistently thwarted to be injured or, in the worst instances, destroyed. Clinical studies of selfobject transferences document from the inside, so to speak, the extensive phase-characteristic remodelling of the mutually enlivening responsiveness of the self and its "archaic"[2] selfobjects. But these analytically recordable transformations only testify to the status of such "responsiveness" as a given: the built-in tendency to connect—by actively approaching and greeting the selfobject, and by responding with joy and pleasure to the selfobject's psychological vitality—reverberates with later self–selfobject experiences over the course of a lifetime (see Lichtenberg's [1983, pp. 48–51] related discussion of pertinent findings).

Primary "Self-Righting" Tendencies: Getting the Selfobject to "Act Right"

The baby normally shows interest in people "out there" from birth on. His physically and gesturally conveyed expectations act as signals that reasonably attuned parents gradually come to understand as "telling"

---

2. I believe the term "archaic," used developmentally, is a misnomer. There are simply phase-appropriate selfobjects of infancy, just as there are phase-appropriate selfobjects at all subsequent stages of life.

them whether or not they are on the baby's "wavelength."[3] Thus, when the mother of a 3-week-old fails to function adequately as a selfobject—that is, fails to meet her infant's expectation that she be spontaneous, that her face and voice work together, animatedly—the infant is taken aback. He backs away reflexively, albeit minutely, and gives his mother a "something is wrong; what's with you?" look.

Mothers (and maternal surrogates) usually respond automatically to the baby's unmistakable signal, and they try anew to give him what he needs and expects. On those less frequent occasions when the mother fails to "get it" the second time, the baby looks at her again, still more surprised, quizzical, and puzzled than distressed, angry, and anxious. He perseveres at setting her right and, if she persists in not acting right, he becomes yet more insistent, redoubling his efforts to reach her. In fact, in the course of these efforts, the baby will literally lean toward her, vocalizing emphatically to get his "point" across.

It is in these progressively more insistent promptings that we see evidence that the baby indeed has a mind of his own and is a "center of independent initiative" (Kohut, 1971). Only when the baby's repeated efforts to regain phase-characteristic control over the out-of-step partner have met with repeated and protracted failure does he literally sag and sink into a "heap," a telling physical analogue to his collapse of initiative. And yet, the baby's state of profound depletion lasts but a moment. Without any intervention on the mother's part, the baby "self-rights," that is, visibly recovers resolve and approaches the mother anew. He sits up once more, leans toward the mother, and begins yet another series of initiatives to reach her. His repetitive behaviors take on the character of a veritable compulsion—the better to get mother to act right!

The baby's tendency toward self-righting by looking at and reaching toward the selfobject is a primary given; it is designed into the baby's self, even as the ability to read the baby's motor, gestural, and vocal signals is designed into the self of the parent who functions as the baby's selfobject (see Beebe & Stern,1977; Call & Marschak, 1976; Carpenter, 1974; Trevarthen, 1977, 1979). Unless the sequence of activities that comprise the self-righting tendency proves utterly unavailing to establish a "fit" with the selfobject, being thereupon submerged in defensive

---

3. See Stern's (1977) microscopic studies of the baby's expectations as signals that enable both baby and parent to correct mismatches until they are again in phase with one another.

measures, this given proves integral to the baby's complementary tendency to self-regulation (Sander, 1980, 1983; Stern, 1985). It is filled in (e.g., via character) over the course of early development, and continues to reverberate over a lifetime.

The Self Restored and Outward Bound: A Lift from the Idealized Selfobject

The crying baby likes to be picked up and put to the parent's shoulder. Within a few seconds or, at most, a few minutes, he ordinarily calms down and undergoes another of those remarkable transformations dependent on the interweaving of inborn givens and selfobject experiences: From his perch on the parent's shoulder, he proceeds from a state of calm to a dramatic "perking up." We see here far more than a "state change." Replenished by the provision of a selfobject function, the baby becomes vigorous, lifts his head, his eyes brighten, and he inquisitively surveys his realm (see Korner, 1974).

It is an inborn given that selfobject functions interact with the baby's endowment in just this way: the baby's self recovers cohesion, firmness, and a sense of in-tune "togetherness" and is able to launch another foray into the world beyond the self–selfobject orbit. This language, to be sure, is partly figurative. The baby of less than 12–16 months cannot yet stand proudly erect and sally forth on his own two legs. Yet, practically speaking, the synergism of givens and selfobject experience has this very effect. Whatever the age, the baby who has received an energizing "lift" from the idealized selfobject is firm and upright as he enters the wider world in phase-characteristic ways.

However, the toddler who can venture into the world inevitably falls down. Indignant and surprised at his misfortune, feeling "betrayed" by his new found capabilities, he turns to his parents (or parenting others), taking for granted, that is, idealizing, their rescuing powers just as, a moment earlier, he was grandiose and took for granted his own powers of erect locomotion. It is the job of those with selfobject functions to see that the baby's physical fall does not lead to a commensurate fall in his self-esteem. They determine whether the baby—or only his pride—is "really" hurt. If the baby has emerged from his fall unscathed, they lend a helping and firming hand, encouraging him to undertake new expeditions while reassuring him of his competence to do so.

The baby may recover from his sense of betrayal in a matter of seconds. Alternatively, the insult to his mind–body self may linger for minutes or even hours. In either event, givens and selfobject experience combine here: the baby self recovers confidence, the baby becomes outward bound once more, and is no worse psychologically for his fall. We see commensurate evidence of the commingling of givens and self-object experience in the newborn who vehemently protests being put down when he still wants to be held up, in the infant on all fours who becomes indignant on losing his balance, and in the slightly older baby who stands by holding the sides of his crib, only to lift his arms to his parents in the unmistakable gesture, "pick me up."

Games Self and Selfobjects Play: Primary Tendencies to Play and Plan Ahead

The 8-month-old infant whose growth occurs in a self–selfobject unit that is working right expects his mirroring selfobjects to light up and applaud. Moreover, he fully expects that his playful overtures to the selfobject will be actively reciprocated. Thus, the baby is normally "full of himself" as he seeks to engage his mother, for example, in the highly ritualized games to which she earlier introduced him. By now an old hand at "cootchie coo," "I'm gonna get you," and "peek-a-boo," the 8-month-old is not content simply to follow the selfobject leader in these pursuits (see Trevarthen, 1977). Instead, looking forward to the joyous denouement of such activities, the baby anticipates what is coming next. As a "planner" who can count on the participation of his partner, he "calls the tune" and he leads his partner on.

   Via this example, we see the playful self as the baby leans toward his mother, takes her hand to play "walking fingers" or "cootchie coo" and soon begins to laugh ahead of time, at the very thought of the games he and his partner will play together. We see, in this same context, the familiar constellation of perceptual, cognitive, and affective givens together with selfobject responses that comprise the baby's self with its species-specific tendency to connect with the mother and to laugh at the joyous outcome of their connectedness.

A DIFFERENT BABY

The preceding examples do no more than illustrate what self psychology has taught us over the past decade: that a primary psychological tendency (a given) propels the normal baby to establish selfobject ties. By offering adequate selfobject responses to the baby's connecting initiatives, parents and others ensure that this tendency will continue through the successive stages of development. This continuation comes by way of the baby's—and later the child's—built-in expectation that, whatever the phase-characteristic frustrations he encounters, he will always be able to reconnect with his selfobjects. In fact, the inevitable transient disruptions of the self–selfobject tie and the efforts of both child and parent to reestablish them, constitute a "repetition compulsion" that spans the whole of childhood and adolescence. It is this repetitive cycle of establishment, disruption, and subsequent reestablishment of the self–selfobject tie that provides the developmental context for the silently working process of transmuting internalization.

It follows from the above that the baby we "see" via the theory of self and selfobject is radically different from the baby we "see" via other psychoanalytic theories of development. Self psychologists, buttressed by recent findings of infant researchers (e.g., Stern, 1977, 1985), do not see an undifferentiated, narcissistic baby, a greedy, driven baby, or a sadistic, envious baby torn between good and bad part objects. Instead, when we observe infants and young children and integrate what we see with what we learn reconstructively from patients in analysis, we discover a self and others "out there" from birth on (Greenberg & Mitchell, 1983). To be more precise, we see in-phase schema of the self and others that are actively constructed from birth. The basic content of these schema—the experiential content that fills in the outlines of the self and of others—corresponds to the particular pattern of satisfaction and frustration to which a given individual's selfobject needs have been subjected. Analysis testifies to the remarkably diverse ways in which such satisfaction and frustration can act as the driving force in positive and negative self states. Our analytic reconstructions, once more, dovetail with what we have learned from the findings of infant researchers. These two avenues of inquiry into the vicissitudes of the early self in relation to its selfobject environment converge into the formulation of the endopsychic state of the self: a baseline of cohesion that is repeatedly disturbed, only to be restored and thereby transformed as development proceeds.

It follows that, for self psychology, the primary psychological task from infancy on is the maintenance of the self. Correspondingly, it is with respect to the developmental and clinical implications of this task that self psychology diverges decisively from psychoanalytic theories that see the primary work of the early years differently, whether in terms of drive taming, separation, the resolution of infantile conflicts, or the overcoming of infantile objectlessness and/or narcissism.

Ego-psychological investigators, beginning with Benedek (1938) and Spitz (1945), have provided examples of gross selfobject failures. Their studies, and the studies they spawned (e.g., Bowlby, 1951; Emde, Gainsbauer, & Harmon, 1976; Sander, 1980; Sroufe, 1979; Stern, 1977), provide telling documentation that givens and experience do indeed go hand in hand. They show, expressly, that repeated frustration of basic needs adversely affects vigor, self-assertiveness, playfulness, and affectionateness; but the ego-psychological framework in which these findings were cast was "pathomorphic" (e.g., Emde *et al.*, 1976). It situated adult psychopathology—including self disintegration—in the baby's psyche, as though sexualization, disintegration anxiety, depression, and rage seen in adults suffering from psychological disorders is a primary part of the normal development of babies. That is, ego psychologists saw the drivenness, rage, and depression of the baby as the embodiment of innate predispositions rather than the outcome of developmental derailment in which selfobject failures disrupted the mobilization of givens of an altogether different sort: the positive, growth-promoting, self-consolidating givens I have illustrated.

Self psychologists do not question the phenomenological immediacy of preoedipal and oedipal drives, of schizoid withdrawal, of object splitting, or of early manifestations of pathological grandiosity. What they do, however, is subsume these phenomena within a new superordinate framework. Following Kohut, they take such indices of apparent psychopathology as symptomatic of a more primary psychic reality: the reality of a self that, in response to a range of selfobject failures and resulting structural deficits may become, variously, depleted, deflated, disillusioned, or prone to fragmentation.

Signs of massive selfobject disappointment are not restricted to the earliest years of life. They may emerge in the later stages of childhood or even in adolescence, when basic needs for support, recognition, and/or confirmation are not adequately met. That is, the emergence of self pathology is partially dependent on the vicissitudes of the selfobjects themselves—or, more precisely, on the vicissitudes of those objects that provide selfobject functions—over the course of the life cycle. Whenever the selfobject becomes too needy, anxious, or depressed to give the self what it needs, the power and structural integrity of self and selfobject alike will suffer, giving way to disintegration products like those catalogued by the ego psychologists of the preceding generation.

This is only to observe that the inner dialectic between self and selfobject does not stop in early childhood. Self psychology places the interweaving vicissitudes of self and selfobject at the center of development from birth to death. To this extent, the self–selfobject dialectic is the "psychical thread"—to borrow Freud's characterization of the legacy of the Oedipus complex—through which we address questions of psychological health and illness throughout a lifetime.

CONCLUSION

According to self psychology, the relationship between "givens" and "experience" is a cogwheeling, spiraling interrelationship of self and selfobject. Developmentally, this viewpoint enables us to "construct" a baby whose inner reality is governed by the vicissitudes of the self in relation to the complementary vicissitudes of the selfobject(s). Clinically, this viewpoint yields a revised outlook on the developmental tasks to be addressed in psychoanalysis. In place of assumptions about primary narcissism, lack of differentiation between self and object, and primal depression and guilt characteristic of earlier psychoanalytic theories, self psychology takes the primary connectedness of self and selfobject from birth on as its point of departure. This baseline condition has, as its normal, predictable sequelae, recurrent disruptions of the self–selfobject tie followed by "self-righting" tendencies by which self and selfobject, in various ways, seek to reconstitute the tie. The anger, anxiety, and/or depletion that are "set right" via the reestablishment of the self–selfobject tie are far different in character from the anger, anxiety, and/or depletion that bespeak a chronic inability to get the selfobject to "act right."

I have summarized several patterns of mother–infant interaction in order to exemplify the inevitability of transient disruptions of the self–selfobject tie, the infant's persistent self-righting tendencies in the face of these disruptions, and the pathological sequelae to disruptions that have not led to empathically in-tune ministrations. I have further emphasized that the self's tendency to make contact with the selfobject not only subserves other needs (e.g., hunger), but is itself a primary "given" that gains expression in a variety of everyday contexts. It is both the existence of self–selfobject ties and the fact of their recurring reestablishment in the face of disruption, that enable the child to metabolize ("transmute") givens and experience into securely internalized functions that gradually fill in the outline of selfhood with which he entered the world.

REFERENCES

Beebe, B., & Stern, D.N. (1977). Engagement–disengagement and early object experiences. In N. Freedman & S. Grand, eds., *Communicative Structures and Psychic Structures*. New York: Plenum.

Benedek, T. (1938). Adaptation to reality in early infancy. *Psychoanalytic Quarterly*, 7:200–215.

Bowlby, J. (1951). *Maternal Care and Mental Health*. New York: Columbia University Press.

Brooks-Gunn, J., & Lewis, M. (1979). *Social Cognition and the Acquisition of Self*. New York: Plenum.

Call, J.D., & Marschak, N. (1976). Styles and games in infancy. In E. Rexford, L. Sander, & A. Shapiro, eds., *Infant Psychiatry* (pp. 104–112). New haven, CT: Yale University Press.

Carpenter , G. (1974). Mother's face and the newborn. *New Scientist*, 61:742–000.

Carpenter, G., Tecce, J., Stechler, G., & Friedman, S. (1970). Differential visual behavior to human and humanoid faces in early infancy. *Merrill–Palmer Quarterly*, 16:91–108.

Emde, R.N., Gaensbauer, T.J., & Harmon, R.J. (1976). *Emotional Expression in Infancy: A Biobehavioral Study* (Psychological Issues, Monograph 10). New York: International Universities Press.

Freud, S. (1905). Three essays on the Theory of Sexuality. *Standard Edition, 7*, 130–245. London: Hogarth Press.

Greenberg, J.R., & Mitchell, S.A. (1983). *Object Relations in Psychoanalytic Theory*. Cambridge, MA: Harvard University Press.

Kohut, H. (1971). *The Analysis of the Self*. New York: International Universities Press.

Kohut, H. (1977). *The Restoration of the Self*. New York: International Universities Press.

Korner, A. (1974). The effect of the infant's state, level of arousal, sex and ontogenetic stage on the caregiver. In M. Lewis & L. Rosenblum, eds., *The Effect of the Infant on its Caregiver* (pp. 105–121). New York: Wiley-Interscience.

Lichtenberg, J.D. (1983). *Psychoanalysis and Infant Research*. Hillsdale, NJ: Analytic Press.

Papoušek, H., & Papoušek, M. (1977). Early ontogeny of human social interaction: Its biological roots and social dimensions. In M.V. Cranach, K. Foppa, W. Lepenies, & D. Ploog, eds., *Human Ethology: Claims and Limits of a New Discipline*. Cambridge: Cambridge University Press.

Piaget, J., & Inhelder, B. (1969). *The Psychology of the Child*. New York: Basic Books.

Sander, L.W. (1980). New knowledge about the infant from current research: Implications for psychoanalysis. *Journal of the American Psychoanalytic Association*, 28:181–198.

Sander, L.W. (1983). Polarity, paradox, and the organizing process in development. In J.D. Call, E. Galenson, & R.L. Tyson, eds., *Frontiers of Infanty Psychiatry*, Vol. 1. New York: Basic Books.

Spitz, R. (1945). Hospitalism: An inquiry into the genesis of psychiatric conditions in early childhood. *The Psychoanalytic Study of the Child*, 1:53–74.

Spitz, R. (1950). Anxiety in infancy: A study of its manifestations in the first year of life. *International Journal of Psychoanalysis,* 31:138–143.

Sroufe, L.A. (1979). The coherence of individual development: Early care, attachment, and subsequent developmental issues. *American Psychologist,* 34:834–841.

Sroufe, L.A., & Waters, E. (1976). The ontogenesis of smiling and laughter: A perspective on the organization of development in infancy. *Psychological Review,* 83:173–189.

Stern, D.N. (1977). *The First Relationship: Infant and Mother.* Cambridge, MA: Harvard University Press.

Stern, D.M. (1985). *The Interpersonal World of the Infant.* New York: Basic Books.

Trevarthen, C. (1977). Descriptive analyses of infant-communicative behavior. In H.R. Schaffer, ed., *Studies in Mother–Infant Interaction.* London: Academic Press.

Trevarthen, C. (1979). Communications and cooperation in early infancy: A description of primary intersubjectivity. In M. Bullowa, ed., *Before Speech: The Beginning of Interpersonal Communication.* Cambridge: Cambridge University Press.

11

Discussion

Models for Transmuting Internalization

ANNA ORNSTEIN

Tolpin's chapter represents a further refinement of her thinking in relation to the theory of the development of the self that she had described
in earlier papers (M. Tolpin, 1971, 1978; Tolpin & Kohut, 1980). These
papers are an invaluable contribution to the psychoanalytic literature
as they have further elaborated on Kohut's views on the development
of the self; especially in light of the recent findings of infant research
(e.g., Demos, 1984; Sander, 1975; Stern, 1977).

In the previous chapter, Tolpin interprets a series of the baby's
everyday experiences (feeding, playing, being lifted up, falling) in a
manner similar to her interpretation of the developmental significance
of separation anxiety and the transitional object (M. Tolpin, 1971). The
description of these infant experiences and their interpretations are models
for the conceptualization of transmuting internalization of the caretakers' selfobject functions. For example, when Tolpin details the caretaker's functions such as "picking the baby up, talking to him, soothing
and holding," she presents a vivid picture of the complex set of experiences that touch on various, interrelated aspects of development, that
cannot be reduced to "satiation of hunger" or the "satisfaction of the
oral drive." Rather, these experiences ought to be considered as pre-
cursors of psychic functions that, through repetition and optimal frustration, become fundamental aspects of the developing self. Even the
casual observer can follow the impact of the caretaker's ministrations:
the baby becomes calm and is then able to nurse. Calming the baby
precedes nursing: a bit of structure building through transmuting internalization takes place before satiation can be assumed to alter the in-

fant's self state; structures that will perform the self-soothing and self-calming functions of the psyche.

Similar to the vivid description of the changes in the baby's self state from hunger and agitation to calm nursing, Tolpin traces the changes in the infant as it is being "lifted up" and perched on the caretaker's shoulder. The change here is not only from agitation to calmness, but the observer can also witness in the baby a "dramatic 'perking up'. . . . Replenished by the provision of a selfobject function, the baby becomes vigorous, lifts his head, his eyes brighten, and he inquisitively surveys his realm" (p. 122).

With these easy to observe, everyday examples of infant behavior, Tolpin draws attention to two interrelated and continually interacting aspects of development; the interdependency between the infant's "givens" and the environment's complementary selfobject functions.

Researchers seem to agree on the compelling nature of infants' behavior and their capacity to engage the adult:

> before the advent of language and other symbolic forms of representations, the infants affective expressive behaviors are the only reliable and valid indicators of the saliency of events for the infant, and thereby constitute the primary medium of communication and meaning. (Demos, 1984)

But what enables the caretaker "to read the infant's" clues? What is the nature of this preverbal communication that Stern (1977) calls "mental state sharing" (p. 72) and what Kohut (1971) called "mirroring?" I believe mirroring, validating, confirming that "confers" meaning on the infant's emotional experiences is possible because primary human affects are universal and retrievable through vicarious introspection (empathy).

The inborn "primary affects" (Thomkins, 1962) and their later elaborations into increasingly more complex mental states, become keys we all use to open the door to the inner world of others. This is the key that caretakers use when providing selfobject functions to the infant and growing child. Empathic selfobject responses have a dual quality; they reflect where the child is at the moment and where he or she would like to be in the future. The adult tests and assesses the baby's affects while maintaining his or her own independent motivational stance and responds by taking both these factors into consideration (Demos, 1984).

What I am touching on here, is the intriguing relationship between the capacity to communicate affects and the development of empathy. Clinicians can be pleased that some of the best minds in the field of infant research are now investigating this area that has great significance not only for our understanding of development, but for clinical work as well. I believe that psychotherapists, similar to caretakers, possess upper and lower tolerance limits for the expressive behavior of their patients and tend to maintain their patients' associations within those limits. This has far reaching consequences for the manner in which affects will be developmentally integrated into the organization of self experiences and for what is possible experientially for the patient in a therapeutic situation.

I shall comment on one other aspect of this paper because of its significance for the theory of pathogenesis. This is related to the infant's "primary self-righting tendencies." These are inborn capacities that "help the caretaker to find the proper attunement." The existence of such inborn tendencies in the infant would support Tolpin and Kohut's earlier (1980) contention that only when the infant runs into repeated empathic failures on the part of the caretaker does it develop defensive, that is, pathological psychic structures. Anger then could be recognized as an additional signal to the environment for help; a secondary event to frustration and not the expression of "the aggressive drive." When ordinary self-assertive measures fail, anger appears as a "breakdown product," giving rise to the development of further defensive structures that protect the immature psyche from total disorganization. However, once defensive structures are in ascendence, the infant can no longer utilize its selfobject environment even when the latter adopts a more empathic attitude toward its need. This sets "a negative" reciprocal interaction into motion in which changed parental attitudes and increased efforts can not readily penetrate the infant's (and growing child's) self-protecting defensive wall.

Classical psychoanalytic theory, based on Freud's reconstruction of the libidinal phases of development, had evolved a developmental theory that is "phasic"; the impetus for psychological growth being provided by the phasic nature of libidinal drive maturation. Most developmentalists have abandoned this model and yet have developed others that still recognize the epigenetic sequence in some form or another. The concept of the developmental lines has been added to the phasic nature of developmental theory based on libidinal drive maturation. Even though landmarks in the developmental sequences that are thereby provided are only loose approximations, they do indicate the kind of developmental tasks that the growing psyche has to master in order to fall within the average expectable range.

Self psychology has not yet been able to spell out the sequences of the various developmental tasks when these developmental sequences and tasks are placed into the context of an empathically responsive selfobject environment. I am thinking of developmental tasks that would not be limited to the establishment of homeostasis, self-cohesion and the development of self-esteem, but would include attachment, the processes of differentiation (especially that of affect), the relationship between affect differentiation and cognitive development, and the development of morality, to name only a few. I agree with Basch (1985) that this kind of comprehensive statement regarding development cannot be achieved through reconstructions in the analytic situation and that we have to depend on the contributions of researchers whose observations are informed by self psychological considerations; that is, developmental studies within the unique and specific environment in which the infant (child) lives.

REFERENCES

Basch, M.F. (1985). Personal Communication.
Demos, V. (1984). Empathy and affect: Reflections on infant experience. In J. Lichtenberg, M. Bornstein, & D. Silver., eds., *Empathy* (Vol. 2). Hillsdale, NJ: Analytic Press.
Kohut, H. (1971). *The Analysis of the Self.* New York: International Universities Press.
Sander, L. (1975). Infant and caretaking environment: Investigation and conceptualization of adaptive behavior in a system of increasing complexity. In E.J. Anthony, ed., *Explorations in Child Psychiatry.* New York: Plenum.
Stern, D. (1977). *The First Relationship: Infant and Mother.* Cambridge, MA: Harvard University Press.
Tolpin, M. (1971). On the beginnings of a cohesive self: An application of the concept of transmuting internalization to the study of transitional object and signal anxiety. *Psychoanalytic Study of the Child,* 26:316–352.
Tolpin, M. (1978). Selfobjects and oedipal objects: A crucial developmental distinction. *Psychoanalytic Study of the Child,* 33:167–184.
Tolpin, M., & Kohut, H. (1980). The disorders of the self: The psychopathology of the first year of life. In S.I. Greenspan and J.H. Pollock, eds., *The Course of Life: Psychoanalytic Contributions Toward Understanding Personality Development* (Vol. 1: *Infancy and Early Childhood*). Washington, DC: National Institute of Mental Health.
Tomkins, S. (1962). *Affect, Imagery, Conciousness* (Vol. 1: *The Positive Affects*). New York: Springer.

12

Discussion

Controversies about Development: Givens and Experience

JOSEPH LICHTENBERG

Theories of development evolve around explicit or implicit questions. One of the first major questions asked by psychoanalysts beginning with Freud was what childhood must be like to account for the development of neuroses and psychoses, One answer was that it must be sensation centered, first orally, then anally, and then in the phallic–urethral or clitoral–urethral area. Another answer is that it must be relationally centered along the lines of pathological conditions: an autistic or narcissistic stage, a stage of symbiosis, followed by a stage of separation–individuation, or a paranoid–schizoid position, followed by a depressive position. Other conceptions speak of an undifferentiated state of id and ego, or of the absence of self and object boundaries, of primary masochism or sadism, autoeroticism, omnipotence, and the like—all patterned after pathological states. Alternatively, infant researchers ask a more phenomenological question: What can the developing child do? They have focused their observations and designed ingenious research techniques to answer this question. The answers have been startling to many analytic theoreticians—while probably less so to mothers—although Brazelton (1980) reports that many a mother says to him, "I didn't know my baby could do that," as he puts the baby through his or her paces.

The following are some of the answers these studies have provided. Neonates will organize the 24-hour time period into discrete mental states of quiescent wakefulness, alert wakefulness, crying, and rapid-eye-movement and non-rapid-eye-movement sleep (Wolff, 1966). They will actively seek many stimuli and with clear discrimination avoid others. They display clearly demonstrable preferences for some stimuli over others—some learned while others seem at first genetically patterned. They will imitate facial expressions of interest, surprise, sadness, and joy (Meltzoff & Moore, 1977). They are able to move their bodies in synchrony with human speech (Condon & Sander, 1974) and develop expectations—for example, that their mother's voice and face go together—and when the expected pattern is violated they respond with distress (Carpenter, Tecce, Stechler, Friedman, 1970). From the feel of something in their mouth they can tell what it looks like without ever having seen it (Meltzoff & Borton, 1979), that is, they abstract properties experienced in one mode (touch) and apply the knowledge to another mode (vision) (Stern, 1985). They register patterns of perceptions and the affective–action responses they make to the perceptions in their memories, and as a result are primed to repeat these patterns when the stimulus is reintroduced for a period of up to 2 weeks (Rovee-Collier, Sullivan, Enright, Lucas, & Fagen, 1980). They work to accomplish a task for the satisfaction it gives, but will continue to practice the skill seemingly more for the pleasure of competence than the satisfaction itself (Papoušek & Papoušek, 1975). They have a far wider repertoire of affects than has hitherto been appreciated (Demos, 1982). I have reviewed these findings of what babies can "do" in Psychoanalysis and Infant Research (Lichtenberg, 1983). These are the givens about which Tolpin writes. I have also used these findings to question existing theories—some that are taken as dogma—and have suggested alternate ways to conceptualize the development of the first 2 years: a perceptual–affective–action pattern organization during most of the first year, an intermediate phase of sign–signal informational exchange, followed at about 18 months by a phase of consolidation of sense of self utilizing symbolic representation in primary and secondary process cognitive–affective modes.

In discussing givens and experience, Tolpin addresses a still more difficult question: what do babies experience? Tolpin writes of joy, bliss, , well-being, majesty, interest, playfulness, curiosity, confidence, angry protest, a "what's with you?" expression, planning, expecting, deflation, anxiety, and depletion—all relating to experience. Tolpin insists that she wishes to describe a *different* experience.

For her claim of a different baby, Tolpin draws on the theories of Kohut. She states that "Self psychology places the interweaving vicissitudes of self and selfobject at the center of development from birth to death" (p. 126). I am in sympathy with the spirit of Tolpin's account of development that begins with the premise that the baby is born into a milieu of empathic responsive selfobjects and that the baby is strong (Kohut, 1984, pp. 212–213). I certainly support the value of a mental model using the self and its vicissitudes as a central construct. My thinking about infancy (and my clinical experience) jibes with Tolpin's emphasis on emotions. I especially appreciate Tolpin's citing the continuity of positive growth inclinations that arise when built-in givens are set in motion by the ordinary experiences of the infantile period. In even the earliest feeding, hungry babies are equipped to be assertive partners in their mother's ministrations. Fussy infants have the innately given capacity to activate exploratory interests and thereby calm themselves. In the attachment play between mothers and infants, the infants quickly learn the patterns of the exchanges and become initiators and avid stimulators when the mothers fall out of step. Crying infants can be restored to a positive state by being picked up (a restoration of attachment connectedness) and, with this lift, by reinvesting their interest in exploring the world around them. The child's confidence in newly acquired skills such as walking can be restored by being set back on the path by mothers after a fall—a combination of being righted and their own self-righting. In 8-month-old infants, the attachment games expand with their greater motor development but, by now, infants are active planners in bringing about an anticipated outcome they desire.

Tolpin's emphasis is on growth and health: asserting, exploring, calming, self-righting, initiating, planning, and anticipating. All these derive from givens and are brought forward under the powerful impact of the experience of a mother who fits in with them and with whom these innate potentials are designed to fit. The inner experience of this mutual fit for both partners is more than can be accounted for by drive satisfaction: it transcends the simple pleasure–gratification level. The inner experience is one that produces an inner state of cohesion of self which is coincident with the result of a self–selfobject experience. Inevitable disruptions of cohesion occur such as failing to sustain attachment activities, unquenched hunger, and falls taken without the lifting parent in attendance. The expectation will have become built in from prior successes that the mother–infant tie will be restored and with it the restoration of cohesion and a renewed self–selfobject experience of fit. Tolpin alludes to the connection between this formulation and the findings in the clinical situation of repetitive disruptions and the res-

toration of cohesion that has been described as "transmuting internalizations."

As Tolpin states, the view of infancy she offers differs markedly
from that put forward by psychoanalytic theories that emphasize conflict,
insatiable driveness, and taming of the primitive, whether sexual or
aggressive. In these theories, much of the infant's observable behavior
receives little attention and the infant is conceptualized as having to
overcome great hypothesized psychic obstacles. The self psychology
view is that infants are endowed by innate givens to fit into a specific
ecological niche within the family group. The experience of a mutual
interaction characterized by empathic responsiveness builds self cohesion and a repository of self–selfobject experiences that invigorate the
self and facilitate the restoration of cohesion after temporary disruptions. In building her case for the relationship between givens and experience, Tolpin uses directly observable behavior and evolves a conceptual framework that I believe, in its essentials, agrees with the findings
of contemporary research on infants. From the review of the extensive
findings of infant research that I have attempted (Lichtenberg, 1983),
I would conclude that Tolpin has not gone far enough in questioning
traditional concepts. She states that "Self psychologists do not question
the phenomenological immediacy of preoedipal and oedipal drives, of
schizoid withdrawal, of object splitting, or of early manifestations of
pathological grandiosity" (p. 125). Rather, she states, these phenomena
are subsumed within a new superordinate framework.

I question each of these assumptions or at least the accuracy of the
language with which they are described. When Tolpin describes the
"driven hunger" of the infant she is using driven as an adjective—easily
verifiable by observation. While questioning the significance of "drives"
she reverts to the traditional terminology when she states "it is not the
drives alone but the baby's biological and psychological givens and his
experiences with parental selfobject functions that form the . . . infantile
self", (p. 119). This mix of concepts is confusing. Hunger and the entire
physiological need and action response state attendant on it are part of
the baby's biological and psychological givens. The regulation of such
psychological needs is part of the fit. I prefer not to call these needs
instinctual drives because it ties us to vestiges of the dual drive motivational theory which is not subsumable under self psychology without
doing violence to both sets of formulations. I likewise take exception
to calling the aversion responses of withdrawal and avoidance "schizoid." This causes the innate and learned patterns by which infants react

in response to dystonic experiences and what is the infants only way to express the dystonicity to become confused with an organized illness pattern of later life when alternate choices of response are possible. Splitting is a more complicated story but little or no evidence supports this conception which occupies an important position in many contemporary theories (see Lichtenberg, 1983; Stern, 1985).

Tolpin also at times describes the infant's observable joyousness and vitality as grandiose, meaning a fantasy of greatness or imperviousness. I seriously question whether, before demonstrable evidence of symbolic representation at around 18 months, we should attribute a fantasy life to the infant and young toddlers. The affect state changes in which joy gives way to distress and then, after restoration, returns to joy are clear observables quite sufficient to support Tolpin's contention of the healthy self-righting inclination built into the infant.

The centerpiece of Tolpin's blueprint for normal development is the selfobject's empathic meeting of the infant self's strong efforts to connect, in all its manifold manifestations. But can a selfobject empathically meet the infant self or does a *mother* try to meet it as best she can and then become a selfobject when and if she succeeds? This may sound picky—we all know Tolpin means the mother (or father) when she says selfobject—but if we all "know" this, then we are missing the point. Self psychology views selfobject functions as an *inner reality,* an *endopsychic experience* of other persons whose functions are part of, necessary for, the normal workings of the body–mind–self. Rather than being a person in the physical world, the selfobject is an inner reality— a subjective experience—that occurs when things go right when there is empathic responsiveness or when, in Kohut's words, there is optimal frustration. The mother is flesh and blood, and I rather miss her human ways and her problems in Tolpin's chapter. I say this first because I believe the term "selfobject," could easily degenerate into a flag waving for selfpsychology or, worse, imprecise jargon that could lose gains made by such fine thinkers as Tolpin. To restate my point, it is valuable to have a concept that refers to a subjective experience of the right note being struck, all systems working, development proceeding, an affect resonated with, a groping being responded to, a needed barrier being provided, as, for example, when Kohut told the reckless driver patient, "You are a complete idiot" (1984, p. 74), a stable, indestructable opposer being there to push off against, self-righting occurring, God in his heaven, and all being right in the world.

In Tolpin's eagerness to illustrate the ways in which the baby is

strong, and thereby not to slip into "pathologizing" normal development, she errs in underemphasizing the problems of mother and baby
and so runs the risk of mythologizing selfobject and self. For example:
she cites the case of a 3-week-old with fussy periods, whose mother
could not calm him but who was transported into joy by the clown rattle.
He indeed had a "selfobject experience," but what was not said is that
many babies during their periods of nonspecific fussiness do not and
will not respond to novel play materials. They are more or less incon-
solable and their mothers have to live through this difficult period. Put
in terms of the theory, these mothers cannot experience their fussy
babies as selfobjects but have to rely on supportive friends, husbands,
Dr. Spock, or their inner resources.

Tolpin's example of "when others of 3 week olds fail to function
as selfobjects" in accord with the infants' expectations is clear, but she
introduces a contradiction in terms by continuing, "When the mother
(or other selfobject) remains impervious. . . ." The impervious, unresponsive mother is clearly not providing the infant a selfobject experience. Furthermore, her example is misleading as a norm for the persistent effort a baby can be expected to exert in order to activate an
unresponsive mother. While all biologically healthy babies are indeed
centers of independent action initiatives, they vary greatly in how much
they will persevere in the face of an impervious mother. In other words,
the variability and changeability in babies is understated in the interest
of a commendable attempt to portray the healthy trends in the mother–
infant pairing.

A mother often does not know whether she is providing a selfobject
experience; she simply does the best she can. Her baby's needs or
temperament may be too much for her at a given time. An outside
observer may also have trouble judging whether the selfobject function
is being fulfilled. For example, Tom at 13 months was reluctant to stop
playing with his blocks when called to dinner. When his mother went
to get him, he started to cry and angrily throw his blocks. She picked
up the struggling toddler, held him to her breast, and calmed him into
silence. Did he experience her as serving a selfobject function? We could
say she did if we knew, as she may have intuitively known, that without
soothing him in this way, Tom would have spiraled into a full-blown
temper tantrum and had a functionally disorganizing experience. We
could say she did not if we knew that Tom would have learned more
about negotiating controversy had his mother sat with him a moment

while they worked out what a call to dinner meant and how they would collect the blocks for the next play period.

Life, like interpretations made or not made in the clinical setting, is a series of uncontrolled experiments, only a relatively small number of which can we know in advance will lead to a selfobject experience. It is with some embarrassment that I relate that the most effective single interpretation I ever made was over 30 years ago, in my first year of psychiatry, and I did not know I was making it. I had chosen to do individual psychotherapy with a woman in a state hospital. She was diagnosed as a paranoid schizophrenic and was the most consistently angry human being I had ever seen. I was harangued by her about a multitude of injustices for some months, until one day as she was haranguing and I was rocking back and forth in my straight chair, I noticed a slight expression of anxiety in her face. Assuming she was troubled by the unsteadiness of my perch in the chair I said, "Don't worry, I won't fall, I'm an expert." In a totally different tone she replied, "Oh, thank God, I was so worried about your wife, I was feeling so guilty about taking you away from her." At that point I almost did fall off my chair in amazement. Her subsequent improvement clearly indicated that through my fumbling attempts at intimacy and my "interpretation," I was experienced by her at that moment as a selfobject.

I will mention one final difference with Tolpin. I place greater importance on a wider range of foreground experience than she. The difference with Tolpin I cite here is one of emphasis. Certain experiences bring out the baby's strengths and contribute to self cohesion. Tolpin's examples center on the ministrations of the mother that lie mainly in the realm of attachment activities. Her emphasis correlates beautifully with the findings of clinical psychoanalysis in which the empathic resonance between analyst and analysand in the intersubjective sphere is paramount for the maintenance of the analysand's self cohesion. But the infant builds inner strength and self expansiveness from other foreground experiences as well. Fundamental is the regulation of physiological needs, if these are not adequately regulated attachment resonance suffers. Of course in the neonate these two interactional realms are difficult to tease apart. Traditionally psychoanalysis has given particular prominence to sexual regulation as a source of cohesion or its disturbance. Self psychology has questioned this, providing evidence that often in the absence of a strong sense of self the individual turns to sexual activity to try to reinvigorate a lifeless self. However, in the baby, sensual pleasure play with others or by himself contributes to an expansive self and builds toward the special sense of certain body parts to be prized with pride. I place considerable importance on those foreground activities in which a toy, the mother, or other humans provide opportunities for children to solve problems and gain competence or efficacy pleasure. In these instances the child is learning the all-important experience of how to become confident in the self as master of expectancies and director of intentions while being alone in the presence of the other—to use Winnicott's felicitous phrase—the other being the unobtrusive parent in the background.

I also place greater importance on what Sander (1975) calls the "inevitable polarities" that require reconciliation. There is much evidence that in ordinary development, despite the best intentions, infants are pressed to use innate responses to dystonic stimuli and that we can observe patterns of antagonism and withdrawal replacing patterns of positive attachment and of assertiveness based on interest and competence pleasure. Learning to regulate aversive responses contributes to the child's ability to manage controversy without self-constricting submissiveness or self-defeating arrogance.

I conclude by providing a hint at another way of conceptualizing what a baby may experience. Affect is the key to experience (to the individual variants in the ever-recurring primary psychological tendencies, in Tolpin's terms), but I would allow the infant 18 months before the step to symbolization, while other theories imply that it occurs immediately. The greatest impediment to understanding the experience of the infant lies in the difficulty for an adult to imagine what it is like to not be able to imagine, but to be able to experience a world richly saturated in sensory perceptions whenever a stimulus presents itself—whether from the external world or the body. Coordinated with these perceptual responses to stimuli are affect activations and action responses—the total experiential unit being a perceptual–affective–action pattern. At first, these arousal states begin and end in the way dreams flash on and off—that is, they are stimulus dependent. They operate totally in an action mode—what is remembered and reactivatable is the entire pattern, which once reactivated can be modified and added to in an action mode until about the age of 9 months, when the "out there," through what I call an "imaging capacity," (Lichtenberg, 1983) is established (like a still shot taken out of a moving picture). Experiencing the surrounding world first in a kaleidoscopic fashion and then sometimes as a fixed particular source of interest, an object of contemplation, gives the infant a different mode of entry into his ecological niche than we have previously conceptualized. Rather than building up representations as primitive symbols, infants build memories of organized patterns of actions which are made significant by the affective response that accompanies the action. This helps to explain the significance of those actions, and most particularly those interactions, that provide the affective response we call a selfobject experience. As these experiences become familiar in memory they are an expectancy eagerly sought, a compelling source of a need to repeat. This is the compulsion to repeat that is liberated in our patient's when our empathic resonance restores a sense of hope that the expectancy may again be met.

REFERENCES

Brazelton, T.B. (1980, May). *New knowledge about the infant from current research: Implications for psychoanalysis.* Paper presented at the annual meeting of the American Psychoanalytic Association, San Francisco.

Carpenter, G., Tecce, J., Stechler, G., & Friedman, S. (1970). Differential visual behavior to human and humanoid faces in early infancy. *Merrill-Palmer Quart.*, 16:91–108.

Condon, W.S., & Sander, L. (1974). Neonate movement is synchronized with adult speech. *Science*, 183:99–101.

Demos, V. (1982). Affect in early infancy: Physiology or psychology. *Psychoanalytic Inquiry*, 1:533–574.

Kohut, H. (1984). *How Does Analysis Cure?* A. Goldberg, ed., with P. Stepansky. Chicago & London: University of Chicago Press.

Lichtenberg, J. (1983). *Psychoanalysis and Infant Research.* Hillsdale, NJ: Analytic Press.

Meltzoff, A., & Borton, R. (1979). Intermodal matching by human neonates. *Nature*, 282:403–404.

Meltzoff, A., & Moore, M. (1977). Imitation of facial and manual gestures by human neonates. *Science*, 198:75–78.

Papoušek, H., & Papoušek, M. (1975). Cognitive aspects of preverbal social interaction between human infant and adults. In *Parent-Infant Interaction.* New York: Associated Scientific Publishers.

Rovee-Collier, C., Sullivan, M., Enright, M., Lucas, D., & Fagen, J. (1980). Reactivation of infant memory. *Science*, 208:1159–1161.

Sander, L. (1975). Infant and caretaking environment: Investigation and conceptualization of adaptive behavior in a system of increasing complexity. In E.J. Anthony, ed., *Explorations in Child Psychiatry* (pp. 129–166).

Stern, D. (1985). *The Interpersonal World of the Infant.* New York: Basic Books.

Wolff, P.H. (1966). *The Causes, Controls, and Organization of Behavior in the Neonate* (Psychology Issues, Monograph 17). New York: International Universities Press.

13

Self Change and Development in the Analysis of an Adolescent Patient: The Use of a Combined Model with a Developmental Orientation and Approach

MORTON SHANE AND ESTELLE SHANE

From the time that Hartman distinguished self from ego in 1950, there has been increasing interest and corresponding conflict within the psychoanalytic community concerning the concept of the self. As Richards (1982) points out in his discussion of a panel on the subject, two broad and antithetical positions can be discerned: one, elucidated by mainstream analysis, holds that no radical revision of theory is required to encompass a consideration of the self, and the other, exemplified by self psychology, maintains that indeed a "radical revision approaching replacement of psychoanalytic theory is necessary because traditional theory is deficient, inaccurate, or in some way limited" (p. 940). Each of these antithetical positions implies that one can conceptualize the psychoanalytic situation without reference to either aspects or the totality of the other, competing theory. Yet it is obvious that self psychology remains dependent upon a great many of the insights contained in classical theory, as Kohut himself maintained until the end of his life (see also Greenberg & Mitchell, 1983, in this regard). On the other hand, while classical analysis does not depend upon self psychology per se, the theory is rendered inadequate by its central assumption of a more or less well-functioning ego in the patient. In particular, it is in the area

This chapter was originally presented at the meeting of the American Psychoanalytic Association, Denver, Colorado, spring 1985, and it was also presented at scientific meetings of the Houston-Galveston Psychoanalytic Society, fall 1985, and the Los Angeles Psycholoanalytic Society, fall 1985.

of deficiencies in self-esteem and self constancy (and object constancy) that traditional theory can benefit from self psychology. One can argue that ego psychology over the past 3 decades has attempted to respond to these issues in terms of deficient structuralization and insufficient cathexes of the self representations; however, these concepts fail to address the two-person psychology aspects (Modell, 1985) in self-esteem regulation and maintenance of self constancy so well elucidated in the concept of the self–selfobject relationship. These theoretical lacunae in classical analysis, related to faulty structuralization, are accommodated in the clinical situation by preliminary psychotherapy, parameters, and the like, with the goal of rendering the patient analyzable (e.g., Weil, 1974). That is, first there is a phase of treatment concerned with structure building and consolidation, followed by a phase of treatment concerned with conflict interpretation and resolution. But, this clinical accommodation to the patient's structural imperfections seems as awkward as the theoretical accommodation referred to earlier. Again, there is inadequate appreciation of the intersubjective (Stern, 1985; Stolorow, Brandchaft, & Atwood, 1983), especially in that area crucial to problems of self-esteem and self constancy, namely, the feelings of being regarded or demeaned, understood or misunderstood, responded to or ignored. Again, it is with just this interaction in the psychoanalytic situation that self psychology has a great deal to offer. As a matter of fact, some— for example, Adler (1985)—have suggested that the therapeutic alliance with such patients is dependent upon the establishment of stable self– selfobject relationships through the development and working through of selfobject transferences. Thus, some analysts in the mainstream permit themselves a free use of constructs from both the classical and self psychological frameworks, in effect employing a combined model of the self. We believe that such a combined model is necessary to any analysis that is balanced and that seeks to take into account both an intact mind in conflict and a deficient self besieged by loss of integrity.

In this chapter, we present clinical material to illustrate this balanced approach. To organize our thinking we utilize what we are calling a bipolar–tripartite model of the self.[1] Yet we are aware that combining models is distinctly unfashionable, and opens one to attack from all sides. We recognize, in addition, that there can be major theoretical and technical difficulties that arise from such efforts. We defend our

---

1. One possible graphic representation of the model described in this chapter can be seen in Figure 1.

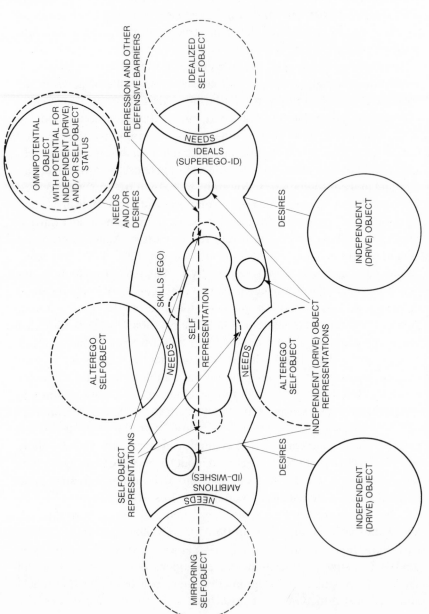

Figure 1. A Bipolar Tripartite Model: A Developmental View of the Self

combined model in two ways. First, as developmentalists, following a developmental orientation and approach (Goodman, 1977), we are committed to utilizing the best in theoretical constructs related to the unfolding of human potential, and self psychological concepts combined with the tripartite model are persuasive to us in this regard. Just as separation–individuation formulations have benefitted classical theory with a focus primarily on the preoedipal period, but also beyond, so, we believe, does self psychology add its unique contributions to an expanded and enriched view of ongoing developmental processes. Second, and perhaps, as we have indicated, more controversial, despite the obvious high level and technical differences in the formulations and approaches behind the tripartite and bipolar configurations, the similarities between their respective models override, in our opinion, the disparities between their informing propositions. If it is true, as Meissner (1984) has pointed out, that psychoanalysts as clinicians work almost exclusively with models of the mind rather than with theoretical formulations, then such a similarity between models is not insignificant. In our combined model, designed to be used in the clinical situation, the sector of ambitions is seen as roughly comparable to the id; the sector of ideals as roughly comparable to the superego; skills as roughly comparable to the ego; and intersectorial imbalances as roughly comparable to intersystemic conflicts. Also, in our model, as in the mainstream model, representations of independent (drive) objects are built up within the psyche; selfobjects, too, have their representations in the psyche, but are conceptualized as variously merged with or connected to the self representation, on a continuum ranging from archaic to mature. It should be noted that in this model objects can be conceptualized as either independent (drive) objects or selfobjects, that is, objects perceived by the individual as either having an independent center of initiative or perceived as part of the self more or less without such a separate center of initiative. The attachment of selfobjects to the self is based on needs that preserve the integrity of the self, whereas the attachment to independent (drive) objects is based on psychological desire, that is, desire conceptualized in the psychological realm of discourse (see Brenner, 1982). Note that while the distinction between need and desire may be a difficult one, it does have an operational utility in the clinical situation. Less than optimal frustration of a need is more likely to be threatening to the patient's self cohesion than such frustration of a desire. Therefore, the analyst is more likely to see the satisfaction of needs in the analysis as legitimate, and less likely to see the satisfaction of desires in the analysis in the same way. (Parenthetically, this distinction we make between need and desire was made explicit by Winnicott [quoted in Greenberg & Mitchell, 1983, p.198] and inferred by Kohut [1971, 1977].) Along with most analysts, we postulate psychological drives as a significant aspect of normal development. How, then, does this view integrate with self psychology's postulation that when drives appear, they represent breakdown products of a fragmenting self? We think that the concept of drive as breakdown product refers not to the normal expression of oral, anal, phallic, or oedipal desires, but rather to a pathological heightening of such normal psychological desire, infused by aggression that is reactive to the experience of frustration or humiliation.

To return to the combined bipolar–tripartite model, the similarity we draw between the three sectors of the bipolar self (that is, ambitions, ideals, and skills, on the one hand) and the elements of the tripartite model (id, superego, and ego, on the other) has been quite adequately addressed by Wallerstein (1983), who also notes these strong parallels. In his comprehensive review of the two systems, Wallerstein points to self psychology's original contributions; however, he does not highlight one distinctive feature inherent in the bipolar model. In our view, the standard tripartite model is enriched by the bipolar concept of a structure-supporting selfobject attached to each of its sectors, thus implying that there is an abiding environmental influence on the significant structures of the mind. We feel this addition is both clarifying and helpful, and it does not represent a contradiction of modern mainstream analysis. For example, Loewald (1978) says there can be no id without the mother, and the superego is never a closed, completely autonomous, fully formed structure from the point of view of psychoanalytic developmentalists (Shane, 1977). The same might be said for the capacities of the ego, that its structure, too, is dependent for support and sustenance upon the environment throughout life—Mahler, Pine, and Bergman's (1975) subphase of "on the way to object constancy" does last a lifetime, after all. But self psychology, with its addition of selfobjects attached to each sector of the self, has expanded this modern ego psychology view of the human being as an open system interrelated with and dependent on the subjectively perceived environment, whereas the tripartite model as invented by Freud (1923) tends to stress instead a maturational striving toward autonomy and independence from the surround.

We see this emphasis on autonomy as a reflection of Freud's well-documented phallocentrism. It is apparent that Freud conceptualized development in terms of the boy, with the girl reduced to counterpart, but we have been struck that the masculine bias in Freudian thinking goes beyond perceiving development within a masculine framework. The mainstream psychoanalytic focus on autonomy as a goal for emotional health, for example, also happens to be a quality that is most often associated with maleness, particularly by men themselves. Freud had the genius and courage to believe that if he discovered in himself a particular tendency or fantasy, however shocking or unacceptable, the discovery must be true for most others as well. We can hardly be surprised, therefore, that he accepted his masculine perception of the world as the perception. After all, gender differences are subtle and have been slow in coming to light.

It is important, then, that Kohut has corrected for some of this masculine emphasis, counterbalancing it with what, in academic psychology, is referred to as a more "feminine" sensibility. Thus, Kohut (1980) questions autonomy as a legitimate goal of development, referring to it as a bias of the Western world. For him, healthy development involves the attainment of mature interrelatedness, not a capacity to stand separate and independent from one's environment. This thesis is reflected in his bipolar model, with its selfobjects embedded in each sector of the self, and remains the essence of Kohut's self–selfobject relatedness, crucial not only to healthy development, but also to an understanding of the analytic venture. In this regard, a general difference is noted in Western culture between how males and females think and relate. For example, in figure–ground studies, most often males perceive the figure, and females, the ground. Related to this, men are more likely to see themselves as independent, competitive strivers, and women to see themselves as interrelated within a social context (Gilligan, 1982). We can agree with Kohut that the emphasis on autonomy is a bias, although not of the Western world, as he says, but rather a bias of the Western male. Moreover, we would insist that just as in the figure–ground dichotomy, no one view is more correct or unbiased than the other, and, in fact, an equilibrium must be reached between autonomy and interrelatedness if we are to maintain as rich, balanced, complete, and correct a vision of development, and of the psychoanalytic situation, as possible.

For these reasons, then, we conceptualize a tripartite–bipolar working model rather than an either/or exclusionary theory. For despite many assertions to the contrary, such a superimposed combined model of the mind, or self, represents, to our view, how mainstream analysts open to self psychological insights are actually likely to think in the clinical situation. It should be noted that in combining these models we are equating the mind with the self, and the model of the mind with the model of the self. By so doing, we obviate the issue of which model is superordinate to which. We also avoid the issue of complementarity, that is, which model seems appropriate for which patient and when.

The model we propose, as with any psychoanalytic model, is but a construct in the mind of the psychoanalyst (Shane & Shane, 1980, 1985). It is useful only to the extent that it provides form and organization for understanding the psychological functioning of a given patient. We must emphasize, of course, that it has to match the patient's conscious and unconscious view of himself in his subjective psychological world, while at the same time remaining consistent with what is objectively known about human development in general, and even about that person in particular. This conception, which utilizes a developmental orientation and approach (Shane, 1977), extends the understanding of the self somewhat beyond the limits of subjective memory, introspection, intersubjectivity, and vicarious introspection, however central all of these are to analytic understanding. Therefore, we see the analyst's delineation of self structure in a particular patient as generated from three sources: the subjective world of the patient; the objective knowledge possessed by the analyst of the patient's life and of human development and human psychological functioning; and the intersubjective experiences within the psychoanalytic situation of transference and countertransference interactions, which interactions provide the most meaningful content of analytic reconstruction and narrative formation. As analyst and patient gradually and collaboratively discover and construct a sense of the patient's self, that self is made part of the representational world of the particular patient as an enhanced psychoanalytic self-awareness. This, in our opinion, is an integral and essential aspect of the analytic process. However, this effort at psychoanalytic self-enhancement, augmented by self psychological approaches, does not supplant the struggle to understand the mind in conflict (Brenner, 1982), but rather encompasses that struggle; hence the use of the combined model.

At this point we will describe the achievement of such a psychoanalytically enhanced sense of self as it emerged in the treatment of an adolescent girl.[2]

Nancy D, age 15, was referred for analysis by her father's analyst because of general unhappiness. The beginning picture of the self of this patient as it was conceptualized in her analyst's mind was based on an observational report supplied by her father, a 50-year-old, charismatic stockbroker and civic leader. He explained that both Nancy and her brother, Douglas, age 17, had been adopted and were currently living with him because of their adoptive mother's alcoholism. He described Nancy as greatly worried about her mother, and as shy, lonely, virtually friendless, at odds with her brother, and doing poorly in school. He said Nancy had been sad all of her life, attributing this pervasive affect to the following: Nancy's mother had been severely alcoholic from Nancy's adoption at birth; he himself had always drunk moderately and had been absent from home a great deal; the parents had fought bitterly and continuously throughout their marriage; and Nancy's older brother was openly hostile, and also uncontrollably physically aggressive with her.

Nancy herself appeared plain in appearance, listless in manner, and a great contrast to her dynamic, outgoing, and self-assured father. She seemed shy, depressed, and anxious, avoiding direct eye contact throughout the sessions. Subjectively, she was able to describe quite clearly her painful and confused feelings concerning her mother, revealing a mixture of fear, pity, and guilt in relation to her. She was afraid that her mother might actually physically harm her while drunk, or at the least embarrass and humiliate her, as she had done so often in the past. Yet she pitied her mother's helpless dependence on alcohol, and, when drunk, her clinging need of others. But Nancy's most intense feeling about her mother was guilt. She felt duty bound to try to help

---

2. It is particularly interesting to look at an adolescent patient when one considers the sources from which the self is discerned psychoanalytically, for it is at this developmental level that all three data sources are, in a unique way, concomitantly in view to the analyst. That is, subjective self-observation reaches an exquisite peak, and the sense of personal history and identity both crystallize. At the same time, while the analytic process can reach adult degrees of complexity, providing plentiful material for transference- and countertransference-based interpretation and reconstruction, technical adaptations retained from child analysis permit some access to objective, historical reports from important others. Thus, the availability of material from all three sources, subjective, objective, and transference–countertransference, permits the delineation of a full and relatively accurate psychoanalytic self.

her while at the same time she was reluctant to try, knowing from past experience that it was of no use. She felt most guilty because, while the court had given her mother custody of her at age 11, at age 12 Nancy had run away to live with her father and brother. She explained that she had been feeling lonely, desperate, and deserted, and that she had packed a suitcase one weekend and "just left." She feared that this "betrayal" had exacerbated her mother's drinking, which was by now life threatening, but she felt she had to save herself.

Nancy remembered that first year away from her mother, with just her father and brother, as the happiest of her life, but after a time Douglas reverted to his old pattern of getting angry with her and then physically hurting her. The situation with her father was more complicated. She revealed little in these first sessions except for great love and admiration for him, referring to him as "perfect."

In time, however, she became conscious of defended against memories and perceptions of him as sexually seductive and emotionally abusive. During one of the earlier sessions Nancy described a day at home. By the time she awoke, her father would have left the house. She and Douglas would have breakfast alone as the housekeeper was discouraged by their father from "spoiling them." After school she and Douglas would be alone again until her father returned, exhausted, out of patience, and needing to retire to his room for "a drink." He would drink until sleepy, have food brought in to him, and she would not see or hear of him again unless she happened to witness his almost nightly sleep-walking episodes. She described these as "funny," but it was apparent that she felt scared of him at these moments as he wandered around in the dark not conscious of what he was doing. When confronted with this, Nancy admitted that the sight of her father in that state was threatening both to her safety and to her wish to see him as strong and in control.   •

In her more optimistic moments Nancy would reveal a secret hope that her father's current relationship with a much younger woman would lead to marriage—to, as she put it, "a family at last"—and a new and more satisfactory mother. At the same time she betrayed her doubts, based on the woman's immaturity, and finally concluded that she was quite sure she would never have a proper mother.

As she talked about her situation during these early sessions, her analyst could observe some of her symptomatology. Nancy was never able to meet the analyst's eyes. Her chronic anxiety was demonstrated by her severely bitten fingernails and her obsessive uncertainty about her own moods and feelings. A typical statement was: "I'm in a terrible mood—well, not a terrible mood—I hate everything—I don't hate everything but I am bored, I'm bored with life. I don't know if that's true or not." Referring to the combined model, it was clear that Nancy's subjective sense of herself was marred by a weak cohesiveness related to a faulty, inconsistent selfobject milieu, as well as by anxiety, depressive affect, and resultant defensive symptomatic doubting.

Her mother came in just once, about a year after Nancy began analysis. She was driven in by her new husband whom she insisted remain for the interview, and she was obviously too drunk to talk very much. She could remember little about Nancy's early childhood, but nevertheless her presence suggested a great deal about the patient's difficult early environment.

A salient feature of Nancy's early life was the fact that she, like her brother, had been adopted at birth. Nothing was known about her biological parents. An even more salient feature was the fact that her adoptive mother's alcoholic problem began the same year she had been adopted, with the result that neither parent was available much of the time. While they could afford to provide household help, they had no sense that consistency was important; consequently people would come and go frequently. As her father described it, the children were left to the care of inadequate and unfamiliar caretakers while he was out of the house and her mother remained incapacitated. This information was essentially unknown to the patient.

Thus, the specific details of Nancy's early history are sparse. Her father did remember that her mother had refused to drive Nancy to nursery school, and neither parent thought to provide a substitute means of transportation, so that Nancy, when she began kindergarten, felt behind the others. Here the life narrative is taken over predominantly by subjective reports from the patient herself.

Nancy went to a progressive, private school from kindergarten through sixth grade. She remembered enjoying school and being miserable when she was forced to remain home. During fifth and sixth grade she had great difficulty eating in school, although she could not say why for certain. She recalled that her teachers would be disturbed by this and would coax and encourage her to eat, and she suspected that perhaps she was looking for their attention. They would write notes about this to her mother, who apparently did not respond. However, her mother was sufficiently in contact with Nancy to have informed her about the facts of life, including providing an adequate preparation for menarche, which occurred at age 11. Nancy remembered beginning to masturbate at about age 10 or 11, and she was never especially awkward about sexual matters. When she began analysis, the patient was in junior high school, felt friendless, was shy with her classmates, and was performing inadequately.

The material just presented comprises content for beginning formulations of the self to this particular patient, contributed mainly from objective and subjective sources. Objective data were provided by both parents, the analyst's initial observations, and a general knowledge of development and mental processes. What emerged was a picture of a deprived infancy and a deprived and troubled childhood with an inadequate and unsupportive selfobject surround. This contributed to symptomatic self-doubting, reflecting an underlying shaky sense of self constancy and self cohesiveness, a low sense of self-esteem, and a pervasive depressive affect. Conflicts were revealed regarding abandonment and guilt over hostile aggression toward her inadequate and frustrating mother, along with a suggestion of fended-off oedipal desires regarding her father, and a weakening of her superego or pole of ideals and standards in relation to attempts to retain an idealized picture of him. Thus the beginning formulation of the self employed concepts from the combined model of the mind.

Turning now to the analysis itself, we will demonstrate the evolution of a psychoanalytic picture of the patient's self as it is enriched by intersubjective data from transference–countertransference exchanges within the analytic process. We will also demonstrate how the patient's own sense of self is enhanced, firmed, and given shape as she is provided, through interpretation, an in-depth appreciation of the unconscious workings of her mind, and as she also experiences the meliorative effects of new selfobject and new developmental object interactions. Only isolated vignettes from the beginning, middle, and end phases of the treatment will be presented as it is possible to do no more than suggest the flow of this 7-year analysis.

Once the analysis got under way, and the initial subjective revelations about her life had been aired, Nancy revealed an unusual difficulty in expressing herself. When in any given hour she had been silent for a time, she would complain of boredom, a recurrent and unpleasant state for her, both inside and outside her analytic sessions. At such times the analyst would attempt to get her to connect the boredom to her life situation in the present as well as in the past (that is, the emptiness she had felt in relation to her distant mother), and, most difficult of all for her, to connect her boredom to her current relationship with the analyst. She was told that boredom is often a feeling that arises to protect against other feelings within her. In one particular hour where this issue came up, Nancy could think of nothing but her boredom, and her fear that her analyst would find her boring in response. Then, only reluctantly, she recalled an experience with her father the night before. His girl-friend, Susan, had come for dinner, and her father, moderately drunk, had carelessly spilled his drink at the table. Nancy hurried to wipe it up, and her father, gruffly pushing her away, yelled, "Keep your fucking hands to yourself!" Susan defended and consoled Nancy, who was both humiliated and frightened at the moment, but later, long after her father's abject apology, still felt miserable because, as she said, she could not bear to disappoint or displease him in any way. She went on to say that when she woke in the morning she had had a headache and she had felt bored all day in school. The analyst told Nancy that it must be hard for her to deal with the mixture of feelings that were stirred up the night before; that she must find it difficult to experience rage and disillusionment with her father whom she loves and needs so much. Also, she was told that she must find it hard to receive comfort from a woman because it reminds her of what she had needed for so long from her mother. Nancy was able to acknowledge that she felt these emotions toward her father, in addition to feeling hurt, and she knew that she had guiltily sought and enjoyed attention from women before, like from her teachers when she would not eat, but what surprised her most was the fact that her boredom served to protect her from these feelings. Once the usefulness of the psychoanalytic concept of boredom as a defense against painful affects was understood, analyst and patient could get to the question of why she was feeling the boredom in the here and now. Could there be some specific emotion she was not examining? Nancy was then able to connect her wish for Susan's comfort the night before with what she both wanted and feared from the analyst, that the analyst would become for her a comforting, mothering person, but, also and inevitably, one who would disillusion her. This transference theme of unconsciously avoiding painful affects related to the frustration of unmet needs was central for the opening phase. It became central as well to a psychoanalytically enhanced understanding of her self as it emerged in the interaction with the analyst and then, as was illustrated in the vignette, was communicated to the patient. Such interpretations, made by the analyst qua analyst, can also be understood as an aug-mentation of the patient's skills or ego capacities, made by the analyst qua alterego selfobject, auxiliary ego, or new developmental selfobject, thereby illustrating the abiding influence of the structure-supporting selfobject on the psyche.

Another aspect of the patient's increasing awareness of herself was Nancy's discovery that she had her own needs, desires, intentions, and preferences, and a legitimate right to feel them. In the past, the determination of what she wanted had always been unconsciously dependent upon first finding out what others wanted from her, her necessity to please was so strong. Her analysis became for her a continuous realization that she had her own thoughts and feelings, and that she was entitled to them regardless of whether they conformed to the wishes of others. To give an everyday instance, she said in one session, "I want to see a movie tonight—well, I'm not sure I want to go—I don't know if Ginger [her friend] wants to go or not—maybe I should just stay home. I don't know." When her doubt and uncertainty were pointed out, Nancy was truly surprised. Yet, as she reflected on it she realized very simply that she could not know if she wanted to go to a movie because she was not sure whether wanting to go to the movie would be at variance with what her friend wanted. In tracing the origin of this particular and persistent quality in her thinking, it appeared, based upon her associations, to be linked to her memories of her mother's arbitrary and unpredictable moods and priorities. Together, analyst and patient could speculate that in order to deal with her mother, Nancy had had all of her childhood to mold herself to her mother's apparent intentions, and her problem became trying to predict them rather than to ascertain her own. This character trait also shaped her interactions with her father, brother, and friends. Inevitably, she responded in a similar way to the analyst, particularly around the question of who her sessions were to benefit, and, in fact, who her analysis was to benefit. This provided an opportunity for exploration within the maternal transference, and thus to reconstruct with some conviction the molding of herself to her mother, that is, her history of needing to provide a selfobject function for her mother, rather than having a mother who provided such functions for her. For example, on one occasion, Nancy's school was going on a 3-day camping trip that would have necessitated her missing a session. While she was quite regretful because it was an opportunity to solidify some new friendships, she unquestioningly told the school she was not going. In talking of this later, she said that she had not realized at first how much she had wanted to go, but, in any case, the analyst had been expecting her and must not be disappointed. In other words, Nancy could not allow herself to know that she wanted something independently and at variance with the apparent wishes of an important other. The repeated work on such instances in the analysis ultimately reduced Nancy's anxiety about object loss, strengthening her capacity to trust and rely on the analyst as one able to give Nancy's needs priority. These meliorative new developmental object and mirroring selfobject experiences led to a firming and individuating of her self-feeling and an enhanced object constancy.

The transference wish that emerged late in the middle phase of analysis was that of being rescued, protected, and seductively overprotected by a loved and admired parent, and, consistent with this both conscious and defended-against wish, Nancy revealed herself to be accident prone and disinclined to protect herself, both characteristics of children and adolescents who are unconciously seeking such care from others. Nancy was soon able to recognize and be fearful of her wish to injure herself in order to get protection. She said: "Sometimes I think I wouldn't mind getting into an accident. I wouldn't want to get killed or anything—but sometimes I wouldn't mind—I wouldn't want people to feel sorry for me, but maybe, yes, someone to take care of me. It is an old, old feeling. I used to dream about it and daydream about it. I still do."

Thus, under the pressure of the intense transference wish, Nancy was able to recover, after the initial defensive negation, a fantasy of being rescued, permitting a reconstruction of her childhood longings. Despite the interpretive reconstructions, Nancy continued to express these wishes. When she became ill, as she often did during this phase of her analysis, she was depressed and bitterly disillusioned that her analyst, along with others, seemed to let her down once again. It required considerable working through before the wish to be helpless and rescued was sufficiently mastered. We see here an instance of intrapsychic conflict or intersectorial imbalance. To elucidate the latter, the strong need to be admired and treasured is at variance with valued ideals of independence. Fear of abandonment and self-inflicted injury serve both as self-punishment and as means to repair threatened selfobject loss, thereby restoring equilibrium and balance to the self.

Connected with this theme, Nancy worked on her anguish over an unhappy and ill-chosen love affair that had occurred the previous summer during a prolonged absence from the analysis. This affair was ultimately understood as her need for a close, exclusive attachment to replace the analyst, combined with an ongoing attraction to boys who would treat her badly, that is, who would desert her as her mother, her father, and her analyst had. Boys who liked her quickly lost their appeal; boys who were ambivalent, who would flirt with her at the same time they flirted with others, were very attractive to her. She would "fall in love" and then feel hurt and rejected when the relationship ended. This masochistic attitude was reconstructed as having positive and negative oedipal meaning. In addition, the dyadic quality to these relationships was recognized and interpreted. Nancy sought a closeness to boys that had pregenital aspects; she wanted to be hugged and to have her back played with by someone whom she could admire and idealize; she wanted to be held, comforted, and stroked. In response to the interpretation that she might want this kind of closeness with the analyst as well, Nancy recalled for the first time an old nighttime ritual from latency days. She would take all of her stuffed animals into bed with her. Each would have to be held, stroked, kissed, and comforted in the same amount to avoid jealousies among them. She would then pretend the bed was a boat rocking in a stormy sea; one animal would be washed overboard, after which a rescue operation was launched. Finally, the animal would be recovered, kissed, comforted more than the rest, and allowed to be the only one to spend the night in her arms. Over time, connections were made between this nighttime ritual and her turning passive into active in relation to her adoptive and biological mothers, as well as her recurrent tendency to be accident prone, her current transference wishes, and her newly emerging sibling rivalry with other patients.

The uncovering of this important memory served to confirm the interpretation of Nancy's rescue fantasies, adding a convincing depth to her evolving life narrative. In addition, the insight contributed to the patient's being able, in time, to work through, and for the most part give up her masochistic character pattern and primitive mirroring self-object hunger, and, eventually, to enter into phase-appropriate and healthy heterosexual relationships.

Toward the end of Nancy's long analysis, her mother's condition worsened, and it became clear that she was dying. Her mother's terminal illness strongly and poignantly revived in Nancy her childhood relationship to her, with the attendant feelings of deprivation, hostility, and guilt, not only over her reactive hostile aggression (Parens, 1979; Shane & Shane, 1982), but also over her oedipal triumph. Interpretation and working through of these feelings ultimately led to a new self integration. For example, early in this period, Nancy had had a major confrontation with her mother during which she berated her for her selfishness and for her "disgusting lying and drunkenness." She came into her hour describing the pride she felt in being able, at last, to stand up to her mother. She said, "I recognize that I am my own person now and have to be my own mother and father." Far from being a momentary response, Nancy's pronouncement turned out to be a reflection of an apparently permanent structural change, confirming both her relinquishment of primitive selfobject seeking and her readiness for new, phase-appropriate, late adolescent, independent (drive) object and selfobject experiences, and a phase-appropriate autonomy. Being able to be a parent to herself involved both transmuting internalizations—that is, internalizations without an object tag—and identifications—that is, internalizations with an object tag to significant others.

During her mother's 4-month terminal illness, Nancy was able to master some of the anger she had felt for her in the past. More importantly, turning passive into active, she had the opportunity to give to her mother again, but this time effectively and without self distortion. Nancy's constant presence allowed her mother to rely upon her, and the latter often verbalized her gratitude. The analyst pointed out both the pleasure in being needed and the comfort she got from having a predictable relationship with a sober mother for the first time. Nancy demonstrated real strength in dealing with her mother's death, and for the following year, worked through in the mourning process her ambivalent feelings derived from a lifetime of troubled interaction.

The final vignette comes from the end phase of the analysis. About 8 months into mourning her mother's death, a week after the first Christmas without her, Nancy had a dream that "it was Christmas all over again." In the dream, Susan, her stepmother, who was now actually being divorced from her father, was trying to take over the festivities, and Nancy felt angry. She was then accused by someone of wrongdoing. In associating to this dream, she said she thought that her stepmother stood for her mother who had died, whom she both wanted to have back and was glad to have gone. She connected the accusation of wrongdoing in the dream with her past wishes to replace both her mother and her stepmother, and her oedipal guilt that both were now out of her father's and her own life. Her further association was to her father's question the week before: "Are you still seeing Dr. Shane four times a week?" She had "forgotten" to talk about the conversation, during which she had responded to her father's question, "Of course I do; I need to!" She was then able to analyze why she had forgotten to mention it: she felt guilty because she knew she needed the analyst and her analysis less than she did before. It was interpreted that, although the analyst remained extremely important to her, there might be some side of her that would like to be free of her analyst as well. Nancy was thoughtful, and responded: "It's ironic; now that I finally trust you, I don't think I really need you as much." It turned out that, as she was mourning her mother's death, she was also beginning to mourn the prospect of losing her analyst.

In fact, Nancy was doing very well and had reached most of her analytic goals. She had largely overcome the developmental arrests and weaknesses that stemmed from inadequate selfobject experiences. In addition, she had resolved the conflicts regarding her mother and father as independent (drive) objects in dyadic and triadic configurations, and had worked through the transference neurosis. Moreover, the fact that the analysis had continued through the mourning process in relation to her mother's death, and facilitated it, enabled this patient to become more conscious of her defended against conflicts and attachments from the many developmental phases that comprised the course of her life to date. A complete and in-depth picture of her self was achieved that matched, largely, the analyst's view of the patient's mind and its functioning.

In this chapter we have attempted to demonstrate that a developmental orientation applied to a bipolar–tripartite amalgam provides an adequate working model of the self and its enhancement in the analytic process. The question that needs to be addressed is, what is added by using this developmental combined model? Simply put, it permits a focus on the totality of the psychological person conceptualized as a bipolar self in intimate interchange with corresponding selfobjects, without sacrificing the indispensable theoretical advantages of the tripartite model of the mind with its intrapsychic representational world, its intersystemic and intrasystemic unconscious conflicts and compromise formations, and specific attachments and attractions to independent (drive) objects. We are convinced that the developmental orientation clarifies the sources of the material by which one devises an in-depth picture of the psychological world of the patient. For example, the fact that this adolescent patient had been adopted and raised by a mother who almost certainly was inadequate to meet her daughter's developmental needs from birth onward and throughout the crucial separation–individuation process, must necessarily have fed into the analyst's conception of the patient, and must, in addition, have influenced, covertly or overtly, the choices and priorities of analytic intervention. We have maintained that dependence upon reconstruction alone, based upon transference interactions and subjective material exclusively, is incomplete; to pursue the analytic task as if this important analytic approach were sufficient unto itself for understanding and interpretation would be misleading, since every analyst has within his or her armamentarium a significant degree of psychoanalytic knowledge about growth and development. As developmentalists, we believe in being conscious of where our ideas about the life course of a given patient originate. Whether these ideas come from what we know objectively about normal emotional and cognitive development and functioning, are heard "objectively" from others regarding the patient, come from a successful reconstruction of the past based on the patient's here and now transference reactions with our concomitant, vicariously introspective and subjective responses, or, finally, come from a patient's preanalytic, naive, subjective introspection, being conscious of their source clarifies the work we do.

REFERENCES

Adler, G. (1985). *Borderline Psychopathology and Its Treatment.* New York and London: Aronson.
Brenner, C. (1982). *The Mind in Conflict.* New York: International Universities Press.
Freud, S. (1923). The ego and the id. *Standard Edition,* 19:1–66.
Gilligan, C. (1982). *In a Different Voice: Psychological Theory and Women's Development.* Cambridge, MA: Harvard University Press.
Goodman, S. (1977). *Psychoanalytic Education and Research.* New York: International Universities Press.
Greenberg, J.R., & Mitchell, S.A. (1983). *Object Relations in Psychoanalytic Theory.* Cambridge, MA: Harvard University Press.
Hartmann, H. (1950). Comments on the psychoanalytic theory of the ego. *Psychoanalytic Study of the Child,* 5:74–96.
Kohut, H. (1971). *The Analysis of the Self.* New York: International Universities Press.
Kohut, H. (1977). *The Restoration of the Self.* New York: International Universities Press.
Kohut, H. (1980). Summarizing reflections. In A. Goldberg, ed., *Advances in Self Psychology* (pp. 473–554). New York: International Universities Press.
Loewald, H. (1978). Instinct theory, object relations, and psychic structure formation. *Journal of the American Psychoanalytic Association,* 26:493–506.
Mahler, M., Pine, F., & Bergman, A. (1975). *The Psychological Birth of the Human Infant: Symbiosis and Individuation.* New York: Basic Books.
Meissner, W. (1984). Models of the mind: The role of theory in the psychoanalytic process. *Psychoanalytic Inquiry,* 4:5–32.

Modell, A. (1985). *Psychoanalysis in a New Context*. New York: International Universities Press.

Parens, H. (1979). *The Development of Aggression in Early Childhood*. New York & London: Jason Aronson.

Peterfreund, E. (1983). *The Process of Psychoanalytic Psychotherapy: Models and Strategies*. Hillsdale, NJ & London: Analytic Press.

Richards, A. (1982). The superordinate self in psychoanalytic theory and in the self psychologies. *Journal of the American Psychoanalytic Association*, 30:939–957.

Rosenblatt, A., & Thickstun, J. (1977). Modern psychoanalytic concepts in a general psychology. *Psychological Issues*, 11:42–43.

Shane, M. (1977). A rationale for teaching analytic technique based on a developmental orientation and approach. *International Journal of Psycho-Analysis*, 58:95–103.

Shane, M., & Shane, E. (1980). Psychoanalytic developmental theories of the self: An integration. In A. Goldberg, ed., *Advances in Self Psychology* (pp. 23–46). New York: International Universities Press.

Shane, M., & Shane, E. (1982). The strands of aggression: A confluence of data. *Psychoanalytic Inquiry*, 2:263–282.

Shane, M., & Shane, E. (1985). Change and integration in psychoanalytic developmental theory. In C. F. Settlage & R. Brockbank, eds., *New Ideas in Psychoanalysis* (pp. 69–82). Hillsdale, NJ: Analytic Press.

Stern. D.S. (1985). *The Interpersonal World of the Infant*. New York: Basic Books.

Stolorow, R.D., Brandchaft, B., & Atwood, G.E. (1983). Intersubjectivity in psychoanalysis. *Bulletin of the Menninger Clinic*, 47:117–128.

Wallerstein, R.S. (1983). Self psychology and classical psychoanalytic psychotherapy: The nature of their relationship. In A. Goldberg, ed., *The Future of Psychoanalysis* (pp. 19–63). New York: International Universities Press.

Weil, A. (1974). Ego strengthening prior to psychoanalysis. *Psychoanalytic Study of the Child*, 28:287–301.

ORIGINAL PAPERS

Applied Psychoanalysis

14

A Psychoanalytic Interpretation of *The Bacchae* of Euripides

JERALD KAY

> All that a playwright requires for drama is a vivid memory from his own childhood and family—especially Greek drama, which is most intensely concerned with intrafamilial conflict.
>
> —Philip E. Slater

INTRODUCTION

Whatever faults may be found with *The Bacchae*, it remains unquestionably one of the most engaging, if enigmatic, plays of all times. Throughout history, and in particular the 20th century, *The Bacchae* has had its share of famous detractors and admirers (Dodds, 1944; Guthrie, 1950; Kitto, 1939; Murray, 1913, 1918; Winnington-Ingram, 1948).

Yet, the psychoanalytic voice has been surprisingly and conspicuously absent in the controversy over this play (Caldwell, 1974, p. 128). That psychoanalysts have tended to ignore *The Bacchae* is particularly surprising since Euripides has come to be regarded as "the greatest emotional colorist" (Sutherland, 1968, p. 92) of the classical world. As

> the first psychologist. . . . [i]t was he who discovered the soul in a new sense—who revealed the troubled world of man's emotions and passions. . . . He created the pathology of the mind. It was impossible for poetry to be written on such subjects before his time, for it was then that men first learned to look fairly and squarely at these things to guide themselves through the labyrinth of the human soul by the light of their convictions that all these demonic passions and obsessions were necessary and logical processes of human nature. (Jaeger, 1965, p. 353)

The few psychoanalytic writers who have examined *The Bacchae*

in any depth have generally limited their commentaries to isolated por-
tions of the play (Devereaux, 1970) or to the Greek concept of madness
and character pathology (Devereaux, 1970; Green, 1979, pp. 167–177;
Roberts, 1975, pp. 33–53; Sale, 1972; Simon, 1978; pp. 113–122).

While many of these contributions have been most creative, they
lacked a comprehensive interpretation that could consistently illuminate
and make sense with the whole of the play. *The Bacchae* is after all a
profoundly complex play. It is more than merely an important document
on Greek religion detailing the 5th-century Athenian worship of Dionysus, or on the power exerted by the religious group over the individual,
or even on the role played by group emotions in social and political life
(Winnington-Ingram, 1948, p. 153). *The Bacchae* has many dimensions:
the contrast between the rational and the irrational–mystical, the conflict between civilization and barbarism, between city and wilderness,
between state and humanity, and between the masculine and the feminine (Sutherland, 1968, p. 91). Seen from a specifically psychoanalytic
perspective, Euripides addressed a deeper, more universal concern:
namely, the vicissitudes of the mother–child relationship and its impact
on personality development. That *The Bacchae* can be understood psychoanalytically, however, does not imply that Euripides consciously set
out to focus on psychological or more specifically on developmental
issues, for as Freud acknowledged: "For its power, art depends on an
appeal that is hidden from the artist as well as the audience. . . . All
psychic texts lie out of reach of the mind that produced them (Rieff,
1959, p. 135).

Despite vociferous criticism from the classicist, the psychoanalyst
need not apologize for his viewpoint. Psychoanalysis

> is the only systematic account of the human mind which, in point of subtlety
> and complexity, of interest and tragic power, deserves to stand aside the
> chaotic mass of psychological insights which literature has accumulated
> through the centuries. . . . The human nature of the Freudian psychology
> is exactly the stuff upon which the poet has always exercised his art. (Trill-
> ing, 1947, p. 32)

The purpose of this chapter is not to examine *The Bacchae* as a
way to understand its author (Reed, 1982) psychoanalytically (although
many critics have tried to view this work as the playwright's 11th-hour
religious conversion after lifelong skepticism toward the Olympian de-
ities), but rather carefully to delineate the author's unifying poetic vision
as it appears in his tragedy. This vision, it will be shown, is entirely
consistent both with what self psychology understands about human

personality and its development and with what is now accepted as an accurate representation of sex-role conflict in 5th- and 4th-century Athenian life (Peradotto & Sullivan, 1984; Pomeroy, 1975). More specifically, the self psychological perspective enables a more comprehensive understanding of the play than that achieved through previous psychoanalytic interpretation. The vantage point of self psychology, it will be argued, also provides deeper and more convincing motivations for Euripides' characters and elucidates more clearly selected universal themes of human nature.

THE PLAY

The Bacchae, along with *Iphegenia at Aulis,* and the lost *Alcamaeon* were produced by his son in 405 B.C., one year after Euripirdes died in exile at the court of Archelaus in Macedon. Ferguson (1972, p. 238) reminds us that all of Euripides' plays were written under the shadow of war and that he loved Athens but loathed her antifeminism, imperialism, and arrogance in war. Euripides was a product of the intellectual changes that were to result in the breakdown of the Athenian society. *The Bacchae* is clearly the most complex of his tragedies and takes place in the City of Thebes, ruled by the young Pentheus, son of Agave, and grandson of Cadmus, the heroic and legendary city founder. The dramatic line of the play unfolds around Pentheus's attempt inappropriately and violently to restrict worship of a new and "obscene" god, Dionysus. He seeks to prevent the women of Thebes whom he views as "serving the lusts of men" from going to the god's celebration and even imprisons the mysterious but attractive priest of Dionysus who, in fact, is the god in disguise. Dionysus escapes by destroying the royal palace and convinces Pentheus to come to Mount Cithaeron dressed as a woman, lest he be recognized, and view the powerful and alluring women celebrating the god's rites. Pentheus climbs a large fir tree with the god's aid and is soon discovered by the Theban women. With Agave leading the group of women, Pentheus is literally torn into pieces. Agave returns to Thebes with what she believes is the head of a young mountain lion on her thyrsus (a staff twined with ivy), only to discover at the end of the play that it is the head of her son, Pentheus. The play closes as Dionysus dooms Cadmus, Agave, and her sister to exile.

EARLIER PSYCHOANALYTIC INTERPRETATIONS

Several psychoanalytic interpretations of *The Bacchae* have been offered previously. These will be reviewed before moving to the current self psychologically informed analysis. The classicist William Sale (1972) chose not to approach the play as religious or miraculous but saw it as a portrayal of a real man and his madness. Dividing the play into six "couch sessions," he analyzes the character of Pentheus. For Sale, Euripides has portrayed the young king at the opening of the play with his character defenses in full flower and through subsequent regressions discloses his core pathology. At the start of the play, Pentheus is a brash and violent young man, at the close he is a frightened little boy, pleading for his mother's recognition. During the interceding "sessions" there is an unfolding of several themes central to understanding Pentheus: a conflict about sex with intense fear and hatred of women; a homosexual attraction to the sexually ambiguous Dionysus; and a profoundly limited knowledge of self. With regard to the latter, Pentheus's superficial introductory self definition to Dionysus, "I am Pentheus, son of Echion and Agave" (lines 505–507)[1] contains the cryptic but basic psychoanalytic premise that what unfolds in the drama derives from the impact of an absent father and the highly conflictual relation to his mother, herself dangerously conflicted in her attitudes about men. Both the voyeurism and transvestism are seen by Sale as compromise solutions permitting Pentheus to satisfy his sexual curiosity about women and to resolve his castration anxiety. Pentheus's nuclear problem is realized in the climax of the play: He wants to be a man, but when he demonstrates his sexuality, symbolized by the erect fir tree (the fir is at first bent low and again made erect in its uprooting), he is dismembered by his mother. While noting the pathogenic absence of the father, often mentioned but never seen, Sale emphasizes that violent rage toward her son is a function of Agave's envy of men, who initially she imitates and then destroys as an expression of her desire to castrate all men. Sale (1977, p. 99) interprets the frenetic dancing of the maenads as representing the alternative, more successful solution to Pentheus's conflict, the sublimated, modulated expression of sexuality and aggression. His failure to choose this avenue eventuates in his unrelenting regression and ultimate destruction.

---

1. Line citations throughout this chapter, except where otherwise noted, refer to Arrowsmith (1958).

Bennett Simon (1978), too, emphasizes the infantile sexuality in *The Bacchae* but views Pentheus's curiosity as a normative attempt to answer such questions as, Is sex murder or eating? Can babies be born from fathers' thighs (as Dionysus was from Zeus) and mothers' uteruses? Where is the father (Zeus and Echion) at birth? Is it safe to witness birth (Semele, Dionysus's mother, is destroyed through fire by the jealous Hera)? What is the role of the father in conception (did Zeus really impregnate Semele)?

Simon describes madness as the blurring between self and other, a confusion between inside and outside, as portrayed through dramatic action between Pentheus and Dionysus (lines 115–116). It is not oedipal sexuality that is so frightening, but the regressive pull, the "wish to be the small boy in his mother's arms." Pentheus's character, Simon feels, is marked by reaction formation with ultimate psychosis, as exemplified by the hallucinations of the palace scene. While the wish to merge is identified as an important theme in *The Bacchae,* Simon examines it not from Pentheus's view, but from Agave's, whom he describes as "merging with the ambivalently regarded child with resultant destructive rage."

For Simon, this play is an elucidation of the basic biological and developmental tension to express and integrate masculine and feminine. Pentheus's psychosis is the result of his inability to accept the feminine through repudiation of the bisexual god.

Weston LaBarre (1970), a psychoanthropologist, notes the centrality of the lost father, but argues that Pentheus's fascination with the father is in fact a fascination with magic—the little boy groping for the magic power of the father. Indeed, Pentheus's transvestism is a traditional component of the Shaman ritual. Dionysus, LaBarre feels, is a more general symbol than masculine–feminine synthesis; he is "the grandiose self—the defense against death." He saw the Dionysian cult worship in the 5th and 4th centuries in Greece as the ghost dance of an Athenian civilization dying from platonism, antifeminism, slavery, and war.

Green (1979) shares much with Simon in his assessment of the play, believing the eminent dramatic question to be that of filiation. Is Dionysus born from a mortal, adulterous woman, or is he the son of Zeus? The revelry on Mount Cithaeron is a classical portrayal of the primal scene—Pentheus's wish to see the sexual activities of adults.

A SECOND ANALYSIS FOR PENTHEUS

As noted earlier, Sale's approach to *The Bacchae* through the character analysis of Pentheus is a most creative one. It is ultimately problematic, however, for the following reasons. First, the overreliance on an oedipal-based pathology makes the climatic scene on Mount Cithaeron unsatisfying. Second, he, and others as well, have failed to investigate or to include in their interpretation the final scene of the play. While there are unquestionably textual problems within that last scene due to lengthy lacuna at line 1329 (Dodds, 1944), it nevertheless provides a rich confirmation of all that has preceded it. Through a striking portrayal of the remorseful Agave comes the verification of the specificity of Pentheus's psychopathology. A new psychoanalysis for Pentheus and perhaps a first one for Agave are, therefore, in order to provide a new interpretation of the play that explains all the parts of this work.

Given the play's sophisticated portrayal of psychopathology, a fitting question might be whether there is a precipitant for Pentheus's psychological dysfunction. If so, does it enhance our understanding of the young king? While the appearance of Dionysus unquestionably speaks to a historical introduction of certain clashing beliefs in Greek culture (LaBarre, 1970), it also represents an important psychological event to the youthful Theban king.

Dionysus, it will be argued, is his mother's and, therefore, Pentheus's idealized image of what Pentheus should be. This idealized image is also a socially corrective one, but it is an image that destroys Pentheus because his mother cannot provide its components. Her intense rage emanating from her consistent personal devaluation prevents this process. Pentheus's conflicts, therefore, are not primarily sexual ones, despite the prevalence of his sexualized fantasies about Dionysus. They become sexual through the idealization process as he prepares to become like Dionysus. Rather, his struggle is one for admiration and affirmation through misguided quests for autonomy and power (lines 319, 390, 400).

Further confirmation for this more basic approach to Pentheus's character analysis comes within the first meeting of Dionysus and Pentheus. Whereas Sale has spoken of Pentheus's homosexual attraction to Dionysus, it is equally plausible to interpret the king's early lines to Dionysus (lines 453–458) as evidence of Pentheus's mounting uneasiness at the appearance of this more attractive and charismatic stranger. Pentheus's comments, therefore, reflect an unsettling recognition that there is a substantial threat to his self-esteem. Pentheus exclaims toward the close of his initial confrontation with Dionysus: "But I say, 'Chain him,' and I am the stronger here" (lines 503–505). Off stage, amidst thunder, lightning, and earthquakes, Dionysus destroys the royal palace and escapes Pentheus's shortlived imprisonment. In his speech to the chorus and leader, Dionysus states on two occasions that he humiliated the young king (lines 616–640). This humiliation is so intense that Pentheus becomes overwhelmed and decompensates, as is symbolized by the palatial destruction. In his regressed state, he hallucinates flames, Dionysus, and a bull, aggressive and sexual breakdown products of an unstable psyche (lines, 618, 623, 629).

Pentheus emerges from the palace ruins and immediately threatens Dionysus again, but is interrupted by a messenger from Mount Cithaeron, who relays a fantastic tale that introduces the all-important theme of feminine rageful destruction. When the village men attempt to ingratiate themselves to Pentheus by capturing his mother, she proclaims: "Hounds who run with me, men are hunting us down! Follow, follow me! Use your wands for weapons." The messenger continues, "At this we fled and barely missed being torn to pieces by the women" (lines 731–764).

Again, Pentheus is troubled by humiliation through the shameful routing of the village men by the women (line 779), and he subsequently calls for retaliation. Dionysus dramatically subverts his plan for revenge and invites Pentheus to see the revels on Mount Cithaeron. What follows, of course, is Dionysus's unexpected enticement of Pentheus. He apparently seduces the king to dress as a woman lest he too be attacked; but in this scene, Pentheus continually pleads not to be embarrassed, shamed, or humiliated (lines 826, 842). He dreads this shame and humiliation, as will be argued later, for this is precisely what he has experienced at the hands of his mother. Dionysus, too, echoes the underlying centrality of this theme (lines 853–854).   •

At this junction in the play it is difficult to account for the sudden and dramatic shift in Pentheus. How easily he accepts Dionysus's offer to dress as a woman and view the rites! Many have criticized this turnaround or labelled it as a contrivance not dissimilar to the use of a *deus ex machine*. But there may be a more satisfying and specific psychological explanation for this event, Pentheus can so readily dress as a woman because Dionysus becomes at that moment a much-needed selfobject. Pentheus no longer needs to pursue his aggressive quest for revenge because he hopes now through a different relationship with Dionysus to acquire a sense of himself as a man. Bagg (1978, p. 11) has noted that Pentheus becomes alive and joyful when he dresses as a woman.

In this respect, Dionysus is able to serve two important psychological functions for Pentheus. First, this scene very dramatically portrays how strong is Pentheus's yearning for a father, a masculine selfobject, one who can appropriately accept and mirror his assertiveness and vitality while permitting "the requisite merger with a source of idealized strength and calmness" (Kohut, 1970, p. 524). His grandfather was simply insufficient to provide a psychological wedge of safety and protection between the young king and his mother. Second, and of much greater importance, Pentheus has at last discovered a way to please a man and simultaneously to become closer in a nonthreatening manner to his mother through a feminine identification. Pentheus realizes this, albeit unconsciously, and is then able to *proclaim through his dressing* that Dionysus is indeed the new king. Pentheus desperately needs to be in the presence of Dionysus to gain the affirmation he never received from his parents. The fact that Pentheus is drawn to Dionysus, and not to another man, indicates not only his deep longings for a father, but for one who is a god, omnipotent and omniscient. Nothing less could soothe the deeply troubled Pentheus. Pentheus becomes Dionysus, the desperately needed new self.

Pentheus accompanies Dionysus to Mount Cithaeron and once there with Dionysus's assistance climbs a fir tree in order to witness the Dionysian ritual more fully. What follows is one of the most frightening events in Greek tragedy.

> And when they saw my master perching in his tree, they climbed a great stone that towered opposite his perch and showered him with stones and javelins of fir, while the others hurled their wands. And yet they missed their target, poor Pentheus in his perch, barely out of reach of their eager hands, treed, unable to escape. Finally they splintered branches from the oaks and with those bars of wood tried to lever up the tree by prying at the roots. But every effort failed. Then Agave cried out: "Maenads, make a circle about the trunk and grip it with your hands. Unless we take this climbing beast, he will reveal the secrets of the god." With that, thousands of hands tore the fir tree from the earth, and down, down from his high perch fell Pentheus, tumbling to the around, sobbing and screaming as he fell, for he knew his end was near. His own mother, like a priestess with her victim, fell upon him first. But snatching off his wig and snood so she would recognize his face, he touched her cheeks, screaming, "No, no, Mother! I am Pentheus, your own son, the child you bore to Echion! Pity

me, spare me, Mother! I have done a wrong, but do not kill your own son for my offense." But she was foaming at the mouth, and her crazed eyes rolling with frenzy. She was made, stark mad, possessed by Bacchus. Ignoring his cries of pity, she seized his left arm at the wrist; then, planting her foot upon his chest, she pulled, wrenching away the arm at the shoulder— not by her own strength, for the god had put inhuman power in her hands. Ino, meanwhile, on the other side, was scratching off his flesh. Then Autonoe and the whole horde of Bacchae swarmed upon him. Shouts everywhere, he screaming with what little breath was left, they shrieking in triumph. One tore off an arm, another a foot still warm in its shoe. His ribs were clawed clean of flesh and every hand was smeared with blood as they played ball with scraps of Pentheus' body. The pitiful remains lie scattered, one piece among the sharp rocks, others lying lost among the leaves in the depths of the forest. His mother, picking up his head, impaled it on her wand. She seems to think it is some mountain lion's head which she carries in triumph through the thick of Cithaeron. (lines 1093–1143)

Sale, for one, viewed this intense scene as a mother's castration of her son. In his interpretation he drew heavily on the imagery of the bent and erect fir tree. It is precisely the overemphasis on this one symbol to explain the entire play that argues for a new theory that would include much more of this scene's richness. A self psychological perspective brings to this crucial scene, and indeed to the entire play, a more experience-near interpretation of the characters in the drama. Moreover, it can simultaneously account for both the violent and sexual imagery in this scene and others as being representative of the breakdown products of the main character's faulty self organization. For example, what has greatest impact in the messenger's description of Mount Cithaeron's events is the portrayal of young Pentheus "treed, unable to escape . . . tumbling to the ground, sobbing and screaming as he fell, . . . screaming, 'No, no, Mother! I am Pentheus, your own son, the child you bore to Echion! Pity me, spare me, Mother!'" Pentheus is alone, isolated with no one to help him. He cannot evoke his mother's recognition. He wishes desperately, as he had all his life, to be admired, separate and unique in his mother's eyes. Her failure has been her inability to recognize his budding, nonpathological grandiosity appropriately. In light of Agave's empathic failure, the fir tree scene speaks much more directly of a little boy's pervasive sense of insignificance vis-à-vis his mother, and not merely of a simple recognition of his sexuality as Sale believes. The content of Pentheus's behavior appears to be highly sexual, but it is a distorted sexual imagery. Nonrecognition is the psychological trauma in the scene; it is both a more basic nonrecognition and the little boy's wish for phase-appropriate oedipal confirmation. The message of this play is forcefully delivered: Maternal nonrecognition ultimately leads to psychological destruction.

Pentheus is the little boy as king—he represents the wish to be recognized and affirmed. He suffered not from excessively close, overstimulating selfobjects but from distant, understimulating parental selfobjects (Kohut, 1984, p. 11). He is not solely the victim of an unresolved Oedipus complex; Pentheus's development was never consolidated at that psychosexual stage. His mother's affirmation was required not only in the oedipal sense but throughout all developmental phases, and her motherly deficits, therefore, are not that exclusively limited. What at first glance appears to be boisterous, competitive strivings on the part of the young king is at closer examination exaggerated, hypermasculine, and threatening behavior that compensates for a neglected self and for psychological vulnerability due to the absence of his father and his mother's unresponsiveness and self-absorption. In the earlier portion of the play, his aggression is clearly a defensive behavior, his response to a fear of psychological disorganization concretized in the form of the threatening Dionysus. Pentheus's consistent violent threats against Dionysus are, as Cadmus, Tyresius, Dionysus and messenger all point out, a sign of lack of wisdom (*Sophia*). Pentheus is a caricature of a man. He is tragic man (Kohut, 1977, p. 132). His aggression as well as apparent polymorphous sexuality are breakdown products of an unstable self. He lacks the attributes of a true leader and a cohesive self-wisdom, empathy, humor, and creativity (Kohut, 1978, p. 199).

An additional comment is in order regarding the alleged castration of Pentheus on Mount Cithaeron. To identify the scene as such is to *interpret* what Agave actually does to her son. The scene more precisely speaks to destruction of a whole body. It is perhaps reductionistic to view this violent scene as exclusively one of castration. It more rightly depicts the destruction of Pentheus's entire being and, therefore, more accurately demonstrates and confirms the actual failure in mothering. In this respect Pentheus is unable to be protected by his new, albeit powerful and partially restitutive relationship with Dionysus. He still must ultimately gain the confirmation he never had from his mother, and this is what draws him to Mount Cithaeron.

Such psychopathology in young King Pentheus ought to be confirmed by a careful character analysis of his mother. An interpretation with integrity should be, as much as possible, supported by and consistent with the dynamics and genetics of Agave and Dionysus as well.

This approach is a sensible one because in many respects the movement of the play is through the theme of mysterious filiation, and even more importantly, insidiously conflicted parent–child relationships.

A FAILURE IN PARENTAL EMPATHY

When Agave makes her first appearance in the play, she unmistakably presents herself as a woman deeply confused about her societal role and, therefore, ultimately, about her self-worth. There can be no question that she seeks the admiration and respect of her father, Cadmus (and all men), through her masculine, aggressive strivings in the hunt:

> Your citizens of this towered city, men of Thebes, behold the trophy of your women's hunting! This is the quarry of our chase, taken not with nets nor spears of bronze but by the white and delicate hands of women. What are they worth, your boastings now and all that uselessness your armor is, since we, with our bare hands, captured this quarry and tore its bleeding body limb from limb?—But where is my father Cadmus? (lines 1203–1210)

> Now, Father, yours can be the proudest boast of living men. For you are now the father of the bravest daughters in the world. All of your daughters are brave, but I above the rest. I have left my shuttle at the loom; I raised my sight to higher things—to hunting animals with my bare hands. You see? Here in my hands I hold the quarry of my chase, a trophy for our house. Take it, Father, take it. Glory in my skill and invite your friends to share the feast of triumph. For you are blest, Father, by this great deed I have done. (lines 1233–1244)

So for Agave, affirmation of her personal value must come from her father, not her husband, through recognition of her masculine aspirations. There is no praise of her motherhood or mothering qualities nor are there comments on her warmth, nurturance, or protectiveness. Her violently masculine deed is a breakdown product of an uncohesive self and an indicator of the source of the pathogenic parental failure in empathy. She clearly was never appreciated or valued for her feminine qualities and aspirations. Agave could gain Cadmus's recognition only through behaving as if she were a man.

What follows in the play is a remarkably sensitive interchange between father and daughter; this is a critical scene because on two very important and different levels it speaks to mother's and son's pathology and the potentially curative or restorative process for each. Cadmus, in a highly moving fashion, gives to Agave what she has theretofore not received: empathic acceptance and understanding. He skillfully leads Agave through her denial to recognition of her horrible deed. Indeed, Devereux (1970) speaks of "Cadmus' flawless psychotherapeutic strategy" and states that this scene is "an important document in the history of human culture: As the first surviving account of an insight and recall-oriented psychotherapy" (p. 35). Step by careful step, Cadmus orients his daughter by addressing the concrete first; by asking questions rather than giving answers; and by encouraging his daughter to look at her son's head (lines 1270–1301).

The theme of "looking" has been represented one more time. Voyeurism, Mount Cithaeron, hallucinatory bulls, visual attractions, and so forth, have been instrumental up to this point in the play. For Agave to look at her son's head is curative of her dissociative state. Because her father has empathically led her through this process, it is also curative of a more nuclear problem—an understanding of her own thwarted needs and their impact on her son. Her dismemberment of Pentheus on Mount Cithaeron represents both his and her own fragmented self. Stage directions call for Agave to "lift up one of Pentheus' limbs and ask the help of Cadmus of piecing the body together. She mourns each piece separately before replacing it on the bier." Then she pleads to Cadmus: "Come, Father. We must restore his head to this unhappy boy. As best we can, we shall make him whole again" (line 329). The emphasis on seeing is developed and completed: to see is to have insight (Winnington-Ingram, 1948, p. 170). Equally important, however, is that without appropriate parental mirroring there can be no cohesive self and self-esteem regulation.

TOWARD A PSYCHOHISTORICAL PERSPECTIVE

Individual psychologies of the main characters in *The Bacchae* are so intriguing and convincing because they reflect universal tensions and conflicts. They also reflect, better than any other Greek tragedy, important interpersonal and intrafamilial problems of 5th- and 4th-century Athenian life. Indeed, it is not a novel assumption that interpersonal patterns appearing in poetic and dramatic treatment of myth mirror directly the modal patterns of a culture (Slater, 1968).

Some general comments on the status of women and the parent–child relationship in Athenian society are in order. It is a fairly ubiquitous belief that the Golden Age of Pericles was one of the high points in western civilization. Architecture, government, sculpture, literature, and philosophy all attest to a creative, sophisticated, and apparently democratic culture. Women, too, we are told, achieved a high point in Greek culture. This assumption is based on the fact that "there is no literature, no art of any country, in which women are more prominent, than in the tragedy, sculpture, and the painting of fifth century Athens" (Gomme, 1937, p. 92). The truth, however, is that women "were legal nonentities, excluded from political and intellectual life, uneducated, virtually imprisoned in the home, and appeared to be regarded with disdain by the principal male spokesmen whose comments have survived" (Slater, 1974, p. 9). Pubescent girls were frequently given away in marriage to much older men. A marriage required giving up at an early age of all that was familiar, including household religion. The marital relationship resembled more an older brother and younger sister relationship. The shallowness of the marriage bond was in glaring contradistinction to the emotional intensity of Greek male friendship (Finley, 1940, pp. 137–138). Homosexuality competed with heterosexuality, husbands spent as little time as possible at home, and childrearing was left exclusively to women: "the Athenian male child grew up in a female-dominated environment (Slater, 1968, p. 7).

While the denigration and rejection of women in Athenian society was pervasive (Ehrenberg, 1951, p. 198; Kitto, 1960, p. 219), it was not without consequences. Slater (1974) argues convincingly that while the social position of middle- and upper-class women was quite low, the psychological influence of women was quite high, and the "Greek males' contempt for women was not only compatible with but insolubly bound to an intense fear of them and to an underlying suspicion of male inferiority" (pp. 10–11). But not all women were feared, only the mature maternal women. In Greek tragedies, young women and virginal goddesses are always benevolent while mature ones are cast as envious and vengeful. Greek literature abounds with tales of madness—none of which is caused by the man, only by women to men. Madness for the ancient Greek came from the mother, and it consisted of unbridled aggression and murder, especially of children (Slater, 1974, p. 27). While there is a general idealization of the paternal figure in Greek myth, the opposite is true for the mother. Greek mythology is replete with witches, but there are no Greek sorcerers.

What is the psychological significance of such feminine oppression,

paternal absence, "marital straining and paternal scape-goating"?[2] The
most important result is the profound level of maternal ambivalence
toward the male child and the tendency of this ambivalence, therefore,
to encourage narcissistic pathology as well as homosexuality, which clearly
exposes the intense underlying wish to be close to a man.

> If the wife resents her husband's superiority, she can punish arrogance (or
> even masculinity) in her son. Such vengeance is especially appropriate,
> inasmuch as the son is the sole means of perpetuating the father's lineage
> and property. Furthermore, lack of a son meant not only lack of an heir,
> but also the disappearance of the family religion and rites, and condem-
> nation of the father to external unhappiness beyond the grave. Since the
> direct expression of hostility toward the husband would be inhibited by
> the wife's dependence upon him, her youth and her social inferiority,
> destructive unconscious impulses toward male children must have been
> strong. Both the impulses and the need to repress them would be increased,
> furthermore, by the greater value assigned to male children. A woman
> who failed to produce an heir for her husband was viewed as not having
> performed her most elemental function, and women could be divorced for
> barrenness. . . . The ambivalence of the Greek mother toward her son
> was, in other words, not a normal reactive ambivalence, involving an ob-
> ject-oriented affection and an object-oriented irritation, but a deeply nar-
> cissistic ambivalence in which the mother does not respond to the child as
> a separate person, but as both an expression of, and a cure for her nar-
> cissistic wounds. Her need for self-expansion and vindication requires her
> both to exalt and to belittle her son, to feed on and to destroy him. (Slater,
> 1974, pp. 21–23)

From the vantage point of self-esteem regulation, it becomes clear
that Pentheus is neither a confusing nor an unexpected character. He
is drawn very true to Athenian life. We see him with his sense of en-
titlement, grandiosity, need for constant admiration, and hyperaggres-
sive and masculine tendencies, as the logical and, perhaps, one prototypical man of his times. Consistent with our knowledge of narcissistic
disorders, Pentheus is a young man with an insecurely consolidated sense
of self, specifically of his assertive, self-confident masculine self. His
preoccupation with force and a concomitant false sense of honor, boast-
fulness, as well as his preoccupation with revenge, all speak to a disturbance in self development emanating from the absence of a father
whom he could admire and who would be proud of him, and from a
mother who took no pleasure in her son's emerging assertive masculinity.

---

2. For a more complete and documented account of the pervasiveness and origin of
these characteristics in 5th- and 4th-century Athenian life from which I have drawn heavily,
see Slater (1968, pp. 23–33, 70–74).

There are a number of seemingly confusing aspects of Dionysus and his religion that become clarified when viewed through the themes of sexual antagonism and maternal ambivalence. These aspects are, What is to be made of the mysterious birth story of the young god? What appeal does his religion have? What psychological function might it serve for women like Agave? How are these reflected in the specific rituals of the Bacchae?

Many authors have spoken to the important theme of filiation. That this theme is so critical is supported by the very opening scene description: "Before the royal palace at Thebes, on the left is the way to Cithaeron; on the right to the city. In the center of the orchestra stands, *still smoking,* the vine-covered tomb of Semele, mother of Dionysus."

In other words, the question of Dionysus's parentage remains a burning issue. Dionysus concurs that this is so through his first lines in the play (lines 1–10, 25–50). The chorus, too, addresses the concern in their first appearance (lines 87–104). There can be no mistake, then, that this theme of filiation is critical.

As the play partially reviews, the myth of the birth of Dionysus is as follows:

> Zeus was Semele's lover. In jealousy, Hera came to Semele disguised as a crone, hinted that her lover was not Zeus, but an impostor, and urged the girl to make him prove his identity by coming to her in all his radiant divinity. Zeus unwillingly did so (Semele had made him swear to fulfill any promise she might exact) and Semele was burned to death by his brilliance. Her unborn child was saved by Zeus and sewn up in his thigh, to be born again from there when ripe for birth. . . . His youth was spent in wandering; at one time he was driven mad by Hera. . . . (Kirkwood, 1959, p. 36)

The Semele–Dionysus myth is a central one in describing ambivalence toward mothers, sexual antagonism, and their resultant psychological conflicts. The myth, as many have argued, should be studied from the assumption that Hera is but the intensely negative aspect of Semele. The birthing myth of Dionysus speaks once again to the Greek man's fear of the overwhelming pathogenic woman. She is considered pathogenic because her destructive attributes lead to a psychological inferno that threatens to destroy the infant. The male child, Dionysus, significantly, is only saved by Zeus, the father—the father who was not available to save Pentheus.

But why kill the child? Simply because it is through the child that the man may be most easily harmed. Many cultures are replete with myths that reflect the "external soul" (Frazier, 1959, pp. 594–604).

While generally a woman's immortality is within (who impregnates her is of little matter), the man's immortality is through his children and, therefore, externalized and vulnerable. Hera's attack on the unborn Dionysus is, therefore, an attack on Zeus. Zeus is omnipotent, but he can be punished and injured through his son for his cavalier treatment of his wife (Slater, 1968, p. 263). Zeus's solution to this problem is to internalize, as a woman can, his immortality, through dispensing with the woman completely and sewing Dionysus in his thigh. He is the father and the mother of his own child and safe from the wrath of women (Slater, 1968, p. 263).

In light of the theme of sexual antagonism, the Dionysian ritual can only be understood as an attempt to solve male–female conflicts. On the one hand, it contains the destructive expression of unmistakable maternal ambivalence: the killing and eating of the human child by women (omophagia). On the other hand, Dionysian religion was an attempt at liberation of the woman, "the greatest gift of Dionysus was the sense of utter freedom, and in Greece it was with the women, with their normally confined and straightened lives, to whom the temptation of release made the strongest appeal. Dionysus . . . 'pricks them to leave their looms and shuttles' . . . nothing is lacking which can serve to increase the sense of exaltation and of shedding the self of everyday life" (Guthrie, 1950, p. 148).

The Bacchae is an object lesson in history: It addresses the folly and destructiveness of certain repressions and, as Weston LaBarre has demonstrated, is precisely what Platonism robbed from classical Greece. Socrates and Plato correlate directly with the appeal of Dionysus. The religion of Dionysus argues against the futile "ghost dance" of Plato, for a full range of emotions and appropriate neurotic defenses in Greek culture (LaBarre, 1970, pp. 517–547). "Dionysean ecstacy fused together what the rest of Greek culture strove so obsessively and superstitiously to keep separate" (Slater, 1968, p. 298).

As Slater summarizes, "Pentheus and Dionysus thus represent two modes of responding to the same phenomenon—Pentheus, the strident male, tries directly to combat maternal malevolence and is destroyed by it—Dionysus, the subtle, defensive female-identifying male (effeminacy) who defeats the mother by overtly placating her and then besting her at her own game of psychological evasion and disruption" (Slater, 1968, p. 301).

It is important to note, however, that Dionysus is not an effective answer to the Greek conflict. While he represents the liberation of important and intense female affects, his solution is a very destructive one: a maternal malevolence that is, in this play, satisfied only by child sacrifice within the performance of the Dionysian rites *away* from the community at large. There can be no resolution as long as the sexes are segregated. By creating a vehicle that produces fear of women rather than admiration, the rites temporarily promote enhanced qualities of femininity and well-being through highly masculinizing activities that dictate ultimately that these qualities can only or partially be achieved through the adoption of the masculine and repudiation of the feminine. In the end, Dionysus perpetuates the vicious cycle of intergenerational hostility.

CONCLUSION

As Philip Vellacott (1975) wrote, in *Ironic Drama*:

> A play of Sophocles called its audience away from the practical decisions, the hates and desires, of yesterday and tomorrow, inviting them to weep and tremble in a world of heroically clarified issues. A play of Euripides, for those who listened reflectively, spoke in a different voice. It confronted the war-weary citizen with yesterday's failure and tomorrow's terror. It held up mirrors in which he could contemplate himself and what he was doing with this world, in an embarrassing, a shocking, new light; yet the mirror-image was often so veiled in irony as to be visible only to those who demanded truth, while those who sought the comfort of self-delusion could still find it. (p. 153)

The Bacchae certainly mirrors Euripides' world as forcefully and faithfully as any of his tragedies. It may stand above the rest in its ability incisively to address the dramatic intergenerational and sex-role conflicts that produced major cultural tensions, and, no doubt, great personal unhappiness. From a psychoanalytic perspective, however, *The Bacchae* is a potent showcase for understanding the psychic consequences of certain dysfunctional parent–child relationships. Through the character of young King Pentheus materializes the tragic effects of failure of parental empathy. Agave's own nonrecognition at the hands of her father interferes with the development of her maternal empathy. She is unable to accept or affirm her son's strivings and uniqueness, and as a result Pentheus lacked a cohesive sense of self and the capacity to regulate his self-esteem maturely. Euripides' poetic vision in *The Bacchae* is not only comprised of historical and cultural insights, but most importantly for the psychoanalyst, has intrapsychic ones as well. It is on this level that, for over 2 centuries, *The Bacchae* has profoundly moved all who have read it or have seen it performed. As Kohut (1977) reminded us, "We can surely still grasp, reverently and admiringly, the formal perfection of the work of the great artists of the past; and we are moved by them because we sense the authenticity with which they express the essence of an age in which the desires and conflicts of the cohesive self of the individual cried for expression" (pp. 288–289).

ACKNOWLEDGMENTS

The author wishes to thank Dr. Rena Kay, Thomas Kohut, and Anna Ornstein for their assistance.

REFERENCES

Arrowsmith, W., tr. (1958). *Euripides, The Bacchae.* Chicago: University of Chicago Press.
Bagg, R. (1978). *The Bacchae of Euripides.* Amherst: University of Massachusetts Press.
Caldwell, R.S. (1974). Selected bibliography on psychoanalysis and classical studies. *Arethusa,* 7(1):116–134.
Devereaux, G. (1970). The psychotherapy scene in Euripides' *The Bacchae. Journal of Hellenic Studies,* 90:35–48.
Dodds, E.R., ed. (1944). *Euripides, The Bacchae.* London: Oxford University Press.
Ehrenberg, V. (1951). *The People of Aristophanes.* Oxford: Basil Blackwell.
Ferguson, J. (1972). *A Companion to Greek Tragedy.* Austin: University of Texas Press.
Finely, M.I. (1959). *The World of Odysseus.* New York: Meridian.
Frazier, J.G. (1959). *New Golden Bough.* T.H. Gaster, ed. New York: Criterion Books.
Gomme, A.W. (1937). *Essays in Greek History and Literature.* Oxford: Basil Blackwell.
Green, A. (1979). *The Tragic Effect: The Oedipus Complex in Tragedy,* A. Sheridan, Cambridge: Cambridge University Press.
Guthrie, W.K.C. (1950). *The Greeks and Their Gods.* Boston: Beacon Press.
Jaeger, W. (1965). *Paideia.* G. Highet, tr. New York: Oxford University Press.
Kirkwood, G.M. (1959). *A Short Guide to Classical Mythology.* New York: Holt, Rinehart & Winston.
Kitto, H.D.F. (1939). *Greek Tragedy: A Literary Study.* London: Methuen & Company.
Kitto, H.D.F. (1960). *The Greeks.* Baltimore: Penguin.
Kohut, H. (1977). *The Restoration of the Self.* New York: International Universities Press.
Kohut, H. (1978). *The Analysis of the Self.* New York: International Universities Press.
Kohut, H. (1980). Summarizing reflections. In A. Goldberg, ed., *Advances in Self Psychology* (pp. 473–554). New York: International Universities Press.
Kohut, H. (1984). *How Does Analysis Cure?* A. Goldberg, ed., with P. Stepansky. Chicago & London: University of Chicago Press.
LaBarre, W. (1970). *The Ghost Dance: Origins of Religion.* New York: World Publishing Co.
Murray, G., tr. (1913). *The Bacchae of Euripides.* London: George Allen & Co.

Murray, G. (1918). *Euripides and His Age.* London: Williams & Norgate.

Peradotto, J., & Sullivan, J.P., eds. (1984). *Women in the Ancient World: The Arethusa Papers.* Albany: State University of New York Press.

Pomeroy, S.B. (1975). *Goddess, Whores, Wives and Slaves: Women in Classical Antiquity.* New York: Shocken Books.

Reed, G.S. (1982). Towards a methodology for applying psychoanalysis to literature. *Psychoanalytic Quarterly,* 2:19–42.

Rieff, P. (1959). *Freud: The Mind of the Moralist.* New York: Viking Press.

Roberts, P. (1975). *The Psychology of Tragic Drama.* London: Routledge & Kegan Paul.

Sale,, W. (1972). The Psychoanalysis of Pentheus in *The Bacchae* of Euripides. *Yale Classical Studies,* 22:63–82.

Sale, W. (1977). *Existentialism in Euripides: Sickness, Tragedy and Divinity in the Medea, The Hippolytus and the Bacchae.* Australia: Aureal Publications.

Simon, B. (1978). *Mind and Madness in Ancient Greece: The Classical Roots of Modern Psychiatry.* Ithaca: Cornell University Press.

Slater, P.E. (1968). *Glory of Hera, Greek Mythology and the Greek Family.* Boston: Beacon Press.

Slater, P.E. (1974). The Greek family in history and myth. *Arethusa,* 7:–44.

Sutherland, D., tr. (1968). *The Bacchae of Euripides.* Lincoln: University of Nebraska Press.

Trilling, L. (1950). *The Liberal Imagination. Essays on Literature and Society.* Garden City, NY. Doubleday.

Vellacott, P. (1975). *Ironic Drama: A Study of Euripides' Method and Meaning.* London: Cambridge University Press.

Winnington-Ingram, R.P. (1948). *Euripides and Dionysus: An Interpretation of the Bacchae.* Cambridge: Cambridge University Press.

15

Discussion

Frenzy and Regeneration in Euripides' *The Bacchae*

HARRY TROSMAN

Dr. Kay has done well to apply the insights of self psychology to a literary work that can be so greatly illuminated by such an approach. Kay's aim has been to delineate the author's unifying poetic vision and to demonstrate that it is consistent with contemporary psychoanalytic understanding of human personality. He has successfully demonstrated that the earlier psychoanalytic approach to this play, in terms of sexual conflict with an emphasis on unresolved oedipal issues, does a disservice to the complexity of the author's intent. For example, the character of Pentheus is to be understood better in terms of self pathology than castration anxiety; the relationship between Dionysus and Pentheus can be understood as an attempt on the part of Pentheus to establish a relationship with a masculine selfobject and to come closer to his mother through forming a feminine identification. Even though he initially attempts to repudiate Dionysus, Pentheus is drawn to the god as a way of augmenting his deficient self. In addition, Agave is seen as a prototype for Athenian women, denigrated and rejected by their society, and thus unconsciously vengeful and hostile toward their male offspring. Seen in the psychohistorical context, the character Pentheus is consistent with that of a man who never had an opportunity to develop a healthy sense of masculinity, or to derive comfort in his relationships with women.

In his chapter, Kay presents a review of the literature that has concerned itself with the play from both a literary and psychological point of view. I would add to his review the fairly new, free version of the play and critical comments by the Nigerian playwright, Wole Soyinka, a work that was commissioned for performance by the National Theater, London, in 1973. I had an opportunity to see the play at that time, and can readily attest to its power and excitement. Soyinka offers an interpretation that places *The Bacchae* within the historical and economic context of the time. Such an interpretation is not inconsistent with the psychological view, and I shall review it briefly in order to highlight the psychosocial context.

The Dionysian evangelical religion was brought to Attica from Asia Minor by peasants displaced from an agrarian economy that was becoming progressively more industrialized. Displaced workers and slaves who were forced to migrate brought their primitive religious beliefs, loosely characterized as Dionysian, with them, and in the face of having to accommodate themselves to new social contexts, continued to maintain a belief in the emotionally loaded, mysterious, and primitive forces of nature. Dionysus, a non-Olympian god who was seen as displaced, having to suppress his own identity, and dispossessed, like the people who were the recent migrants to mainland Greece, was an appropriate deity for worship. The cult of Dionysus thus united men and women who were essentially socially deprived and exploited. The religion enabled the adherents to feel themselves inseparable from the forces of nature itself, and essentially to draw strength from communal participation and self-renewal. In Soyinka's version of the last scene of the play, the head of Pentheus is mounted on a stake as the spout for a fountain. From the head flows not blood but wine, from which the Bacchae, including Agave, drink. I believe Soyinka catches the true intent of Euripides here in that the characters, particularly Agave, accept that the final link in Agave's insight is the recognition that leads to a sense of communion with the forces of nature and the need for regeneration and reabsorption in the dynamic forces that underlie human productivity and creativity. In the more specific context of self psychology, we might think of this kind of identification with the community as an additional transformation of narcissism, perhaps even a stage worthy to rank with creativity, empathy, humor, wisdom, and the capacity to contemplate impermanence. The mature selfobject bond, which binds man to his fellow humans in terms of a shared identity, may be a further transformation of narcissism, which finds satisfaction in the solidarity of communal rite and feeling.

At this point, I would like to return to the play itself and continue to explore the opportunities offered by an understanding of the play through the use of self psychological concepts. In doing so, I am immediately struck by the force of Dionysus as a charismatic figure. Quite clearly, he symbolizes the power of blind, instinctive emotion, and he is for others a stimulus for intense merger and loss of separate identity. The pull is so great because those who are attracted to his orbit become incarnations of the god themselves. They willingly lose themselves in the intensity of the merger and slavishly subject their own personalities to that of the will of the god. This recalls, in the clinical context, the propensity of certain individuals to give up their own wills readily and to adopt that of another whom they consider more powerful, more perfect, and more awesome. Kohut (1959) described this constellation in his paper on introspection and empathy as a state of *Hörigkeit*, when he tried to give some emotional meaning to that weak-kneed term bandied about in the 1950s and '60s—"dependency." The effect of the godhead on others, particularly on Pentheus, is best understood psychologically in terms of the regressive potential inherent in narcissistic interests. With Pentheus, we see that his sexual orientation is only weakly cathected in terms of latent homosexuality, voyeuristic heterosexuality, and narcissistic preening and self-adornment. Pentheus reacts to Dionysus both as a father figure and as a homosexual object, but not consistently because his interests are essentially objectless. His libidinal interests are easily absorbed by his narcissitic preoccupations. Sensing and tempted by the regressive pull, he initially rejects the Dionysian vision. He cannot recognize the primitive or the irrational within himself. He tries to deal with the Dionysian element within his own personality by repression, vertical split, and disavowal. Because his own self is so poorly structured, he readily gives up his masculinity and adopts a feminine self. He becomes a transvestite, and from this he slips back to a wish to be carried around in his mother's arms. His eventual dismemberment, and literal somatic fragmentation, is the last step in this narcissistic regression.

In addition, we are presented with the deviations that result from unmodulated idealization. We are dealing with a psychological situation in which excitement somehow must be integrated within the context of the total personality. This, too, is a narcissistic issue expressed in economic terms. How much excitement can one experience without losing all sense of self? How much emotional intensity is necessary for the full development of a consolidated self? Today we recognize that both the Apollonian and the Dionysian aspects of human personality are essential components. Too great a reliance on either one leads to rigidity or fragmentation and an absence of the kind of restitution that the play promises as the divided parts of Pentheus are brought together in order to form a consolidated whole.

Finally, we may note the prevalence of narcissistic issues in the allocation of specific dramatic functions among the characters themselves. We note that at the beginning of the play it is Dionysus who is pursued by Pentheus and is taken prisoner by him. At the end of the play, it is Pentheus who is victimized by Dionysus. At times, it seems that we are not actually dealing with real characters who are understandable in terms of ordinary human psychology, instead we are dealing with a fictional world that has laws unto itself and is put together in order to create certain effects upon the audience. We note that at first our sympathies are with Dionysus. Then when the tables are turned and Pentheus is torn limb from limb, we feel that he does not deserve his fate and that he is subjected to a punishment far worse than the crime he wished to commit. Taking into consideration the world that the play presents, I question how meaningful it is to conceive of the character of Pentheus as an individualized figure who was not empathically responded to by his mother in childhood. For me, Pentheus cannot be understood in genetic terms that may be appropriate in the real world. The tragic impact of the play is greatly heightened by the view that Agave, as we see her, is a loving mother, a view demonstrated by the anguish she feels when she comes to her senses. She dismembers her son not from lack of empathy but because she is so intoxicated by her intense excitement she has lost her capacity for reality testing. We are made to sympathize with Agave when she realizes what she has done, and we see too that she is subjected to the punishment that comes from the whim of the god.

In a word, we are dealing with fictional constructs best understood in terms of the formal devices of the play. *The Bacchae* is the product of the mind of a great dramatist who wants us to realize that, if we neglect certain buried aspects of human psychology, we cannot survive. In this sense, Euripides is a fine forerunner for the views that Freud himself shared and taught to us.

REFERENCE

Kohut, H. (1959). Introspection, empathy and psychoanalysis: An examination of the relationship between modes of observation and theory. *Journal of the American Psychoanalytic Association*, 7:459–483.

16

The Empathic Vantage Point in Supervision

JOHN A. SLOANE

"I see nobody on the road," said Alice.

"I only wish I had such eyes," the King remarked in a fretful tone. "To be able to see nobody! And at that distance too! Why it's as much as I can do to see real people, by this light!"

—Lewis Carroll, *Through the Looking Glass*

The scribes and the Pharisees sit on Moses' seat, so practice and observe whatever they tell you, but not what they do; for they preach but do not practice. They bind heavy burdens, hard to bear, and lay them on men's shoulders.

—Jesus, *Matthew* 23:2–4.

My interest in the use (as distinct from the teaching) of the empathic vantage point in supervision arose out of my work with residents in the University of Toronto Department of Psychiatry over the past 10 years. As one might imagine, I encountered quite wide variations of interest in, aptitude for, and sophistication with psychotherapy, and I was often forced to recognize that there were considerable limitations on what I could hope to achieve with any given resident. In my initial eagerness to transmit my hard-won psychoanalytic knowledge and experience (including the importance of the empathic vantage point in psychotherapy) and to see those views put to wider use, I found myself offering an abundance of empathic observations and dynamic interpretations of the patient, vignettes from my own experience, explanations of theory, suggestions of technique, and occasionally confrontations of what seemed to be countertransference problems of the student.

What I then discovered, to my chagrin, was that the residents with whom I was moved to try the hardest to impart all my pent-up wisdom were the very residents who, in their own interactions with their patients, assumed the most authoritatively "knowledgable" and directive roles and were most often intrusively unempathic toward those who entered *their* offices for help. This, of course, inhibited their patient's spontaneous self expression in ways that looked very much like the same stubborn resistances that I felt myself faced with in them.

At first, this was cause for me to redouble my efforts to explain patiently and ever so tactfully why what they were doing was inadvisable, and why doing it my way would be better. I sat forward and tried to convince them that they needed to sit back and listen to what their patients were trying to say or unable or afraid to say, rather than trying so hard to be helpful or prematurely knowledgeable. But alas, this too came back to haunt me as I all too often heard the familiar ring of my own supervisory style in the way the residents then told their patients how to live and to conduct *their* relationships with other people. Once again, my residents were unconsciously refusing to do as I told them but instead were obediently treating their patients as I was treating them just as, in the other direction, they often treated me as they were being treated by their patients (Eckstein & Wallerstein, 1972; Gediman & Wolkenfeld, 1980; Searles, 1955). At this stage, I often felt like saying, "For God's sake, don't do as I do, do as I *say!*" but was able to restrain my omnipotent impulse long enough to savor the irony, and ponder the paradox.

Like many others (Gediman & Wolkenfeld, 1980), I found myself unable to affect this unconscious process by rational persuasion, and became steadily more aware that a limiting factor was who the resident was, rather than what he knew. I too was part of the problem in much the same way as Stolorow, Brandchaft, and Atwood (1983) describe in their paper, "Intersubjectivity in Psychoanalytic Treatment," in which they say, echoing Winnicott, "there is no such thing as a difficult patient. There are only difficulties that arise in the unique intersection of two subjectivities. . ." (p. 127). I also felt, with Hunt (1981), that my mandate as a supervisor did not automatically include the right to make unsolicited and therefore intrusive interpretations of the resident's "problems," as Eckstein and Wallerstein (1972) appear to recommend. Since I could not beat it, I decided to join forces with this unconscious parallel process, by doing unto my residents (within limits) as I would have them do unto their patients (and, for that matter, unto me).

In other words, I tried to take my own advice and listen from an empathic vantage point, as described by Kohut (1959, 1977), Lichtenberg (1981), Ornstein and Ornstein (1985), Schwaber (1981), and others, to what it was like for them to be with their patients and to be with me (the latter especially whenever there seemed to be a block in communication). I paid much closer attention to *their perception* of their patient and of themselves, and the feelings aroused between them, how they made sense out of them, what else they were reminded of, how they felt naturally inclined to respond and why, what consequences they anticipated, what other choices they felt they had, and so forth. Throughout this I attempted to maintain what the Ornsteins (1985) refer to as an "openness to new configurations of inner experience" (p. 44). In short, I tried to let them teach me the nature and value of their experiential reality and in doing so, I often became aware of things that they did better than I, or at least, that expanded my own understanding in ways that could easily have been overlooked if I had been too intent on my own agenda.[1] My efforts to teach *them* became restricted to only those things that were "optimally responsive" (Bacal, 1985) and immediately relevant to their empathically perceived position, and that invited them to imagine one or two steps beyond where they already were.

The more I was able to discern, acknowledge, appreciate, help put into words, or place in a larger context something of value in what my residents experienced as naturally and authentically *their own* (even when very different from mine), the more confident and competent they became with their patients and the more willing they became, in supervision, to reveal their own thinking and feeling. At the same time, they seemed to become more capable of adopting an empathic vantage point with their patients, which in turn brought more usable material into supervision. In short, they learned to listen best by having someone listen to them.

In other words, a generative empathic process (Shafer, 1959) seemed to be set in motion that was productive of genuine growth in both resident and patient. As Gediman and Wolkenfeld (1980) point out, both psychotherapy and supervision are helping processes, both require

---

1. In my opinion, a prescribed curriculum of what ought to be learned by residents at different stages of their training is better reserved for reading lists, lectures, and seminars rather than as a preconceived agenda for the supervision itself, the content of which will vary enormously from resident to resident. The only agenda the supervisor needs is to attend to the nurturing of whatever innate capacity the resident may have for *listening* to the unexpected richness and complexity of people's feelings, motives, and meanings. In doing this, he draws on the whole of his own experience in whatever order it is called upon by the unfolding interests and abilities of the particular resident with whom he is faced.

involvement, exposure, and risk to the self, and both rely heavily on multiple identificatory processes. They state, "the scope of exposure of the self for the therapist in supervision is far more narrow, but not necessarily less profound" (p. 248). This, I believe, is far more often than has so far been appreciated at the root of what Eckstein and Wallerstein describe as problems in learning. Therefore, it may be that Kohut's self psychology can help a good deal in understanding and improving the supervisory *process* and should not be confined as yet another theoretical or technical content to be taught.

The supervisor's multiple functions in relation to the resident can be used as rationalizations for unconscious motives and attitudes that impair his receptivity to what is emotionally significant and potentially valuable to the resident. It is the latter that must be attended to and built upon in each session. However, the supervisor's role as teacher, responsible for the inculcation of established knowledge, as spokesman of a particular theoretical position (including that of self psychology), as administrator, bearing institutional responsibility for the welfare of his resident's patient, as professional evaluator, concerned with the quality and reputation of the discipline, the institution, and himself, can render him temporarily or chronically unempathic with a given resident. The value of what we have to offer can all too easily blind us to the latent value of what is already there. Depending on the resident's situational, characterological, or transferential vulnerability to narcissistic injury, this can sometimes quite dramatically interfere with the resident's self cohesion, empathic capacity, therapeutic effectiveness, and his willingness and ability to express himself in and learn from supervision.

Attention, therefore, to the supervisor's countertransference can often help him to anticipate such problems before they arise, and can help to illuminate them when they do. This, in conjunction with empathic attention to, and genuine appreciation of the resident's own needs and assets, as well as to his at times unavoidable frustrations, disappointments, and narcissistic injury at the hands of the supervisor, can provide a means of reorienting oneself to the sometimes bewildering, multidimensional complexity with which the supervisor is faced (Gediman & Wolkenfeld, 1980). At crucial moments, and even sometimes for prolonged periods, the empathic point of view may be the only one that will allow access to an affectively comprehensible grasp of the situation the resident faces with his patient, which is always significantly different from the situation the supervisor would face with the same patient. It enables the supervisor to speak with the resident in a way that he can experience as close to, and respectful of where he is, and of what he is striving toward rather than as beyond him and unreachable, beside the point, intrusive, or implicitly devaluing of his abilities. Empathic attunement helps the supervisor offer what he knows in a way that is authentically assimilable into the resident's own preexisting emotional and cognitive schemata or emerging therapeutic self. As Ornstein and Ornstein (1985) point out with regard to analysis, "The analyst's efforts to identify the patient's subjective experiences accurately, and the patient's reactions to feeling understood, are both central for the subsequently emerging explanations to become experience near and emotionally meaningful as well" (p. 51). The same is true of supervision.

With residents whose "therapeutic self" is more firmly established, or with those who, by virtue of their experience, share more of the supervisor's assumptions about the nature of therapy, it paradoxically becomes possible to "teach" more, challenge, confront, and criticize more, suggest more, reveal more of one's own experience, and identify "problem" areas of countertransference more. Such residents can take in, evaluate, debate, and integrate what is offered without experiencing such supervisory activity as intrusive, harshly critical, superior, or otherwise unempathic.

ASPECTS OF THE SUPERVISOR'S COUNTERTRANSFERENCE

I would now like to consider some aspects of the supervisor's countertransference, which I will define, paraphrasing Wolf (1983), as all the psychological needs mobilized in the subjective experience of the supervisor by virtue of his participation in a triadic process with his resident and his resident's patient. In particular, I want to consider those aspects that relate to the central assumption shared by both parties, on which the supervisory relationship is based. This assumption is that the supervisor, like Moses, is more knowledgeable than his supervisee and will impart that knowledge to him. Unfortunately, although this assumption is reasonably serviceable in areas of knowledge or technical skill that exist at an arm's length from the "self" (and is also necessary up to a point in psychotherapy), it is one that may carry with it an almost automatic narcissistic insult when it comes to issues of how best to relate to, understand, influence, and help other people psychologically. Psychology is the one field in which almost everyone regards himself, consciously or unconsciously, as an expert. This is especially true of psychiatric residents. Furthermore, residents often arrive with therapeutic knowledge that includes a dim view of psychoanalysis, sometimes with very good reason. Even when a supervisor succeeds in persuading such a resident, he may inadvertently undermine the resident's self-esteem if he persuades without due consideration for what the resident already knows, or thinks he knows, or does not yet know he knows. When the supervisor, for example, feels particularly certain that he knows something about the patient that the resident does not, it is usually because the resident has the capacity to convey, consciously or unconsciously, an affectively real picture. It is important to recognize this and to credit the resident (although not necessarily always explicitly) with what he is able to bring, whether it is something he has been able to observe and report or is conveyed by means of unconscious identification with and reenactment of the patient's behavior (Gediman & Wolkenfeld, 1980; Searles, 1955). In the latter case it is a matter of expanding the resident's awareness and appreciation of his own resources.

However, most supervisors who spend many long hours listening to patients, and carefully considering their needs to be heard and understood while their own similar needs are largely eclipsed, look forward to the opportunity afforded by supervision to express how *they* see things, especially when eager and seemingly receptive residents offer that rare experience of appreciative recognition. Similarly, the ego need for efficacy, to "make things happen" actively (White, 1963), is also set in abeyance in much of our therapeutic work and when given the apparently legitimate chance actively to direct someone who is asking to be directed, it is often tempting to abandon the more humble and less gratifying task of trying to hear and comprehend what is already happening, and why.

Object-related needs[2] to refind or repair a lost or damaged object can likewise give rise to a pressured concern with understanding the patient, while inadvertently overlooking and thereby devaluing the resident whose need to be understood may be less apparent but no less vital to the outcome of the triadic process. The resident may feel himself to be treated as an extension or mere agent of the supervisor, and feel his self-esteem, self cohesion, and autonomous ego functioning compromised as a result.

---

[2] In my opinion, it is possible to use a self psychological framework in such a way that the content of what is empathically perceived may at times be usefully described in classical, ego-psychological or object relations terms. However, justification of this view is beyond the scope of the present chapter.

Iatrogenic intensification of unnecessarily painful envy, rivalry, and/or defensively exaggerated idealization of the supervisor may ensue. Gautier (1984), in a significant paper describing a painful process of supervision from the point of view of the supervisee, provides ample illustration of this point, although he does not reach the same conclusions.

Object-related needs, when evoked in the supervisor by the resident's own dilemma rather than by the patient's, may stimulate responses in the supervisor that implicitly express a view of the resident as needy, deficient, and injured. To act on this assumption unconsciously while consciously trying to be helpful and realistic may tactily confirm and entrench the resident's weaknesses and sense of inadequacy rather than his strengths. The same can be said, it is worth noting, of empathic overidentification with the resident's need for approving recognition, at the expense of empathically recognizing his readiness to bear confrontation, or open constructive criticism, which at the same time can convey respect.

On other levels, there are competitive impulses stimulated by residents who seem possessive of their patients, who want to display how well they can do without the supervisor's help, or who seem unconsciously bent on keeping the supervisor out of the bedroom of the actual affective interplay between resident and patient even though good psychotherapeutic work may in fact be taking place. There are also, of course, wishes to implant and propagate one's own original ideas or cherished psychoanalytic traditions through the resident, which can impinge in ways that, more often than not, defeat their own aims.

Aggressive motives (and reaction formations against them), are mobilized by the frustration of these narcissistic and object-libidinal aims, resulting in impulses to protest, destroy, forcefully overcome, or otherwise remove whatever in the resident is experienced as an obstacle to these supervisory ambitions. This can sometimes be expressed as an unempathic and therefore fruitless recommendation that the resident seek therapy.

Superego pressures are at work as well, and attach themselves to apparently legitimate vehicles. The supervisor's sense of professional responsibility to the resident, the patient, the institution, the profession, or the public may recruit powerful unconscious forces that prompt the supervisor to disregard the limits of his power to influence a complex process that should include a clear recognition of the personal boundaries, autonomy, and limitations of each member of the triad. Ultimately, the locus of responsibility for the patient resides in the core of the patient's self; for the resident's conduct of the therapy, in the core of the resident's self; and for the supervisor's interventions, noninterventions, and their anticipated effects or lack of effect, in the supervisor's self. As in therapy, the supervisor is primarily responsible for creating a climate, or structure in which growth, learning, and optimal functioning can take place. He cannot make them take place. In my experience, he can best create this structure by not getting in the way, and by respecting the potential of the unseen core of the resident (and of the patient), its resourcefulness, strengths, limitations, boundaries, and its vital need and right to a viewpoint different from the supervisor's (Lewis, 1978). That core, as Kohut (1977) has so convincingly demonstrated, can best fulfill its potential in an empathically receptive and responsive selfobject environment in which it is possible to acknowledge the inevitably occurring empathic failures.

To recapitulate, it is important to be aware of the powerful, multiply determined investment the supervisor has in being, and being seen as knowledgeable and effective. He can then discriminate an expression of these needs from an accurate empathic assessment of the resident's genuine readiness to hear and use what he has to say. The value of imparting accumulated and established knowledge is such a fundamental assumption in all Western teaching, and the wish to do so is so deeply rooted in all developmental levels, that it can easily go unnoticed and unquestioned. However, with most residents this can, at times, significantly impair the supervisor's empathic receptivity. Monitoring the resident's affective self state and the state of what he knows, or almost knows, does and is almost able to do, as well as where and how he experiences a need for help is the starting point of whatever the supervisor might attempt to teach. This, it seems to me, is a radically different focus from that of Eckstein and Wallerstein (1972), who explicitly recommend focusing on "problems" that they try to confront and correct.

Such empathic attention to understanding the resident requires that the supervisor be deeply motivated to immerse himself, that is temporarily lose himself in, or merge with, the Other. This, in conjunction with regressively intensified needs to grasp, to see clearly, to know, to have an effect, and to be appreciated by the object of his primary concern set the stage for some troublesome countertransference phenomena that are worth describing in some detail. These may not be as counterproductive as they first appear when viewed "objectively." In fact, they may even be an integral and useful phase of the empathic process in work with narcissistic disorders. In what follows, I describe my own experience as an analyst and, less frequently but no less significantly, as a supervisor. At first, I regarded these experiences as ideosyncratic pathological impairments of my autonomous ego functioning, and nothing more. I have, however, come to the conclusion that they represent something of considerable value both in the analytic setting and in the supervisory one.

When the supervisor attempts to take into account the resident's, the patient's, and his own self states and their triadic interactions (Gediman & Wolkenfeld, 1980), as well as the usual dynamic, technical, and theoretical issues of supervision, the potential for overloading or frustration of needs that are fundamental to the maintenance of his own self cohesion is considerably increased. Added to this is the unspoken, but powerfully felt affective exclusion, and/or engulfment (under- or overstimulation), encountered in narcissistic disturbances (in the patient, resident, or supervisor) when one comes too close to the infantile core. In this case a kind of "critical mass" is reached where the risk of regressive disorganization or loss of the supervisor's "nuclear self" seems unavoidable except through making implicit demands on the resident for recognition and/or for idealized performance (Wolf, 1983). If the supervisor refrains from making such demands for selfobject functioning, which at that moment are not naturally forthcoming, he may find himself becoming sleepy. Such sleepiness is partly a defense against and partly a restorative phase of a regressive process of otherwise painful fragmentation and depletion accompanied by alarming and embarrassing confusion and amnesia. On rare occasions, actual psychic annihilation or abrupt loss of consciousness may occur with a sensation of falling into a kind of "black hole," engulfing void, or what Green (1975) has referred to as a "blank psychosis."

These phenomena appear to be a regressive response to the absence of usable ego nutrients and narcissistic supplies in a situation in which one is totally absorbed in the task of empathically trying to get hold of something or someone that is not yet there. Everything one can conceive of saying or doing in such a situation seems utterly wrong or futile, including remaining silent. In these circumstances one does not have the option of turning to something or someone else. It is, of course, sometimes possible to rise above such a situation to an objective vantage point and reflect on things theoretically. One can also distract oneself and the resident with some side issue or aspect of the situation with which one feels competent, in a manner analogous to the infant's turning to part objects on losing a more globally experienced "wholeness-in-relatedness." In so doing it may be possible to maintain the vital illusion of knowing, seeing, having, and of efficacy (White, 1963), much to the relief of both supervisor and student. Such relief can be costly, however, as it may short-circuit empathic attunement and the creative emergence of new self-expression on the part of the resident and of the patient whom he unconsciously represents.

Wolf (1983) comments, "defenses against regression can interfere with the analyst's empathizing." Gediman and Wolkenfeld (1980) also observe and recommend "fluctuations in ego functioning and controlled regression" in the supervisor. However, none of these authors appears to advocate the degree of internal loss of control that I am suggesting. A better word for what I am recommending, therefore, might be Bion's (1963) term "contained" regression, although I consider what is contained to be *primarily* fragments of my own dissolving self, rather than projected bits of the resident or patient, even though these also play their part.

What under ordinary circumstances appears to be rational and adaptive supervisory competence and helpfulness may therefore at other times be motivated by a defensive need to escape or master a feeling of disorganization, exclusion/engulfment, and loss of internal control with the immanent subjective risk of excruciating embarrassment or annihilation. On the other hand, what appears to the supervisor internally to be chaotic madness, or death, and externally as sleepiness or simply failure to provide an average expectable response, may be an essential phase in the creative process in supervision. In other words, it appears to be a painful but necessary receptive pre-stage of the discovery or creation of newly emerging and vital material or gestalts— pseudopodia of the true self of the resident and/or patient. For this to occur it is necessary, for me at least, to contain an almost unbearable feeling of "wrongness" and a nearly irresistible impulse to assert myself (interpretively, didactically, or inquisitively). Instead of such self-assertion, I try to maintain a trusting attitude, and allow myself not only to "see nobody on the road," as Alice did, but also to be nobody on the road. In other words, I try to hold myself, or allow myself to be held in a state of slipping or being swept into nonbeing and apparent nonrelatedness. In this way I am much less likely to get in the way of the next step in the emergence of that particular resident (and patient). As Winnicott (1968) states about therapy, "If only we can wait, the patient arrives at understanding creatively and with immense joy, and now I enjoy this joy more than I used to enjoy the sense of having been clever" (p. 86), and, I would add, the sense of having *made* something happen.

The next step may be the resident's more openly expressed frustration, anger, disappointment, curiosity, need for assistance, or other spontaneous self-expression that can both revitalize the supervisor and help to illuminate some hitherto unseen (repressed or split-off) aspect of the triadic system. Or, the supervisor's hypnoid state may permit the unconscious reception of cues from the resident (and through him, the patient) that break through into the supervisor's consciousness in the form of dreamlike images, sensations, affects, or "crazy" ideas that may have surprising relevance to what is happening (Thompson, 1980). In other words, such sleep-like states seem to facilitate unconscious reception and reorganization of empathically perceived data into new configurations that on awakening can become clear in a way that no amount of rational effort could have accomplished. For this to occur, however, one must be accepting of the phasic occurrence of these altered states, and neither become too objective, too scornful, too afraid, too ashamed, or too guilty about them, nor too sure that one knows what they mean or contain in advance. I do not advocate the deliberate induction of meditative trance states, but only that one refrain from actively preventing or interrupting them when they are spontaneously and, as it were, hypnotically induced in response to the flow (or blockage in the flow) of material from the resident. This may occur at precisely those times when something is about to emerge that the resident cannot bear to have observed, judged, or misperceived, and therefore he unconsciously nullifies the presence of the supervisor.

It is my contention that rather than fighting off or analytically rising above such states of mind, or prematurely attributing them to pathological projection, unconscious hostility, "resistance," or a learning problem on the part of the resident, the supervisor can allow himself to feel, and risk appearing dozy, ignorant, incompetent, and powerless. If he can tolerate this empty-headedness and profound uncertainty and maintain a readiness to receive and appreciate whatever presents itself, then the supervisory process is likely to be reordered spontaneously, without the perpetuation of resistances, which are so easily prolonged and intensified by too much effort to overcome them.

This may lead to a subjectively interminable hiatus, however, that corresponds with a "stage of hesitation" in the resident or patient, to use Winnicott's phrase (Davis & Wallbridge, 1981), in which there is nothing to be said. One can only tolerate not knowing or even nonbeing in the faith (Eigen, 1981), or trusting infantile/maternal expectancy that something of value will happen to shed light on the situation. This waiting is akin to what Keats called "Negative Capability, that is when man is capable of being in uncertainties, Mysteries, doubts, without any irritable reaching after fact and reason" (1966, p. 329). It is also related to what St. John of the Cross refers to as the "cloud of unknowing," (Happold, 1963, pp. 60–61) as well as to Taoist or Buddhist meditative states.

> The Way is a void,
> Used but never filled:
> An abyss it is,
> Like an ancestor
> From which all things come.
>
> It blunts sharpness,
> Resolves tangles;
> It tempers light,
> Subdues turmoil.
> —Lao Tzu, *Tao Te Ching*

Nature would appear to abhor even an intrapsychic vacuum, and if the supervisor can keep from abhorring himself, while containing his own inner vacuum, then something significant often enters the void of its own accord. I am not suggesting that we assume the role of Bodhisattvas or that we rely solely on a "mystical" process, but that we recognize, at certain crucial moments, the limits of our conscious vision, reason, and active mastery, and trust the triadic unconscious process, and at times quite literally "give our*selves* over"[3] to it, as Freud (1912) himself suggested.

A spontaneous impulse, idea, or gesture (Davis & Wallbridge, 1981) may then appear within moments, bringing the supervisor back and reorienting him, or it may occur in the next supervisory session, provided the first session ends with both participants in a state of puzzlement rather than with a false sense of closure, that is, without the comforting illusion of knowing more than they do. In the following session, the resident often comes in with new material that he has recalled or discovered in himself or heard for the first time in the patient. At this point, the supervisor, if he is alert, may be able to recognize and appreciate this material as an important key to further dynamic understanding that has come from or through the resident rather than

---

3. Italics added. Freud was referring to the more limited conception of "unconscious memory," rather than to the unconscious as such, but I believe the principle is the same.

being handed down by the "super-visor." At this point then, the supervisor can respond to the new material with relevant questions, tentative interpretations, theoretical elaboration, and so forth. In other words, a more or less didactic phase can follow as a natural consequence of some vital truth that has arisen in the resident, rather than as premature effort to supply him with one. The resident then has the ego-consolidating, or self-affirming experience of having discovered something of value and of having evoked an interesting and relevant response from his supervisor, rather than being the passive recipient of an impressive but not very useful lecture, confrontation, or interpretation. This sequence, if repeated, tends to nurture rather than inhibit the resident's authentic self-reliance, and his reliance on his patients instead of perpetuating excessive dependence on, compliance with, or internal defiance of supervisory "authority."

CASE ILLUSTRATION

It is difficult, in a brief illustration, to capture the fluid quality of the three interweaving streams of experience, both real and imagined, that constitute the supervisory situation. Also, of course, one example cannot illustrate all aspects of the complex empathic process I have been attempting to describe. I will, however, try to present sufficient experiential data to make it possible for the reader to understand what I am referring to and to draw his own conclusions. I will present material from several consecutive supervisory sessions with a therapist in her 2nd year of a psychiatric residency. She had been treating the patient (a 29-year-old woman) for a year prior to the sessions described. She had been in supervision with me for 7 months, but we had been discussing her work with this particular patient for only 3.

The patient comes from a very disturbed family, the youngest of three siblings born to a severely alcoholic, erratic, and abusive mother who was apparently considered to be so mentally incompetent that there was talk of declaring her unfit and of giving this last baby up for adoption at birth. She was, however, kept in the home at the insistence of her "warm, supportive, steadfast," but otherwise passive father, who seemed to "understand" without actually talking about feelings. The "best times" were when the mother was hospitalized, as she often was, and the father "cared for them alone." At such times they were free of fear and of the very painful embarrassment caused by the mother's chaotic presence.

The girl, during her early teens, was also the victim of ritualized physical abuse by her older brother. The sister, 10 years her senior, was "never very close." She seems mainly remembered for a disturbingly intrusive comment, when the patient was 14, that she thought the patient was a lesbian.

The patient, despite and because of such a climate at home, developed an outgoing, engaging personality with a good sense of humor, and became quite competent at work and at school (encouraged, but also to some degree burdened by her father's expectations). She also came to regard herself as a "mediator" in the home, better able to "calm her mother" (and her explosive brother) than anyone else.

Her presenting symptoms were many, but her central concern was with abdominal pains that had been severe enough to require laparotomy. She was, however, greatly relieved when someone recognized that her symptoms were the result of stress, and recommended psychotherapy. She then acknowledge wide fluctuations in self-esteem, preoccupation with becoming overweight, sexual identity confusion, and an inability to maintain close relationships—especially with men. She "never felt whole" with men nor did she feel herself able to "supply what they needed," although she still dreamed of "getting married and having children." Relationships with women could be closer and physically affectionate, but she was inclined to become irritable and to alienate them. At such times of rejection and disinterest from a "girlfriend" she suffered fragmentation, with either overexcitement or depletion to the point of exhaustion and being unable to stay awake.

In therapy, these same self-state disturbances fluctuated in response to variations in the therapist's availability and empathic attunement. As a result of the therapist's naturally empathic, enquiring approach, the patient had been able to develop an idealizing transference. She was openly admiring of her therapist's calmness, competence, and what she saw as the therapist's "interesting life" (as a doctor in the kind of institution where she remembered visiting her mother).

In the sessions immediately prior to the ones I wish to describe in more detail, the therapist had cancelled an appointment. In the next session, the patient expressed "a lot of negativism" about her schoolwork and a sense of "being in the wrong profession" as well as generalized impatience with "stupid people who give her no support." She readily agreed when the therapist commented that she thought the therapist was "one of those," and added, "but what really bothers me is that I'll never get to know you away from this office." The session ended with the patient, sadder but calmer, hinting that she had "a lot of feelings she didn't understand."

In the next supervisory session, the therapist began by reporting that the patient had come in anxious and had avoided eye contact (as the resident was also doing with me), and commented that she was consciously aware of "not wanting to direct the session." She was also mindful of the patient's tentative expression of as yet unknown trans-ference affect in the previous session, and was hoping to find an op-portunity to come back to it. The patient, however, was initially preoc-cupied with her failure to live up to her father's expectations in her school performance, and while she had begun the session animated, she became more and more "flat and perplexed" as the session proceeded. The therapist "decided to let it go on."

At this point in the therapist's narrative to me, I too was becoming sleepy and perplexed and also decided to let it go on, although I had a vague, uneasy feeling that the resident needed, and was nonverbally inviting me, to comment. She also seemed, however, to be struggling to find her own words (or so I thought) while keeping her own feelings and opinions hidden in a way that kept me from understanding what was going on and even from "seeing a way in." There followed, for me, a period of confusion, clouded consciousness, and almost total amnesia for previous sessions and even for the therapist's words of mere moments before. One of the patient's phrases stuck with me for a while causing some concern, "rolling downhill like a snowball, bouncing off one tree and then another," then I lost it again. This uncomfortable limbo lasted most of the rest of the session. I recall a fleeting moment when the therapist was describing the patient's referring to a "girlfriend," when I wondered whether the therapist's own sexuality, or concerns about her own sexual identity were being aroused in some way by the patient's material. I vaguely felt that it would be intrusive and out of place to inquire about it. I also could not be certain that it was not my own sexual inhibition or sexual identity confusion that was being mobilized, but which was beyond my ability to analyze in that context. I sank back into oblivion again as I continued to try to attend to the flow of material, hoping to be reawakened and revitalized by some unexpected self-revelation.

I "came to" momentarily when the therapist was reporting, with more affect, an interpretation she had made to the patient, "You really wish someone would take care of you." To which the patient replied, "God no! It should be reciprocal! Besides, I get to the point that I don't want to be taken care of." This interchange had, it slowly dawned on me, followed a dream the patient had just reported in which she was "seriously injured and dying, but didn't let it be known," which is what I had been experiencing internally as it was being described.

The therapist continued her report of her interpretation, or empathic paraphrasing, of the patient's dream (and of my state of mind as well as her own), "You're there, but don't make it known; you're in need, but don't ask." The patient replied, "I don't think one should *have* to ask. There's an aura around someone who needs unless they wear a phenomenal mask."

I then slipped back once more into my own abyss from which I felt unable to reach out for help, or *to* help, and here again my otherwise automatic notes become illegible. At one point I had a fleeting, but vivid hypnagogic image of a "moldy orange" and was aware of vague apprehensions about the resident whose cautious distance and emotional deadness seemed to have an ominous quality. In fact, she seemed to have the same fearful, self-critical, self-doubting, depressive quality with which I was familiar from a few months previously when her inner struggle was such that supervisory activity on my part proved quite fruitless.

I should mention parenthetically that I regard this resident as having an excellent emerging capacity for analytically oriented psychotherapy, with an unusually good sense of phrasing, tact, and timing in her interventions with her patients. She has, however, only tenuous self-confidence in the light of her own high standards, and relative inexperience. Since she had come a long way in overcoming her reticence about exposing her ideas and expressing her feelings in supervision, I was loathe to intervene at that moment in any way that might be felt as critical or intrusive, or that might intensify her self-consciousness and inhibition ("resistance").

Therefore, when I was conscious at all, I found myself confused, uncertain, unable to take in or process what she was saying, somewhat frustrated and disappointed with her frequent strained silences, and feeling very much "on the spot" in the face of her tentative, fearful, and expectant glances in my direction.

In retrospect, it seems that it might have been easy and advisable to break the ice with some simple inquiry, but at the time I was quite incapable of finding the words. I also trusted my empathic sense that any question, knowledgeable-sounding confrontation, interpretation, or "helpful" theoretical exposition would come across as intrusive, critical, or "superior." Any activity from my side, in other words, seemed likely to leave the impression that "the problem" was hers, when in fact, at that moment, it seemed to belong as much to me as to anyone else in the triad. Consequently, I held my tongue and hid my embarrassing internal chaos and guilt over my own failed competence. In doing so, I was sustained by a faith, born of past experience, that if I did not interrupt, something new and useful was very likely to appear.

At this point, it might be useful to provide the resident's account of this supervisory session as she recalled it a week later.[4]

> I came to supervision that day feeling relatively unprepared. I had been unable to spend the customary half hour rereading my notes and collecting my thoughts about the session with the patient. I was eager to discuss this particular session because it had been somewhat disjointed and I did not feel I had a grasp on what was happening in it.
>
> During the first few minutes of the supervision hour I began reviewing the session in detail, hoping to discover, or have my supervisor discover the "key to the session." I'm reminded here of a well-known author's analogy of the student's approach to poetry, hunting for the hidden meaning like searching for the prize in a box of Crackerjacks. In my review I certainly could not find "the prize" and I think my puzzlement began to show in my presentation since I paused frequently. Then I developed a growing awareness that the usual clarifications and questions were not forthcoming from my supervisor. I looked up and my mentor was "nodding off." This had many associations with similar past events that I recalled later, but at the time, all I was consciously aware of was a mounting feeling of unease. I felt an uncomfortable empathy with that state of trying to recover consciousness when all one wants to do is sleep. I felt inadequate: somehow, probably as a result of my state of relative unpreparedness and puzzlement, my manner was providing a stimulus that was subthreshold to that required to maintain a waking state in my listener. I was frustrated at not having the usual rewarding session and also at not knowing what to do.
>
> Then the absurdity and humor of the situation struck me. I laughed, closed my notes, and said, "This is painful!" You replied, "What is?" and I explained that I knew how painful it was to be fighting sleep like that. You were somewhere between REM and stage one, but you commented, "*You* were empathizing with *me*!"
>
> Then you said the time was up, that you didn't know what else to say, except that you thought something I had said about "slowing the tempo" sounded right. You just reaffirmed what I had said.

From my own point of view, again, I recall resisting the urge to

_____

4. I am grateful to the resident who provided this material at my request following the *next* supervisory session. Her knowledge of my "special interest" was therefore not a factor in what subsequently transpired.

comment further with something like "sometimes such confusion is necessary" because I felt that doing so would be primarily for the purpose of saving face, in other words maintaining a mask of being more knowledgeable than I actually felt. Such seemingly innocuous remarks, I have found, tend to dispel the darkness and disorder prematurely, and create a false sense of security and closure that inhibits subsequent creative combination and emergence.

In the following session, the resident arrived wearing a colorful, attractive new sweater with a bold, expansive pattern. She was in a talkative, outgoing, even exuberant mood and began with the enthusiastic remark, "Much more early material came out than it ever has in the past!" She went on to describe how her patient had arrived, jokingly but grandly announcing, "I'm an inspiration for those patients out there." The patient was shy about proceeding but with a simple, well-timed interpretation to the effect that she was afraid the therapist would find what she had to say trivial, she was able to speak of her wish to be "needed and special," and to be able to "help others in a reciprocal way." She also expressed her fear of "intimacy," a word supplied by the therapist, much to the grateful delight of the patient. She then went on spontaneously to assert and inquire of herself, "whether I'm a homosexual or not must go back to something that happened when I was an infant."

There followed, for me, another phase of drowsiness, confusion, and feeling "out of touch," which this time dissolved spontaneously enough for me to interrupt my resident with the comment, "I have the feeling that you want to present this material in such a way that you will get to hear my reactions before saying what *you* think and feel." The resident agreed, and then went on to describe how she had asked the patient what she (the patient) imagined had happened when she was young. Then the water burst emotionally, both in supervision and in the reported therapy session.

The patient recalled, with some feeling, that there were no pictures of her as a baby, and that she never felt she was a "welcome being," speaking again of being "almost put up for adoption." Then came an outpouring of "phenomenal anger" (resident's words) with her mother, as well as with her father for not having her mother committed.

"For Christ's sake, she's sick! Throw her away for a while! And yet he stood by her! I supposedly took more abuse than I can remember—I had casts, and broken limbs! Father told me all that when I asked him to tell me about my childhood when I was 13. I know it must be true because he's not the type to make me hate my mother even more."

At this point I asked the resident how she had been feeling as she listened to this. She exclaimed, "I was impressed that her anger had a really vicious intensity! It reminded me that she often used the word 'vicious' to describe her own behavior toward people she sees as vulnerable. But this was the first time I had experienced it full force!"

"Could you feel it with her or did it alarm you?"

"I felt I was gradually distancing myself from it."

"Did you feel yourself to be the target of it?"

"Yes, especially when it got to closer parallels to what's happening now. . . . But she didn't seem to be just angry with her mother, she seemed not to want to believe it was true, that her mother had actually done those things, so I said, "You seem to be indicating some warmth for her as well." But the patient recoiled with revulsion and said "No! No! Don't use that word '*warm*'! She understands nothing! She's completely off the wall! She has a terrible time even conceiving an idea, or a concept!"

The therapist persisted, trying several times to get the patient to acknowledge the warmth she was sure was there. I then persisted, myself, in saying that while I thought she was probably quite right in what she was saying, that she might be prematurely insisting on the warm side of her patient's feelings because she found the patient's hatred alarming and "didn't want to believe it" herself, preferring to "hold on" to the warmth. She replied, "I guess so, I did begin to feel that my repetition of 'warmth' was a bit sadistic."

As the supervision hour was drawing to a close, I asked, "How did you feel at the end of the session?"

"I wished supervision was right away, although I wasn't drained, in fact, I was excited in many ways. It struck me how embryonic therapy was; it's taken a whole year to get to this. It seems therapy has just begun."

I replied that I thought "embryonic" was a good word for it, because what the patient was expressing, I thought, was a very early and fundamental quality of rage at the unavailability of the kind of mutually responsive, enjoyable, and empathic nurturing that is so essential to growth. There was also a freshness and liveliness of affect that I found very promising. I also assured her that many of my patients take a good deal longer than a year to get to such a point, and that it was a credit to her receptive work that the patient was expressing herself as freely as she was.

The following therapy session was a difficult one beginning with a "steady stream of what was wrong in her life." In the midst of this the patient spontaneously expressed warm feelings more openly toward the therapist, and fears of being a "total depressant" to her. "All I do is come out with all this crap, but I have a wonderful side of me that you don't see." The resident then commented to me that she does indeed see that side of her, but that the patient has "no constancy" of that image of herself. I suggested that such a formulation had the makings of a good interpretation, if the opportunity arose.

DISCUSSION

Much could be said about this material from a theoretical point of view, especially regarding the projective–introjective interplay that underlies the parallel process as well as the empathic capacities of each member of the triad. I would like to draw attention, in the present context, to the process that would appear to be facilitated by the supervisor's taking the resident's experience rather than the patient's as his primary empathic concern, and by limiting his "teaching" to what springs naturally from affectively alive material. My attention to my own motives for possible interventions, combined with my introjective identification with the resident and through her with her patient, resulted in a phase of painful internal regressive decompensation that I endured in the confident but uncertain expectation that, like labor, it would end and that the outcome would be worth the wait. I believe that the supervisor's willingness to wait passively in circumstances such as these, and to contain his own and the resident's unspoken distress, as well as his willingness to fail and be seen as failing, allows the resident to come through on her own, as she did in this case, with a mixture of humor, concern, and protest that then, and only then, allows the supervisor to respond in a relevant and welcoming, but not necessarily uncritical, way. The movement then flowed naturally from her side, in a way that may have contributed to her openness, in turn, to the patient.

It cannot be stated with any assurance that some other intervention on my part might not have resolved the impasse earlier, or that it would not have resolved in any case, or that some other intervention might not have resulted in more learning or insight. It is my belief, however, that what unfolded in the later sessions can be taken as verification that little was lost and much may have been gained by my being "in empathic attendance" rather than resorting to verbal forceps or instruction. Such a sequence of events is a regularly observable phenomenon that provides, in my opinion, replicable empirical validation of the usefulness of operating for a time in what feels and looks like an irrational and incompetent manner. At such moments of profound uncertainty, it may be more productive than it appears to err on the side of a passive, feminine mode of waiting to be taught, rather than of a phallic-active mode of teaching.

The supervisor's functions, then, include not only didactic elements, but also selfobject functions, mediated by empathy, of mirroring responsiveness, idealizable calmness, and strength despite his own "not knowing," as well as idealizable empathic understanding and knowledgeability when needed. If the resident experiences the supervisor's knowledge as relevant, helpful, and not out of reach, then it becomes more available for internalization and less likely to provoke unmanageably intense and therefore unconsciously destructive hatred, envy or rivalry, and their various defensive consequences. The supervisor can be an idealizable model of someone who "knows a good thing when he sees it," rather than an expert who always "knows best." To teach clearly what is known, he must see clearly what is as yet unknown, and have faith that what cannot yet be seen holds promise of becoming an ally in the therapeutic task.

The consequences of this supervisory stance are several. They include the resident's usually self-limiting tendency to establish a regressive selfobject transference of either a mirroring, idealized, or combined sort. This would appear to be the natural accompaniment of good-enough empathic attunement. It is limited to some extent by the supervisor's open acknowledgment, when appropriate, of his own limitations to assist the resident in understanding the genetic dimension of his own experience. It is also limited by focusing inquiry and comments around the way in which the resident's experience reflects the patient and the patient's genetic dimension (Hunt, 1981; Searles, 1955). For the most part, the resident's need for the supervisor's mirroring and idealized functions are not interpreted as such except when difficulties arise that can be traced to relative failures in empathy on the part of the supervisor. This includes, of course, those times of ignorance and apparent "absence" or inability to respond when the resident might have been experiencing a need or expectation that the supervisor be knowledgeable. The experience of openly identifying and resolving such communicative difficulties by tracing them to unacknowledged frustration or disappointment with the supervisor can be a very useful experience for the resident, especially when it sheds light on a parallel phenomenon between patient and therapist. The resident is then in a much better position to deal with his patient from understanding born of personal experience, rather than from experience-distant theoretical considerations alone (and in this I would include didactic advocacy of self psychological formulations).

There is, I believe, a process of transmuting internalization of both supervisory functions and empathic capacities that occurs as a result of this interplay in a manner that is analogous, on a smaller scale, to the now-familiar process in analysis, described by Kohut (1977) and others. The relatively infrequent meetings, as well as the time constraint of the supervisory contract tend to limit the degree to which a regressive self-object transference occurs. But it also limits the degree to which it can be worked through when it does occur. This makes the termination of supervision a potentially troublesome disruption for both resident and patient, which must therefore be anticipated and carefully addressed.

Sometimes residents who were initially skeptical or afraid of a psychoanalytic approach and who find their own position understood, respected, and built upon rather than displaced in supervision, begin to take a more active interest in the literature and to entertain the idea, on their own, of seeking further supervision, personal therapy, or analysis. When such interest arises spontaneously, it can then be responded to with appropriate suggestions and referral. When the issue of personal therapy comes up in this way, rather than as an intrusive imposition or judgment from above, it is experienced as a discovery of a need within, in the context of a possibility of being understood and helped from without.

At the very least, such an empathic approach tends to minimize the likelihood of the resident's conducting overintellectualized, pseudopsychoanalytic therapy on the one hand, and on the other, going on to antagonistic disparagement of analysis, which has been intensified by narcissistic injury at the hands of supervisors who, in their efforts to teach, may not practice what they preach. This approach may fall short of providing a systematic exposure to psychoanalytic theory and therapeutic technique. The supervisor, however, can take some satisfaction from having been a catalyst during one limited phase of an ongoing process of evolution in which the key determinant of the resident's performance as a therapist and well-educated expert will be the vitality of his own internally arising interest in listening to his patients and to himself, and in pursuing further training. Active integration of the resident's capacity to use himself to the fullest advantage is thereby made more likely. Such an approach may even be able to contribute in a small way to the creation of a climate of mutual respect and cooperation between colleagues of differing viewpoints and talents rather than to the splitting apart of people with a common cause.

REFERENCES

Bacal, H.A. (1985). Optimal responsiveness and the therapeutic process. In A. Goldberg, ed., *Progress in Self Psychology* (vol. 1, pp. 202–227). New York: Guilford Press.

Bion, W.R. (1963). *Learning from Experience.* New York: Basic Books.

Davis, M., & Wallbridge, D. (1981). *Boundary and Space, An Introduction to the Work of D.W. Winnicott.* New York: Brunner/Mazel).

Eckstein, R., & Wallerstein, R.S. (1972). *The Teaching and Learning of Psychotherapy* (2nd ed.). New York: Basic Books.

Eigen, M. (1981). The area of faith in Winnicott, Lacan, and Bion. *International Journal of Psycho-Analysis,* 62:413–433.

Freud, S. (1912). Recommendations to physicians practicing psychoanalysis. *Standard Edition,* 12:111–120.

Gautier, M. (1984). Countertransference and supervision: A discussion of some dynamics from the point of view of the supervisee. *Canadian Journal of Psychiatry,* 29:513–519.

Gediman, H.K., & Wolkenfeld, F. (1980). The parallelism phenomenon in psychoanalysis and supervision; its reconsideration as a triadic system. *Psychoanalytic Quarterly,* 49:234–255.

Green, A. (1975). The analyst, symbolization and absence in the analytic setting. *International Journal of Psycho-Analysis,* 56:1–18.

Happold, F.C. (1963). *Mysticism: A Study and Anthology.* New York: Penguin.

Hunt, W. (1981). The use of countertransference in psychotherapy supervision. *Journal of the American Academy of Psychoanalysis,* 9:361–373.

Keats, J. (1966). *The Selected Poetry of Keats.* Paul de Man, ed. New York: New American Library.

Kohut, H. (1959). Introspection, empathy and psychoanalysis. *Journal of the American Psychoanalytic Association,* 7:459–483.

Kohut, H. (1977). *The Restoration of the Self.* New York: International Universities Press.

Lewis, J.M. (1978). *To Be a Therapist; The Teaching and Learning.* New York: Brunner/Mazel.

Lichtenberg, J.D. (1981). The empathic mode of perception, and alternative vantage points for psychoanalytic work. *Psychoanalytic Inquiry,* 1:329–355.

Ornstein, P.H., & Ornstein, A. (1985). Clinical understanding and explaining: The empathic vantage point. In A. Goldberg, ed., *Progress in Self Psychology* (vol. 1, pp. 43–61). New York: Guilford Press.

Schwaber, E. (1981). Empathy: A mode of analytic listening. *Psychoanalytic Inquiry,* 1:357–392.

Searles, H.F. (1955). The informational value of the supervisor's emotional experiences. *Psychiatry,* 18:135–146.

Shafer, R. (1959). Generative empathy in the treatment situation. *Psychoanalytic Quarterly,* 28:342–373.

Stolorow, R.D., Brandchaft, B., & Atwood, G.E. (1983). Intersubjectivity in psychoanalytic treatment, with special reference to archaic states. *Bulletin of the Menninger Clinic,* 47:117–128.

Thompson, P.G. (1980). On the receptive function of the analyst. *International Review of Psycho-Analysis,* 7:183–205.

White, R.W. (1963). *Ego and Reality in Psychoanalytic Theory.* New York: International Universities Press.

Winnicott, D.W. (1968). *Playing and Reality.* London: Tavistock, 1971.

Wolf, E. (1983). Empathy and countertransference. In *The Future of Psychoanalysis* (pp. 309–326). A. Goldberg, ed., New York: International Universities Press.

17

Self Psychology and Somatization: An Integration with Alexithymia

WILLIAM H. RICKLES

A revision of the psychoanalytic theory of psychosomatic conditions is long overdue (Deutsch, 1980). Although a prominent topic in the 1930s, '40s, and '50s, the theory and practice of psychoanalysis for psychosomatic conditions now occupies very little attention in the psychoanalytic literature. The most obvious reason is pragmatic: an average, expectable course of psychoanalysis or psychoanalytic psychotherapy is not beneficial for most psychosomatic cases and often is associated with exacerbation of the medical condition (Kellner, 1975; Sifneos, 1975). Exceptions are notable (Engle & Schmale, 1967; Sperling, 1978; Winnicott, 1966) and probably are attributable to some undetermined but gifted application of psychoanalysis.

Despite these difficulties and the shift of therapeutic techniques to pharmacological and nonanalytic methods, a small number of analysts have continued to accrue observations about psychosomatic conditions, which have coalesced under the term "alexithymia", or "alexithymic syndrome" (Krystal, 1977; Marty & M'Uzan, 1963; McDougall, 1974; Nemiah, Freyberger, & Sifneos, 1976; Rickles, 1981; Sifneos, 1973; Taylor, 1977). These findings are beginning to shed some light on the propensity of some people to fall ill medically when subjected to environmental stress, disappointment, object loss, or humiliation, while others under the same conditions may become heroic, depressed, psychotic, neurotic, or creative, or may act out. Further, we are beginning to understand, with psychoanalytic tools, why such people often have so much difficulty getting well and why some are prone to develop

---

This chapter was originally presented at the Sixth Annual Conference on the Psychology of the Self, Los Angeles, California, 1983.

protracted illness such as the chronic pain syndrome. (Pain is another topic that has attracted little psychoanalytic attention and is intimately involved with most psychosomatic conditions, therefore necessitating its inclusion in any theory of psychosomatic conditions.) Attempts to integrate this literature with classical psychoanalytic theory have been significant but not satisfying (e.g., Krystal, 1982), and do little to delineate what is needed in the way of average, expectable psychoanalytic technique to render these common conditions more accessible to psychoanalysis.

Self psychology has emerged on the psychoanalytic scene as an extension of psychoanalytic theory and technique that provides an understanding and approach to the modulation–prevention of nonpsychotic, emergency, and depressive affects (Levine, 1983). Additionally, self psychology has provided the concepts of selfobject and selfobject relationships, modeled after Winnicott's transitional object, that are particularly necessary for control of these disorganizing and immobilizing experiences in borderline and narcissistic personality disorders (Kohut & Wolf, 1978). Although these states resemble the highly somatized affects of panic and depressive resignation, self psychologists have not considered the role played by selfobject relationships in somatization, conversion, and medical illness except in passing (Goldberg, 1982). Accordingly, locating alexithymia within the concepts of self psychology may help point the way for psychoanalysis to reenter the scene of psychosomatic conditions, including chronic pain, with technical and theoretical tools for safe and effective application of psychoanalysis to psychosomatic illness.

Self psychology has defined a new class of character pathology called disorders of the self or narcissistic personality disorders. The similarities of observable traits and psychoanalytic explanatory concepts between these disorders and alexithymia attract comparison:

1. Both disorders of the self and alexithymia are considered to be states of personality deficiency.

2. Both present considerable difficulty to treatment with American standard psychoanalysis because of a paucity of repressed, unconscious conflictual fantasy available for interpretation.

3. Denied dependency on others for maintenance of psychological and/or psychophysiological equilibrium characterizes both.

4. Psychoanalytic study of each condition has related the pa-

thology to disturbances in the maternal relationship during the 2nd to 3rd years of life.

5. Most importantly, psychoanalytic understanding of alexithymia and disorders of the self draw on Winnicott's understanding of transitional objects and transitional phenomena as a pivotal paradigmatic model (Palombo, 1982).

It is the thesis of this chapter that alexithymia is a subcategory of self disorders. Inasmuch as the hypothesis that alexithymia predisposes toward (*not causes*) psychosomatic breakdown has received some empirical support (but is by no means present in every case of psychophysiological illness or somatization), examining the relationship may provide the beginning for a self psychology theory of psychophysiological breakdown and somatization. Because of the context of this chapter, I assume that the reader is considerably more familiar with self psychology than with alexithymia. Accordingly, I give a more detailed explication of the alexithymia literature.

OPERATIONAL DESCRIPTION

While working as consultation–liaison consultants, two Boston analysts, Sifneos and Nemiah, began to write about the consistent difficulty they found in relating as analysts to patients they were called to see in psychosomatic consultation. This difficulty took the form of a paucity of affective description and intrapsychic awareness in these patients that effectively blocked the usual means of psychoanalytically oriented, psychosomatic consultation. Sifneos termed this deficiency in usage of affective words "alexithymia," from the Greek word stems meaning "without words for feelings" (Sifneos, 1973). Associated with this verbal deficiency, they reported a tendency for these patients to describe their lives in pragmatic, functional terms without reference to emotion, fantasy, and intrapsychic or interpersonal meaning. Dream reports were found to be scanty. A stiff, wooden posture and carriage completed their description of alexithymic patients (Nemiah, 1978).

In Paris, psychosomatic patients were described similarly with an emphasis on their tendency to think in operational, descriptive, or task-oriented terms without reference to feelings or interpersonal meanings (*pensée opératoire*). The Parisian authors, Marty and de M'Uzan (1963), describe their patients as having a basic inhibition and constriction of object representation characterized by an absence of daydreams and fantasy (de M'Uzan, 1974). These patients seldom remember their dreams, but when they do, the content is sparse and little more than a recital of day residue. Their object relations are described as rigidly conventional and seem to be based on seeing others as stereotypes and "reduplications" of themselves. The capacity for empathic experiencing of objects in their "singularity" is almost totally missing.

In a comprehensive psychoanalytic paper describing her experience with the analysis of alexithymic, psychosomatic patients in Paris, McDougall described these analysands as seemingly normal and free of neurotic or psychotic symptomatology. Instead, she noted that they would manifest facial movements, gestures, sensory–motor experiences, or pain when the psychoanalytic material would have led her to expect neurotic defenses (McDougall, 1974).

Thus, the clinical picture of alexithymia seems to describe a group of people who are not psychologically minded and who relate to others in rather rigid, emotionally stunted, nonempathic ways. They are bereft of intrapsychic conflict and fantasy or have a great handicap in expressing themselves with verbal, affective terms and utilize nonverbal "body language" instead. These descriptors are compatible with narcissistic personality disorders if we assume that, as a consequence of the constriction in affective, interpersonal communication, the characteristic hypersensitivity of narcissistic personality disorders to personal slights, humiliations, and disappointments is not expressed in the usual way but is channeled into nonverbal, somatized behavior. Indeed, McDougall finds somatization to be a common response to narcissistic injury (McDougall, 1980a). One additional observation suggests a self disorder associated with alexithymia. Commonly, the self as experiencing agent is avoided. Indefinite pronouns such as "it," "one," or even "you" are used instead of "I." Bodily parts are not owned but are referred to as "the hand" or "the foot."

> A 50-year-old woman whose creativity in sculpture had attracted national attention suffered from severe, painful vasospastic attacks associated with Raynaud's disease of the hands. Her important creative outlet was threatened by this progressive disease, which rendered her hands cold, painful, and prone to pathological ulceration. As she described her illness, she referred to "the hands" and "the pain" rather than the more active and self-acknowledging "my hands" and "my pain." At times, she would totally disavow her experience with the phrase, "the pain in the hands," rather than stating, "I feel pain," or "My hands hurt."

Affects may be treated similarly.

> A 45-year-old man with ulcer disease, psoriasis, and chronic hepatitis would

avoid all direct expression of affect toward the analyst by waiting until a
feeling subsided and then say, "There was some anger about that."

The similarity is more compelling when we review the intrapsychic situation.

THE INTRAPSYCHIC DEFICIENCY IN ALEXITHYMIA AS COMPARED WITH NARCISSISTIC PERSONALITY DISORDERS

McDougall has written extensively on her analytic experiences with
alexithymic psychosomatic patients (McDougall, 1974, 1980a, 1980b,
1982). She describes a deficiency in symbolic thinking and concludes
that these patients have a diminished capacity to form symbols arising
either by a foreclosure or neglect during a critical developmental phase.
Rather than dealing with preverbal experiences by eventually symbolizing and rendering them safe via verbalization or fantasy formation,
she suggests that the alexithymic psychosomatic patients have prematurely lost touch with these archaic experiences, and consequently these
experiences have no access to preconscious or conscious thought.

Krystal (1977) has extended his analytic study of drug abusers and
concentration camp survivors to include psychosomatic patients. He
often finds clinical alexithymic features common in all. His work emphasizes a further characteristic shared by many with self disorders,
namely, a deficiency in self care and self-soothing. Krystal adduces
evidence that this problem in mental and physical self-soothing and self-
regulation is the result of an unconscious prohibition and belief that
such caretaking activities are the providence of the primal maternal
object and she alone. He traces the difficulty to a premature rupture in
infantile omnipotence.

In *Analysis of the Self,* Kohut also describes an intrapsychic deficiency in fantasy that he interprets as a true deficiency in self-soothing
and psychic stabilizing functions of the self representation. Kohut directed his remarks to the problem of addiction when he wrote: "The
drug . . . serves not as a substitute for loved or loving objects or for a
relationship with them, but a replacement for a defect in psychological
structure" (1971, p. 46).

THEORIES OF DEVELOPMENTAL ETIOLOGY

McDougall describes her alexithymic psychosomatic patients as having tranquilizing mothers rather than satisfying mothers (McDougall, 1974, 1980a). These mothers are very attentive to the child's bodily needs but neglect psychic development. The pressure on the child to accede to her and forego his or her investment in emotional development is enormous; as the mother abandons hope that the father will satisfy her own self-object needs, she turns to the child narcissistically to fill this void in her psychic world.

Lefebvre (1980), working on a psychosomatic unit in Canada, re-ports that the "psychosomatic vulnerability" is increased in patients who suffer traumatic experiences at Mahler's (1968) separation–individuation phase. He finds that the patient, at the time of somatizing, is in a relational mode that is similar to that of narcissistic personalities, and that "confrontation with such self–other differences provokes a relational and economic impasse which lends itself to 'giving up' affects and somatically experienced regressive disorganization" (p. 8). Because they experience individuation of their body from the mother as tantamount to killing the mother–body–self, intense annihilation anxiety ensues in these situations.

McDougall (1974) and also Rickles (1981, 1983) have suggested that a part of the complex skein of the alexithymic is related to transitional phenomena emanating from Winnicott's (1975) developmental phase of transitional object attachment. The mothers of these patients seem to be threatened by the child investing soothing capability into the teddy bear or blanket and thereby making developmental steps to take over and internalize the soothing and regulating functions previously furnished by the mother. Elaboration of the child's relationship with the transitional object promotes a capacity for illusion and fantasy formation (Tolpin, 1971; Winnicott, 1975). These requisite mental functions for symbol formation and creative play are exactly the functions so deficient in alexithymia.

Kohut and Wolf (1978) seem to be describing a very similar series of events. They posit an insecure and vulnerable sense of self deriving from an empathic failure on the part of the parents to respond to the 18-month-old child's need for validating the mirroring of his mental productions and acceptance of his idealizing projections. In this context, minor, nontraumatic failures in these two parental functions lead to "transmuting internalizations" and, by accretion, an autonomous self.

Absent or not-good-enough mirroring and ideal modeling leads to life-long dependence on others or selfobjects to carry out soothing and self-esteem regulating functions of the personality. Winnicott (1975) also emphasized that parental acceptance of the child's illusions and projections onto the transitional objects are extremely important during this phase of mental development.

COMPENSATORY FUNCTIONS

Several authors have described alexithymic patients as using projective identification as a primary mode of relating to objects in order to compensate for their inability to use fantasy and symbolization to deal with affective reactions (McDougall, 1982; Taylor, 1977). The inner world is denied importance, and the mind and body are treated as though they require little or no maintenance operations (Nemiah, 1978). This disregard of mental or physical hygiene and the acknowledgment or recognition of the consequences of such neglect allows the alexithymic patient to respond to work or love relationships in heroic, grandiose measures regardless of the price exacted on their own body and soul as well as the feelings and/or physical well-being of others.

Self pathology promotes retention of an unevolved grandiose self, but the individual must constantly seek idealized selfobjects to maintain this energizing structure. Additionally, ordinary interpersonal experiences require the consistent availability of a mirroring selfobject to maintain a self experience and avoid anxiety (Kohut & Wolf, 1978). Thus, both conditions are described as turning to the object to compensate for personality deficiencies (or in psychoanalytic terms, structural deficiencies) in order to provide (1) self-soothing, (2) self-regulation, and (3) positive self experiences.

MECHANISM OF SYMPTOM FORMATION

Since it is seldom possible to arrange an object world in precisely the fashion the alexithymic psychosomatic patient needs to carry out necessary self-regulatory functions, two types of breakdown are typical. In the case where personality dynamics predispose to manic defenses and obsessive goal-oriented behavior, some alexithymic patients will create lives that are fast-paced and highly demanding. A state of chronic arousal obtains that, because of the deficiency in self-regulation and awareness of inner experience, may persist for years without significant relief. Such a lifestyle could predispose the individual to Selye's physically disabling General Adaptation Syndrome and the many associated somatic disturbances (Selye, 1956).

Likewise diseases or symptoms of chronic central nervous system (CNS)/autonomic nervous system (ANS) arousal may develop according to genetically (ontologically) or environmentally determined organ/system susceptibility. Coronary artery disease offers a documented example of this mechanism of symptom formation. The relationship between the Type A behavior pattern and myocardial infarction in men is probably the most studied and scientifically established psychophysiologic relationship in the literature (Matteson & Ivancevich, 1980). Type A behavior is defined as a behavior pattern that includes: (1) a perpetual sense of time urgency; (2) striving to accomplish more and more in less time; (3) a driven and competitive attitude; (4) easily evoked hostility, overt or covert; (5) chronic impatience; (6) unease with inactivity or relaxing; and (7) overvalue of doing and deprecating of experience or being. Evidence has been advanced suggesting the alexithymic personality patterns may support their chronically aroused lifestyle (Defourney, Hubin, & Liminet, 1976–1977; Rickles, 1983).

When life has been kinder and projective identification demands on objects have been moderately well met, the alexithymic will be psychophysiologically stable until some accident, determined either by providence or the unconscious, introduces an intrapsychic experience that cannot be rapidly eliminated. Usually this inescapable experience occurs in the form of physical pain, but narcissistic injuries may be equally persistent. The painful intrapsychic experience festers like a psychic splinter and, if not relieved, proceeds to create a shattering breach in the psychological defenses of the alexithymic. Because of the rigid nature of the alexithymic's defenses and paucity of psychological means of dealing with unrelieved pain or disability, psychophysiological regression often occurs in which somatization of affect is a major mode of response (Schur, 1955). Along with regression comes demands for dependency and physiological preparation for nurturing experiences. Shattering of the alexithymic's thin, rigid shell of experience and defenses creates a devastating loss of self-confidence and, like Humpty Dumpty, "All the king's horses and all the king's men [and all the king's doctors and psychoanalysts!] can't put Humpty together again." Chronic psychophysiological regression and chronic states of anticipated nurtur-

220 Original Papers: Applied Psychoanalysis

ing, such as the chronic pain syndrome (Blummer & Heilbrine, 1980) and Alexander's (1950) diseases of blocked dependency gratification often obtain when these conditions are met. Transient threats to the alexithymic's equilibrium produce episodic somatic disorders that either run their course or abort when the threat is relieved.

In their outline of self pathology and therapy, Kohut and Wolf (1978) delineate primary and secondary disturbances of the self. These include psychosis, borderline states, narcissistic behavior disorders, and narcissistic personality disorders. Both psychotic and borderline patients are seen as having serious damage to the self that is permanent and protracted. In contradistinction to the psychotics, the experienced behavioral manifestations of a defective nuclear self in borderlines are covered over by complex defenses. While the nuclear self in schizophrenia is noncohesive, the borderline develops some defensive structures, but the establishment of an autonomous self has been thwarted by the intrusion of the parental selfobject.

According to Kohut and Wolf, "when the nascent self of the child required the accepting mirroring of its independence, the selfobject, because of its own incompleteness, fragmentation, and fears, insisted upon maintaining an archaic merger" (p. 415). These intrusive merging selfobjects are reminiscent of the satiating mothers who do not allow development of autonomous means of regulating tension or pain (McDougall, 1974, 1980). Likewise, the narcissistic behavior disorders that include symptoms of perverse, delinquent, or addictive behavior are also found in the alexithymic literature and are understood as suffering from deficiencies in self-care and self-soothing functions (Krystal, 1977).

The narcissistic personality disorders experience only temporary break-up, enfeeblement, or serious distortions of the self; the symptoms (e.g., hypochondriasis, depression, hypersensitivity to slights, lack of zest) are not primarily concerned with the behavior of the individual, but with the psychological state of the mind. Thus, the symptom of self pathology can be understood as either permanent or reactive, defended or not; and, in the case of the reactive group, classified as symptoms of action versus symptoms of mental state.

Viewed from this matrix of theoretical and clinical perspective, the alexithymic with a propensity to somatize would seem to be compatibly defined as a self disorder that utilizes development of somatic symptoms as a major mode of dealing with permanent or temporary enfeeblement of the self rather than, or perhaps as part of, the symptoms of psychosis, provocative projective identification, behavioral acting-out, or changes in states of mind. Four common symptom clusters obtain in narcissistic personality disorders: (1) the *understimulated self* who is consistently occupied with stimulating activity to avoid internal emptiness; (2) the *fragmenting self* who loses a sense of continuity of self in time and cohesiveness in space, resulting in profound anxiety and hypochondriacal concerns; (3) the *overstimulated self* who constantly harbors tension-producing, grandiose fantasies but guards against longed-for merger experiences because of a threat to self equilibrium; and (4) the *overburdened self* that lacks the self-soothing capacity that protects one from the traumatic spreading of unchecked disturbing emotions. In each of these cases, one finds a precarious system for the modulation of arousal and dependency gratification. Chronic or acute disturbances in the precarious balance of self-regulation might be expected to produce somatic disorders of hyperarousal (e.g., migraine, hypertension, coronary artery disease) or dependency nurturing frustration (e.g., asthma, gastric ulcer, colitis, dermatitis) in susceptible individuals.

SYNTHESIS

Studies of alexithymic conditions and self disorders have attempted to organize clinical experience with patients who seem to be unable to regulate their own affective life without considerable help from other people, chemical substances, or other things, such as their own psychological productions, bodily parts, and functions. Deficiencies in personality function are seen as the problem in both. Further, the problem has been found to arise in the stage of infant development concerned with separation–individuation and the creation of autonomous self-regulation through the development of symbolizing and fantasy functions of the personality. Alexithymics have been found to be stuck in relatedness that is similar to the infantile relationship with a transitional object (Horton, 1981). Self psychology has used a similar paradigm to describe selfobject relationships to people, things, and so forth, that provide a means of self-regulation and soothing. Disorders of the self are explained in terms of the vicissitudes of selfobject relationships.

The narcissistic state of consciousness detailed by Bach (1977) poignantly describes the difficulties found in alexithymia, including defects in (1) perception of self, including body self; (2) language and organization as expressive of thought; (3) personal sense of agent and intentionality; (4) regulation of mood; and (5) perception of time, space, and causality. More recently, Basch (1983) has delineated the differences in denial versus disavowal defenses. In an eloquent and detailed paper, he shows that denial is best understood as a psychotic defense that interferes with reality testing. Disavowal produces a split in consciousness and only eliminates the meaning of the experience, not the reality of the experience itself. Thus, the capacity to symbolize, think, and experience "psychologically" are damaged. Such a defense mechanism, used in characterological excess, exactly describes self pathology and alexithymia.

Accordingly, I propose that disorders of the self have a previously unrecognized but powerful role in the development of somatic illness. As with neurosis, the psychosomatic illness overshadows the more subtle pathology of the self and has been unrecognized in most psychoanalytic studies of somatization. If this proposal is correct, then we are in a better position to understand the common dismal failure of psychoanalytic therapy for psychosomatic conditions. Psychosomatic patients may be understood as suffering from a self disorder that leaves the individual highly vulnerable to unregulated swings of CNS/ANS arousal or depression. If the individual is so unlucky as to have inherited a potentiality for developing medical illness in response to hyper- or hypoarousal, then these pathophysiological manifestations will regularly become part of his or her life experience. Secondary elaboration of these somatic experiences will be used as symbolic equivalents (Segal, 1957) and integrated into the defensive structure. In the case of neurosis, such experiences will be symbolized and will respond to interpretation. In self disorders, somatic symptoms are devoid of symbolism and do not respond to interpretations. Attempts at interpretation result only in narcissistic injury and no therapeutic gain. Because of a split and subsequent defect in self experience as agent and self as observer, the individual cannot see this connection and cannot use defense/resistance oriented psychoanalysis in a constructive way. Perhaps we can understand in this way why the average, expectable psychoanalysis is so problematic for psychosomatic patients. Further, we may understand why Sperling (1967), a very idealizable and strong therapist, and Winnicott (1966), the discoverer of transitional objects and the "holding environment," were more successful. The detailed connection between self pathology and somatic illness requires considerable elaboration before safe psychoanalytic work can be undertaken with life-threatening psychosomatic conditions. To begin this endeavor, the final section of this chapter will deal with the nature of the relationship between the self, a phenomenal entity, and the body, a physical entity.

THE BODY AS A SELFOBJECT

Kohut (1978) defined the self as an "independent center of initiative" and "recipient of impressions" (p. 414). Only a moment's reflection is required to perceive that terms such as "body–self" are meaningless. There is no initiative or perception in a physical body; only a psychic entity can initiate or perceive. The descriptors have no meaning for physical entities. Accordingly, the body is not an agency of the mind or self, but a very special physical object that impacts the self and can receive self or object representations like any other object. Because of the unique Siamese-twin relationship between the body and the self, it is necessary and proper to designate the body–selfobject relationships as special and unique from all others including intrapsychic object relationships. Further, because the body and the self have such an intimate and mutually interdependent need-fulfilling relationship, I propose that all body–self relationships partake of selfobject relationships. Accordingly, in the individual suffering from a self disorder, the body may be treated either as a mirroring selfobject or as an idealized selfobject. In either case, as with other selfobjects, if the body functions in such a way as to appear to have an independent center of initiative, the same types of narcissistic injuries and compensatory reactions that have been described in other types of selfobject relationships (Levine, 1983) will obtain.

> Jane was 23 years old and going places in a hurry. While amassing an outstanding scholastic record, she also worked full time. Her ambition was to make a million dollars before she was 30, and her youth and energetic personality supported her, thus requiring her to pay little or no attention to health maintenance. Fatigue, hunger, and intercurrent illness were dealt with quickly and easily without much fuss. When her car was rear-ended and she developed a severe whiplash injury with all the attendant chronic symptoms of pain and limitation of activity, she was furious. She explained that her injury was not her fault, and she had no time to spend in physical therapy, traction, hydrotherapy, or learning self-relaxation techniques to aid in healing herself. The pain and disability as well as the treatment were felt to be intrusions visited upon her by independent centers of initiative. The other driver, treating physician, and adjunctive therapist, as well as her body, all constituted narcissistic threats to her continuing actualization of her grandiose self.

Because of the special symbiotic relationship of the self and the body, unique consequences devolve that are unseen in the unusual selfobject relationships. In borderline but compensated patients, breakdown of a symbiotically invested body–selfobject might be the basis of life-threatening, malignantly progressing conditions such as ulcerative colitis, status asthmaticus, status epilepticus, malignant hypertension, or eclampsia. A detailed understanding of the selfobject quality and vicissitudes of the body–self relationships should provide a powerful aid in understanding and treating conditions such as psychosomatic illness, including chronic pain, physical mutilation, being accident prone, and also suicide, addictions, compliance problems in medical treatment, anorexia nervosa and other eating disorders, sports injuries, clumsiness, and so forth, to name only a few.

SUMMARY

This chapter has attempted to show the parallels and differences between the alexithymia and the self pathology literature according to operational definitions, nature of the intrapsychic deficiency, etiology, development of compensatory functions, and mechanisms of symptom formation. This comparison has facilitated the development of an outline of a selfpathology theory of psychosomatic disorders and somatization. The way is opened for exploration of the vicissitudes of the relationship between the self, a psychic entity, and the body, a physical entity bearing a unique relationship to the psyche, which is accurately described in terms of selfobject relationships. The implications for therapy of medically ill analysands are considerable.

ACKNOWLEDGMENTS

This contribution is presented under the auspices of the Interdisciplinary Group for Advanced Studies in Borderline, Psychotic, and Narcissistic Disorders.

REFERENCES

Alexander, F. (1950). *Psychosomatic Medicine: Its Principles and Applications.* New York: Norton.
Bach, S. (1977). On the narcissistic state of consciousness. *International Journal of Psycho-Analysis,* 58:209–233.

Basch, M.F. (1983–1984). The perception of reality and the disavowal of meaning. *Annual of Psychoanalysis*, 11:125–154.

Blummer, D., & Heilbrine, M. (1981). The pain-prone disorder: A clinical and psychological profile. *Psychosom.*, 22:395–402.

Defourny, M. Hubin, P., & Liminet, D. (1976–1977). Alexithymia, pensée opératoire, and predisposition to coronopathy: Pattern 'A' of Friedman and Roseman. *Psychother. and Psychosom.*, 27:106–114.

de M'Uzan, M. (1974). Psychodynamic mechanisms in psychosomatic symptom formation. *Psychother. and Psychosom.*, 23:103–110.

Deutsch, L. (1980). Psychosomatic medicine from a psychoanalytic viewpoint. *Journal of the American Psychoanalytic Association*, 28:653–699.

Engle, G.S., & Schmale, A.H., Jr. (1967). Psychoanalytic theory of psychosomatic disorder. *Journal of the American Pyschoanalytic Association* 15:344–365.

Goldberg, A. (1982). The self of psychoanalysis. In B. Lee, ed., *Psychosocial Theories of the Self* (pp. 3–22). New York: Plenum Press.

Horton, P.C. (1981). *Solace: The Missing Dimension in Psychiatry*. Chicago: University of Chicago Press.

Kellner, R. (1975). Psychotherapy and psychosomatic disorders: a survey of controlled cases. *Archives of General Psychiatry*, 32:1021–1028.

Kohut, H. (1971). *The Analysis of the Self*. New York: International Universities Press.

Kohut, H., & Wolf, E. (1978). The disorders of the self and their treatment: An outline. *International Journal of Psychoanalysis*, 59:413–426.

Krystal, H. (1977). The self-representation and the capacity for self-care. *The Annual of Psychoanalysis*, 6:209–246.

Krystal, H. (1982). Alexithymia and the effectiveness of psychoanalytic treatment. *International Journal of Psychoanalytic Psychotherapy*, 9:353–378.

Lefebvre, P. (1980). The narcissistic impasse as a determinant of psychosomatic disorder. *Psychiatric Journal of the University of Ottawa*, 5:5–11.

Levine, H.B. (1983). Implications of self psychology. *Contemporary Psychoanalysis*, 19:153–170.

Mahler, M. (1968). *On Human Symbiosis and the Vicissitudes of Individuation*. New York: International Universities Press.

Marty, P., & de M'Uzan, M. (1963). La pensée opératoire. *Revue Francais Psychiatrie*, 27(Suppl.):1345–1356.

Matteson, M.T., & Ivancevich, J.M. (1980). The coronary-prone behavior pattern: A review and appraisal. *Social Science and Medicine*, 14(a):337–351.

McDougall, J. (1974). The psychosoma and the psychoanalytic process. *International Review of Psycho-Analysis*, 1:437–459.

McDougall, J. (1980a). A child is being eaten, I: psychosomatic states, anxiety neurosis, and hysteria—a theoretical approach; II: the abysmal mother and the cork child—a clinical illustration. *Contemporary Psychoanalysis*, 16:417–459.

McDougall, J. (1980b). *Plea for a Measure of Abnormality*. New York: International Universities Press.

McDougall, J. (1982). Alexithymia: A psychoanalytic viewpoint. *Psychotherapy and Psychosomatics*, 38:81–90.

Nemiah, J.C. (1978). Alexithymia and psychosomatic illness. *Journal of Clinical Ed. Psych.*, 39:25–37.

Nemiah, J.C., Freyberger, H., & Sifneos, P.E. (1976). Alexithymia: A view of the psychosomatic process. In O. Hill, ed., *Modern Trends in Psychosomatic Medicine*, (pp. 430–439). London & Boston: Butterworth.

Palombo, J. (1982). The psychology of the self and the termination of treatment. *Clinical Social Work Journal*, 10:15–27.

Rickles, W.H. (1981). Biofeedback and transitional phenomena. *Psychiatric Annals*, 11: 23–41.

Rickles, W.H. (1983). Personality characteristics of psychosomatic patients. In W.H. Rickles, J.H. Sandweiss, D.W. Jacobs, R.N. Grove & E. Criswell, eds., *Biofeedback and Family Practice Medicine* (pp. 155–174). New York: Plenum Press.

Schur, M. (1955). Comments on the metapsychology of somatization. *Psychoanalytic Study of the Child*, 10:119–164.

Segal, H. (1957). Notes on symbol formation. *International Journal of Psychoanalysis*, 38:391–397.

Selye, H. (1956). *The Stress of Life*. New York: McGraw-Hill.

Sifneos, P.E. (1973). The prevalance of "alexithymic" characteristics in psychosomatic patients. *Psychotherapy and Psychosomatics*, 22:255–262.

Sifneos, P.E. (1975). Problems of psychotherapy of patients with alexithymic characteristics and physical disease. *Psychotherapy and Psychosomatics*, 26:65–70.

Sperling, M. (1967). Transference neurosis in patients with psychosomatic disorders. *Psychoanalytic Quarterly*, 36:342–355.

Sperling, M. (1978). *Psychosomatic Disorders in Childhood*. New York: Jason Aronson.

Taylor, G. (1977). Alexithymia and the counter-transference. *Psychotherapy and Psychosomantics*, 28:141–147.

Tolpin, M. (1971). On the beginning of a cohesive self: An application of the concept of transmuting internalization to the study of the transitional object and signal anxiety. *Psychoanalytic Study of the Child*, 26:316–352.

Winnicott, D.W. (1966). Psycho-somatic illness in its positive and negative aspects. *International Journal of Psycho-Analysis*, 47:510–516.

Winnicott, D.W. (1975). *Through Paediatrics to Psycho-Analysis*. New York: Basic Books.

18

Self Psychology and the Problem of Suicide

DAVID E. REISER

TWO CASES

"R.C."

Whenever Richard Cory went down town,
We people on the pavement looked at him:
He was a gentleman from sole to crown,
Clean favored, and imperially slim.

And he was always quietly arrayed,
And he was always human when he talked;
But still he fluttered pulses when he said,
"Good-morning," and he glittered when he walked.

And he was rich—yes, richer than a king,
And admirably schooled in every grace:
In fine, we thought that he was everything
To make us wish that we were in his place.

So on we worked, and waited for the light,
And went without the meat, and cursed the bread;
And Richard Cory, one calm summer night,
Went home and put a bullet through his head.

—Edwin Arlington Robinson

"J.P."

John Peters was a 3rd-year medical student at a prestigious West Coast medical school when, seemingly out of the blue, he took his own life. He was 25, at the top of his class academically, and a great source of pride for his two prominent professionally accomplished parents. He was adored and respected by his classmates.

As he began his junior year, however, he felt overwhelmed. He feared he could not learn enough, quickly enough, to be perfect. On the day of his death, he had difficulty inserting an IV into a young child. An intern on the service encouraged John to stop being so rough on himself and

227

suggested he take the afternoon off. John left the ward, went to his parent's house, sealed the garage, and gassed himself with carbon monoxide.

These two vignettes—one old, one all too recent, one drawn from literature, the other from real life—make several points. The first concerns the impact that self psychology has already had on our clinical thinking. Most readers of this chapter will instantly discern that a disordered self may somehow have contributed to the untimely deaths of these two individuals. Only a decade ago, the work of Kohut was still controversial, and even suspect. In the beginning he elucidated the psychodynamics of a subgroup of patients he called "narcissistic," a diagnosis presumed at first to be rare. In 10 years self psychology has expanded into a movement. We still have not discerned the outer boundaries and sheer variety of contexts in which this new paradigm sheds useful light.

My second point concerns the prevalence of disorders of the self. The American poet Edwin Arlington Robinson wrote "Richard Cory" in 1896. This leaves little doubt in my mind that self psychology existed at the height of the Victorian age, precisely when Freud was making his great discoveries concerning repressed sexuality, the Oedipus complex, and the unconscious. *Studies in Hysteria* was published just one year before "Richard Cory." Richard Cory's anguish might arguably be classically oedipal; conceivably, he committed suicide from intense guilt over his success, unconsciously connected with his wish to castrate his father and marry his mother. Yet, it is more likely that, whatever oedipal conflicts he had, some excruciating disorder of the self led Richard Cory to snuff out his life.

Suicides like John Peter's are very disturbing. They are particularly excruciating because they leave us feeling so helpless. John's suicide seemed so sudden, so unpredictable. Beyond his usual fretfulness and chronically high level of perfectionism, John had not seemed different in the weeks prior to his suicide. There had been no vegetative signs, no veiled threats, no alteration in his personality, or eating or sleep habits. None of the clues we rely on to alert us to impending suicide were there. There simply was no prodrome.

I propose that John's suicide, and many others like it (for we are currently in the midst of an epidemic of suicide in the young), could not have been predicted—at least not by the signs and symptoms that clinicians traditionally apply to suicide. This is because all such signs and symptoms are derived from our understanding of depression. While depression always has been, and will continue to be, a major cause of suicide, we must stop thinking of it as the sole cause. Rather, many suicides—perhaps the majority of suicides in the young—are not due to depression as we traditionally think of it, but instead are due to disintegrations of the nuclear self. In other words, I believe that the current epidemic of suicide in the young is best explained from the new perspective of self psychology.

Psychiatry has traditionally used two explanatory and predictive models to deal with the problem of suicide. The first is psychoanalytic (structural–drive theory). Beginning with Freud's classic monograph on *Mourning and Melancholia*, analytic theorists have developed explanatory models of suicide based on the roles of aggression, guilt, conflict, ambivalent identification with the lost object, and rage turned against the self. These formulations are of profound importance and continue to serve us well when we deal with classical depressions.

The second major model has been the biological. This model emphasizes family and personal history and, especially, the presence of biological markers: altered vegetative signs, sleep disturbance, weight loss, psychomotor retardation, and ruminative obsessional thinking centering on themes of badness and guilt.

The new suicides—if I may refer to them that way—are not explained by either of these models. Vegetative signs are the exception. Actual object loss is not very common. Shame and mortification appear to be far more prominent than the traditional affects of remorse and guilt. Prodromal signs are abbreviated or entirely absent.

As a consequence, we find ourselves baffled and helpless in the midst of these sudden, "out of the blue" suicides. How can we begin to understand them? How can we develop a theoretical formulation that will lend some sense to these "senseless" tragedies? The psychology of the self points a way, though it does not offer any miracles or pat, easy solutions. These "new suicides" will continue to thwart us in our attempts at prediction. They will remain chillingly unforeshadowed in too many cases. In part, this unfortunate truth is explained—though not remedied—by the formulations of self psychology. Almost by definition, an impaired nuclear self is one prone to rapid fragmentation or sudden disintegration in the face of disrupted narcissistic homeostasis. The suddenness with which regression occurs is itself almost pathognomonic. Thus, the psychology of the self may illuminate our understanding of the "new suicides" but still not lead to easy answers. In some ways these "new suicides" are analogous to such medical catastrophies as a ruptured aortic aneurysm, or an intracranial bleed in the

Circle of Willis. Perhaps the contribution of self psychology to an understanding of this type of suicide is similar to the contribution of angiog-
raphy and CT scans in vascular conditions. We can sometimes detect a
time bomb before we have the capability to defuse it. A more sanguine
view, of course, would hold that a successful analytic treatment of the
self disorder can lead to a strengthening of the nuclear self. However,
many of the most grave self disorders never present in time for adequate
treatment. Among individuals who do seek help, many *can* be helped.
A few may still commit suicide despite the best of our efforts.

In the remainder of this chapter I wish to put forward my central
thesis that "narcissistic" suicide is not a homogeneous entity. I believe
that suicide can occur as a consequence of disintegration in several
different types of nuclear self. In my view, these nuclear "selfs" are
characterized by different levels of developmental arrest, different narcissistic vulnerabilities, and especially by different dynamics in the relationship between the self and its selfobjects. I propose to delineate
five such "selfs."

1. The Endangered Self
2. The Enraged Self
3. The Vulnerable Self
4. The Grandiose Self
5. The Mirroring Self

This chapter is offered as a clinical contribution. It is beyond my
intention, and quite frankly beyond my reach, to attempt to advance
theory. At the same time, I think we all need to be cautious at this stage
in self psychology's development. As its popularity grows, we must be
sure to reassert continually that this is a scientific movement within
psychoanalysis, not a new "popular" psychology. I get nervous when I
go to the newsstand and see magazines with titles such as *Self* and *New
Self*. Therefore I feel an obligation to anchor my labels to key elements
of self psychological theory. Without this, their value would be highly
questionable. Thus, I advance three preliminaries: my definition of the
self, my definition of the selfobject, and finally my hypothesis that the
relationship of the self to its selfobjects has developmental vicissitudes.

The definition of the self that I invoke here is based on a paper by
Kohut and Wolf (1978). They state, "The patterns of ambitions, skills,
and goals, the tensions between them, the program of action they create,
and the activities that strive toward the realization of this program are

all experienced as continuous in space and time . . . they are the self, an independent center of initiative, an independent recipient of impression." This definition, like all such, may not be the final word on the subject; however, it can serve our purposes here. What holds a self together, any self, is the selfobject. Much work on the selfobject has been done by Marian Tolpin and Ernest Wolf, among others, yet it is difficult to find a precise definition of the term. Perhaps recognizing this difficulty, Wolf resorted to metaphor in one description, successfully I believe:

> One may compare the need for the continuous presence of a psychologically nourishing selfobject milieu with the continuing physiological need for an environment containing oxygen. It is a relatively silent need of which one becomes aware sharply only when it is not being met, when a harsh world compels one to draw the breath in pain. And so it goes also with the selfobject needs. As long as a person is securely embedded in the social matrix that provides him with the field in which he can find the needed mirroring responses and the needed availability of idealizable values, he will feel comfortably affirmed in his total self with its ambitions and goals. In short, he will feel himself strong and, paradoxically, relatively self-reliant, self-sufficient, and autonomous. (1980)

Wolf makes a further observation about selfobjects that is central to our purposes here. He notes that there is a developmental line for self–selfobject relations, commencing at birth and continuing through childhood, perhaps beyond. This point deserves considerable emphasis. It suggests that perhaps selfobjects are required throughout life. Furthermore, the specific functions and nature of the selfobject obviously vary, based on stages of development. It is only a step from here to the inference that developmental arrests at different points in life can lead to different stages and types of self–selfobject relationships.

In the exposition that follows, I have attempted to differentiate among self–selfobject relationships. I present my formulations in a developmentally ascending hierarchy, from earlier developmental arrests to later fixations. One must appreciate that the formulations are still tentative and their place on a continuum hardly ironclad.

THE ENDANGERED SELF

Isaac Hyde was 50 years old at the time of his self-enucleation. He had spent the majority of his life in a state hospital in Colorado. Deinstitutionalization led to his release into the community. He mostly hung around the Greyhound bus station off of Main Street.

Isaac had one glass eye, the result of childhood trauma. When people threatened him, he would pluck the glass from its socket and roll it between thumb and index finger. This invariably achieved its desired goal of increased interpersonal distance. The episode in question, however, was different. Distraught and severely delusional, Isaac enucleated his other eye with a butcher knife. He could give no reason for the act, but I learned that the mutilation followed Isaac's liaison with a new waitress in the bus terminal's all night coffee shop. The waitress had taken an interest in Isaac and attempted to strike up a friendship. Sexual exploration began and led to intercourse—the first for Isaac in decades. After this, his self-enucleation occurred.

The Endangered Self is, I believe, seen primarily in schizoid and schizophrenic conditions. This tormented, primitively organized self is in perpetual conflict between the wish for human contact, with its threat of engulfment and annihilation of the self on the one hand, and autism, with its terrible separateness and isolation, on the other. Schizophrenic patients quickly learn the danger of excessive closeness and intimacy. Thus, many survive in isolated, schizoid lifestyles, like Isaac. But sooner or later the dreadful loneliness catches up and drives the schizophrenic patient to seek human contact, despite the risks. Usually patients try to do this in controlled, ritualized ways. Isaac's nightly coffee at the bus station was an instance of this. It worked until someone overwhelmed him with excessive intimacy.

It is hazardous to make too many quick inferences about this very primitive type of self and developmental genetics. I am cautious about glib extrapolations regarding early mothering in the pathogenesis of schizophrenia since the ravages of the disease process itself so maim and distort the entire psychological apparatus. What does seem clear, based on clinical observation, is that such individuals function with an almost literal inability to establish self–selfobject bonds. Almost by definition, the selfobject is universally used by the self to establish narcissistic equilibrium. In these severely disturbed individuals, however, it appears that the human intimacy required for even minimal self–selfobject connections is simply too hazardous. As a consequence they try instead to relate to *things*, to customary street corners, all night bus stations, favorite park benches. Quietly, stealthily, at the very borders of humanity, they try to smuggle in minimal human contact. Unable to establish even limited ties to selfobjects, they are forever at risk and forever alone.

THE ENRAGED SELF

Barbara Lockwood was an attractive 23-year-old nursing student when she presented at a university neurology clinic complaining of headaches. She was examined by a psychiatry resident rotating through Neurology. The diagnosis turned out to be a small stroke as a result of using oral contraceptives. While the resident performed a breast exam, the patient became curious about him and learned that he was a psychiatrist. She complained of interpersonal difficulties and he offered her psychotherapy, which she readily accepted.

The psychotherapy was soon characterized by erotic overtones and a lack of focus. She expressed much anger, especially at men. Masochistic sexual practices were also reported.

The resident soon was seeing the patient three times a week. She began calling him at home and appearing in the emergency room. Which each escalation, the resident offered more contact. The patient's life outside of therapy became chaotic—she picked up men who beat her and drank heavily.

The patient came into the office one day screaming, "You Goddamn son of a bitch, I ought to kill you!"

The resident took a vacation. Upon his return, he discovered that his patient was in intensive care, following a digitalis overdose. A psychiatric consultation had been obtained during his absence. The patient told the consultant of her therapist. "I love him, but I hate him more." For the first time, the consultant learned that the patient had been repeatedly beaten by her father, subjected to incest, and chased around the house with a knife. This had gone on with the approval of the patient's mother, who would shout, "Give it to her good, Joe!"

The Enraged Self is often lumped into the diagnosis of "borderline," an increasingly indiscriminate and carelessly used term. I believe that the dynamics of patients such as Barbara Lockwood might be better understood from the perspective of self psychology. Specifically, I hypothesize that these patients had parents—especially mothers—who early in life projected onto their children their own "bad self." Then, upon confronting this disavowed and despised introject, the parent would turn on the child and attack it ruthlessly.

These are battered, starved, and hideously abused children. One of the most compelling examples in our current culture is Christina Crawford, the adopted daughter of Joan Crawford, who wrote a bestseller that later became a film entitled, *Mommie Dearest*. As the book and film make clear, Joan Crawford projected onto Christina all the disavowed, hated parts of her narcissistically imperfect self. She then attacked the child, physically and psychologically, in paroxysms of unpredictable rage. During one wrenching scene in the film, Joan Crawford has just experienced a narcissistic injury in her career. She enters Christina's room that night in a virtual daze. Waking the child up from a sound sleep, she screams, "No more wire hangers!," a nonsensical reference to the type of coat hanger in the child's closet. She then batters the girl mercilessly.

These are the children that Shengold (1975) refers to as the victims of "soul murder." Yet, a number of them somehow survive. They manage this, I believe, by forming deeply ambivalent, hostile–dependent relationships with a succession of selfobjects that replicate the original disturbed parent–child dyad. In the lives of these children, the same selfobject that had to be depended on for parenting, security, and survival was also the selfobject that attacked the child unpredictably—a vicious and overpowering enemy. It is hard to overestimate the intense ambivalence that this love–hate, self–selfobject relationship evokes. On the one hand these children, if they are to survive at all, must invest considerable positive narcissistic cathexis in even the worst parent. This includes idealization, adoration, surrender, and worshipping love, although these same parents are also the enemy. Thus, psychological and perhaps literal survival depends on the child's capacity to simultaneously idealize *and* ward off the parental selfobject—an enormous and enormously confusing task.

What becomes of these children when they grow up? It is almost inevitable that the closer they get to another person, the more that person will simultaneously become the object of intense defensive rage. Such rage is readily understandable. As children these people depended on their rage to survive; as adults, they unconsciously view all attempts at intimacy as a replication of the self–selfobject disturbance of their childhood. Love, in other words, is simultaneously a lifeline and an assault. Thus the patient in this vignette says of her therapist, "I love him, but I hate him more!"

Such patients are extremely difficult to treat and no one treats them exceedingly well. Certain clinicians treat them exceedingly badly; these narcissistic, grandiose therapists see in such patients an opportunity to act out unanalyzed Pygmalion fantasies. These patients are very sensitive to this and perceive it, correctly in some senses, as an attack.

THE VULNERABLE SELF

No one really expected Mrs. Rubin to take her life. At 47, she was well known to the residents of University Hospital. Chronically hypochondriacal, she had undergone 17 surgical procedures—most of them laparotomies. She had been transferred from therapist to therapist over the years.

Once a month, a psychiatry resident listened for a half hour to her list of bowel complaints. Actually, more was known of Mrs. Rubin's institutional life (she had a huge chart), than of her own life. One note indicated that her mother had suffered from tuberculosis, and had been in and out of sanitariums throughout the child's life, dying when the patient was 17.

Every summer when she was passed on to a new resident, she would appear in the emergency room, having overdosed on one medication or other, usually a prescription from the departing resident.

One summer, Mrs. Rubin had an especially difficult transfer. The new resident seemed cold and unsympathetic to her.

That weekend she died of a respiratory and cardiac arrest following an ingestion of Valium, Darvon, and alcohol. She had only taken a handful of pills, but in combination the dose proved lethal.

There exist in every clinician's caseload patients who might best be described as chronically empty, unfulfilled, and needy. The specifics may vary, but these patients often display common characteristics. First, there is a vulnerability to separation. They do not fare well when the therapist takes a holiday or when children grow up and leave home. Along with this, there is usually chronic misery. These patients do not seem overtly enraged or hateful but they are rarely very content or happy either. Often there is hyponchodria, obesity, poor general health without specific maladies, and a chronic litany of sighs and complaints. One is tempted to think of them as "pathetic."

These patients threaten suicide intermittently, attempt it periodically, but succeed only rarely, usually by accident. One senses that the attempts are a plea. We refer to such attempts often as "gestures" or "acting out."

We know what plagues these patients—it is almost a psychiatric cliché—"separation anxiety." But what does that mean in self psychological terms? I believe that we are referring here to a group of patients whose self pathology originated in the separation–individuation phase of development described by Mahler (1972), especially the practicing subphase, and the subphase of rapproachment. In such individuals there is a lifelong confusion between growth, and abandonment. Unlike the Enraged Self, the Vulnerable Self does not rely on aggression as an integral tool for preserving identity. This does not mean that aggression is not present; rather, a distortion of aggression is at work in these individuals.

We can only speculate regarding the complex genetics that lead to a confusion between aggression in the service of independence, and aggression as a provocation for abandonment by the parental selfobject. We do know from Mahler's work that a very exquisite and flexible parental empathy is required with the rapproachment-phase child, who one moment needs to regress and cling, and the next needs to cast-off and push away. I suspect that mothers who had rapproachment difficulties of their own may in turn become faulty selfobjects for their children, transmitting confusion in the child over the struggle between autonomy and abandonment.

Regardless of the theoretical complexities, this confusion between growth and dread of separation might explain a common clinical observation: Regression in these patients often occurs after a phase of therapeutic progress. Not only do these patients fall apart during vacations, they tend to experience intense separation anxiety after taking significant strides forward. The termination phase must be handled especially carefully with these patients. Above all, during termination the newly cohesive nuclear self will be tested. The therapist—as a self-object—must help the patient achieve individuation without simultaneously threatening separation and abandonment. For years, clinicians have sensed that some patients cannot cleanly, unambiguously terminate. We keep them in our caseloads if only to see them infrequently, perhaps exchanging letters and Christmas cards. In the past some of us have felt guilty for not effecting a "proper" termination. From the perspective of self psychology, in the treatment of the Vulnerable Self, we may have been doing just the right thing.

THE GRANDIOSE SELF

I shall not elaborate here on the grandiose self. This is of course the original nuclear self disturbance that Kohut (1971) described in his early work on narcissistic personality disorders, and whose treatment he described in depth in his first book, *The Analysis of Self*. This is the self that depends on selfobjects for mirroring, applause, perfect empathy, and idealized, heroic behavior. The fragmentation that the developmentally vulnerable bipolar self experiences when the selfobject fails to meet these needs is well described—an often catastrophic fragmenting occurs, which is characterized by severe feelings of internal emptiness, rage, and pressure to act out, often in extreme forms, to relieve the unbearable pain and tension of the disintegrating self.

In his early work, Kohut believed these individuals to be relatively uncommon. I think it is now clear, as the applications and relevance of self psychology have expanded, that there are many different types of disordered selfs, the classical "narcissist" being just one, though certainly an important one.

We also know the very real risk of suicide in patients suffering from this disturbance. A number of suicides in the young, as well as countless more "accidents," may best be understood in terms of pathology in this type of self. Thus, the enraged adolescent who experiences a humiliating fight with his father, downs a six-pack and drives his motorcycle into an embankment at 120 miles an hour may well be experiencing a fragmentation of his nuclear self secondary to faulty mirroring.

Many of the characters played by the 1950s cult hero, James Dean, seem to be prototypical of this type of disturbed self. *Rebel Without a Cause* is probably the classic example. It is worth noting in this regard that James Dean is currently experiencing a renaissance of hero worship among the young. He takes his place beside such mythical figures as Jim Morrison of the Doors, Jimi Hendrix, and others—diverse celebrities whose common bond may be found in the fire of their grandiose rage, and their premature deaths a shared premature death, either through suicide or overtly destructive behavior.

THE MIRRORING SELF

I return finally to the case that began this chapter—John Peters. I first became aware of a particularly poignant form of disordered self during a complex phase of my own professional development. At a certain point, I found that I was working with a number of grown children of psychiatrists. Fortunately, my work with these patients coincided with the final 2 years of my own analysis. This was important since I am the son of a psychoanalyst. Clearly, the struggles and conflicts of my patients were significant for me.

These children, several of whom were already in medical school or psychiatric residency training, did appear to have some kind of self disturbance. I acknowledged this with much personal discomfort. Each seemed haunted by chronic depression, an inordinate addiction to praise and admiration, and a harsh, unrelenting, self-imposed standard of perfection.

I saw all the "pathology" Kohut (1971) described in my patients— the longing for empathy and mirroring, the tendency to idealize and then feel bitterly disappointed, the need always to be on stage. But the other side of Kohut's early case histories, the darker side, the sense of mordant, inner emptiness, the shell-like affective impoverishment, the

profound inner conviction of these patients that they are phony, fraud-
ulent, and incapable of real love, I did not discern. With the help of
sophisticated supervision, and my own analysis, I was able to trust my
observations and get past certain stereotypes that were rampant at the
time. Many people then were especially troubled by the apparently rigid
distinction between "narcissism" and "object love." This turned out to
be a false polarization that Kohut's later work did much to mend. Then,
however, it was *au courant* and it confused me. For despite the ster-
eotyping, I found most of my patients to be lively, sensitive, bright, and
truly likable young men and women. They were capable of highly differentiated empathic responses to the people around them, and were
able to articulate their perceptions with great insight and feeling. The
psychiatry residents I worked with were uniformly at the top of their
class, and talented, perceptive, effective psychotherapists. These patients certainly were not the empty shells, the "as if" personalities I had
been accustomed to equating with "narcissism."

Above all, these children, now grown, were able to love, and love
deeply. They were, in fact, exquisitely sensitive to others, even too much
so. Sometimes, it seemed to me, they functioned as though they had
empathic radar banks running down both arms. Their chronic depression
came not from an inability to love, but from the inability of these children, as adults, to turn their own exquisite empathy inward. Though
they were highly attuned to the authenticity and significance of emotions
in others, they seem strangely oblivious, even ridiculing, of emotions in
themselves. They appeared to be at their best only when they were
mirroring the desires of others.

The plight of the Mirroring Self has been sensitively described by the
Swiss psychoanalyst, Alice Miller:

> What are the reasons for this kind of narcissistic disturbance in these gifted
> people . . . ? In all of these people I found a childhood history that seems
> significant to me.
>   There existed an amazing ability on the child's part intuitively, that is
> unconsciously, to perceive and respond to the need of the mother or of
> both parents, that is to take on the role which had unconsciously been
> assigned to him. This role secured love for the child, that is narcissistic
> cathexis by his parents. He could sense that he was needed and this gave
> his life a guarantee of existence.
>   This ability is then extended and perfected. Later these children not only
> become mothers (confidants, comforters, advisers, supporters) of their own
> mothers, but also take over the responsibility for their siblings and even-

tually develop a special sensitivity to the unconscious signals of the needs of others. No wonder that they often choose the psychoanalytic profession later on. Who else, without this previous history, would muster sufficient interest to spend the whole day trying to discover what is happening in the other person's unconscious? (1979)

This then is the Mirroring Self. It is a child of often exceptional gifts who functions like a chameleon trapped upon a tapestry of bright and variegated color, a tapestry whose threads are the emotional needs and requirements of others.

I have long since come to believe that this disturbance goes far beyond psychoanalysts and the children of analysts. For reasons that are unclear to me, and must include social and cultural factors, we appear to be producing a literal bumper crop of these young people. I believe that pathology of the Mirroring Self type was responsible for John Peters's suicide, and is responsible for many other suicides among the most talented, beautiful, and admirable of our young people.

Psychological chameleons that these children are, they quickly intuit the narcissistic needs of anyone and everyone around them. Whoever is with them, whoever cathects them, they sense how to return the image that the other person wants to see. For the depressed mother, these children are the empathic, endlessly forbearing therapist. For the ambitious father, they are the hard driving, academically successful student. For the teacher, they are the disciple; for the football coach, the dedicated athlete.

These children are, in short, indefatigable, infinitely adaptable, creative, ready-and-willing selfobjects for any and all selves who reach out to them and wish them to function in this role. They are mirrors for us all.

More curious still somehow, this condition emerged out of childhoods that were not overtly pathological; yet the experiences of these children must have been deeply flawed in some way. How else could these young people have come to live so completely focused on performance, on the good opinions of others, so totally devoid of any empathy for their *own* simple right to be? How else could they have ended up acting as though they believe that unless they are performing as selfobjects for others, their own needs of acknowledgment and existence simply do not count?

Our current culture abounds with examples from art and literature of this type of self. These include the characters in J.D. Salinger's work—Franny, Seymour Glass, Holden Caulfield. The work of poet Sylvia

Plath is a case in point, as is that of Anne Sexton. A wonderful and especially complex movie entitled *Harold and Maude* offers a subtle, but unmistakable example of a young man suffering with this self pathology. Harold's character also makes it very clear how important repressed narcissistic rage is in these individuals.

The dynamics of this type of self have yet to be elucidated. Furthermore, the epidemic of this affliction in young people today should not be explained away through simplistic formulations. Though such is the standard image invoked, it is far too glib to state that *all* such young people are the products of cold, unempathic parents who present a phony facade to the world while they are actually narcissistic and totally self-serving.

These young people often seem unable to find solace, serenity, and peace in stabilized self–selfobject relations of their own. Instead they compulsively yield themselves as selfobjects in relationship after relationship, until they are exhausted, dangerously enraged, or broken-hearted. When this exhaustion occurs simultaneously with a significant narcissistic defeat (for the perfectionism in these children is ruthless and unsparing), then we witness a painful disintegration of the self, a subjective experience of depthless inner loneliness, pain, and suffering. It is at such times that these young people seem driven to take their own lives.

In this chapter I have attempted to elucidate five different types of disturbances of the self, catagorizing them according to different types of needs within the self, and different relationships in the self–selfobject dyad. I have attempted to suggest that a conceptualization along a developmental hierarchy may be possible, but I also acknowledge that I regard these first approximations as highly tentative. Finally, I have emphasized the existence of a particularly poignant and mysterious type of disturbed self, the Mirroring Self, an affliction of society's brightest and most beautiful young spirits that too often leads to unbearable inner pain and the compulsion to seek peace through the ultimate act of self-destruction.

REFERENCES

Kohut, H. (1971). *The Analysis of the Self*. New York: International Universities Press.
Kohut, H., & Wolf, E. (1978). The disorders of the self and their treatment: An outline. *International Journal of Psychoanalysis*, 59:413–426.

Mahler, M. (1972). A study of the separation–individuation process. *Psychoanalytic Study of the Child, 26,* 403–424.

Miller, A. (1979). The drama of the gifted child and the psychoanalyst's narcissistic disturbance. *International Journal of Psychoanalysis,* 60:47–58.

Shengold, L. (1975). Soul murder. *International Journal of Psychanalytic Psychotherapy,* 3, 366–373.

Wolf, E. (1980). On the developmental line of selfobject relations. In A. Goldberg, ed., *Advances in Self Psychology* (pp. 117–130). New York: International Universities Press.

Theoretical Problems

19

British Object Relations Theory and Self Psychology

BERNARD BRANDCHAFT

The period of 1930–1965 was marked by the emergence in Great Britain of the first sustained attempts to reexamine the fundamental precepts upon which psychoanalysis had been based. It was motivated by disquiet on the part of a large number of respected and dedicated analysts with the limitations in therapeutic results that were so clearly and frankly acknowledged by Freud (1937) in his final summation, *Analysis Terminable and Interminable*. The turbulence led to a flowering of creative genius within psychoanalysis. That it occurred when and where it did is undoubtedly due in large part to particular characteristics of British intellectual life with its long tradition of open-mindedness, restless curiosity, and tolerance for diversity. Some of the more impressive results of this reappraisal, agonizing in many ways for its supporters and its opponents alike, are to be found in the diverse body of work come to be identified as object relations theory.

In the United States psychoanalysis was generally spared the bitterness and ferment that occurred in Britain as "certain of Freud's discoveries, and the particular manner in which psychoanalysis transmits them, become the legacy of his pupils and collaborators" (Steiner, 1985, p. 78). The training institutes of the American Psychoanalytic Association, as a result of whatever complex, historical, cultural, and personal factors, embodied a different attitude than that widely held in Britain and exemplified by Marjorie Brierly. "The aim and task of analysis is to be eclectic and flexible," she wrote. "I approach every patient with a full quota of implicit rather than explicit theoretical and technical preconceptions. . . . But I am more inclined to alter my preconceived notions to fit the patient's new pattern than to cut the pattern to fit my notions." She concluded, . . . "we cannot crystallize psycho-analysis: we cannot keep it fixed in any shape or form however desirable these may appear at any given time. Analysis cannot live unless it grows, and it cannot grow without modification" (Brierly, 1943, quoted in Steiner, 1985, pp. 42–43).

The development of self psychology raises for American psychoanalysis the fundamental questions about the psychoanalytic process that were here deferred. Naturally it has stimulated increased interest within the American psychoanalytic community in the earlier contributions of the British innovators. Kohut himself curiously failed to acknowledge any influence of object relations theorists on the development of his work and this has subjected him to severe criticism.[1] Some critics have maintained that there is little that is original in the basic theoretical and clinical contributions of self psychology not to be discerned in earlier work, especially that of Balint, Fairbairn, Winnicott, and Guntrip. Consequently an attempt to consider some of these various developments within an historical perspective might add clarity to this discussion.

There is a further purpose to be served by an attempt to answer the question of what is unique in Kohut's contribution to psychoanalysis, for the influence of British innovators (with the exception of Klein) upon their colleagues has remained relatively limited as has the continued development of their basic concepts. Hence the prospect that the innovations begun by Kohut may have a wider impact depends upon whether his work will be found to have added something sufficiently unique and significant as to prove more enduring. If in fact Heinz Kohut has made it possible for us to see and understand more of human experience and the psychoanalytic process than before, it is important that this growing body of work follow its trajectory toward the realization of its own potential.

I

It seems appropriate to begin this discussion with the following text:

> I wish to acknowledge my debt to my psycho-analytic colleagues. I have grown up as a member of the group, and after so many years of interrelating it is now impossible for me to know what I have learned and what I have contributed. The writings of any one of us must be to some extent plagiaristic. Nevertheless I think we do not copy: we work and observe

---

1. In *The Analysis of the Self* (Kohut, 1971), for example, there is only the most cursory reference to the work of Balint and Winnicott and none to others herein considered.

and think and discover, even if it can be shown that what we discover has been discovered before. (Winnicott, 1965, p. 11)

A review of the work of the British theorists by anyone also familiar with Kohut's writings will reveal that many of the observations and resultant contributions overlap. All were made possible by crucial departures from dominant psychoanalytic doctrines of the time and place. Each innovator consequently suffered, was isolated and stigmatized as a threat to psychoanalysis, even though it would be hard to find a psychoanalyst who did not agree in principle that only the open communication of divergent clinical experiences together with the formulation and testing of new hypotheses can enable our science to escape "senescence".

The area of observation that occupied the focus of each of the British innovators was that which Freud had described as having "remained hidden from us at the outset" because psychoanalytic research took "neurotic symptoms for their starting point" (1914, pp. 75–76).

It was inquiry into the period of infancy, at first under the impetus of Melanie Klein's application of Freud's methods of investigation to the analysis of small children, that led to the conceptualization of basic psychological configurations not envisaged by Freud. Subsequently each of the innovators attempted to chart from his clinical work the foundations of the infant's psychological organization and to offer hypotheses about how these are laid down. Each came to recognize that defects or arrests in this area were not confined to a small group of patients, but rather tended very widely and radically to shape later development and determine its course. Such primitive deficits were frequently concealed beneath psychoneurotic symptoms and covered over by psychoanalytic procedures that failed to mobilize and address them openly in the therapeutic endeavor.

It was in Melanie Klein's work that the infant's relation to its objects first came to occupy the focal point of investigation and brought about fundamental revisions of psychoanalytic theory. This first object relations theory evolved under the influence of Freud's recent elevation of the death instinct to the status of a primary force in development and pathogenesis. Hence Klein's new concepts of intrapsychic structure were based upon the child's libidinal and destructive relationships to internalized objects. She believed the primary psychological motivation to be the child's annihilation anxiety due to the death instinct and that this led to the necessity to secure a libidinal relationship with "good" internal objects as the essential basis for normal development. The course of this relationship she described in terms of progression from the paranoid schizoid position to the depressive position. This course was largely determined, as she saw it, by the child: its ability to modulate primitive defenses of splitting and projective identification, the relative strength of its libidinal and sadistic instincts that promoted or interfered with processes of fusion, and finally various ego capacities as the infant's ability to tolerate guilt feelings and to engage in reparative acts to its "good" objects damaged in its omnipotent destructive fantasy. Each of the British theorists with whom we shall be concerned subsequently focused on a different, if contiguous, aspect of relations between the infantile self and objects as it emerged in the psychoanalytic process. Balint's interest was in "the basic fault" and its relationship to the development of object love, which he considered to be the primary area of developmental disorder and the most fundamental goal of development. His unique contribution to treatment is described in the core concept of "the new beginning." Fairbairn's most innovative attempt was to disentangle developing object relations theory from its embeddedness with instinctual theory (Guntrip, 1968, p. 410). His preeminent focus was on schizoid factors and splits in the personality that he regarded as "the basic position in the psyche" and the fundamental impedimenta to growth. Winnicott's stress was on the area of development before differentiation of self and object had taken place and out of which it would emerge. He specifically came to emphasize the importance of mother and infant as an indissoluble psychological unit in his thesis of "good-enough mothering" in contradistinction to instinctual factors. He described the conditions necessary for "true self" formation, for him the primary goal of development, as well as the interferences that gave rise to the core pathology of the "false self."

In retrospect, each of the object relations theorists in his own time as did Kohut, made bold attempts to revise, more or less radically, psychoanalytic metapsychology from the perspective of his own clinical experience. Through personalized thinking each made individual contributions to revisions of concepts of endopsychic structure that anticipated or paralleled many of the findings fundamental to Kohut's self psychology. This independent concordance by investigators beginning from differing premises and widely separated geographically speaks against current judgments that self psychology is a passing fad. However, Kohut and the object relations theorists were each a product of his own times, and only within that context can the uniqueness of the contributions be appreciated.

II

It is difficult to convey how rigid were the barriers that existed between the psychoanalytic worlds of the United States and London at the times when the developments we are considering were taking root. The languages that were being used might just as well have belonged to a different linguistic heritage for the extent to which each was understood by the other. Many important London psychoanalysts, absorbed in the ferment and bitter controversy attendant upon the introduction of new ideas, considered psychoanalysis as practiced in the United States to be oblivious to significant advances in the field. No psychoanalyst practicing in Great Britain, for example, could fail to have been influenced by the clash of doctrines and personalities that preoccupied the entire second generation of psychoanalysts after Freud, as Vienna came to be replaced by London as the center of psychoanalytic education and activity. Perhaps the continued preoccupation of British psychoanalysis and the fallout from the controversies that began more than half a century ago[2] helps explain why no more than a handful of British psychoanalysts, at most, appear to have familiarized themselves with Kohut's work. In the United States the leaders of psychoanalysis, for their part, did not understand as being psychoanalytic at all the diversity of developments taking place in London that bypassed the bearer of Freud's mantle, his daughter Anna. Although controversy dominated psychoanalytic education and discussion in Great Britain beginning in the 1920s and continuing almost unabated to the present, no authoritative presentation of these issues was even permitted in the teaching at any training center within the American Psychoanalytic Association until relatively recently, and even today such courses are very few and far between. American psychoanalysis still remains relatively inoculated against the work of the British schools and thus self psychology is the first serious and broadly based diversity encountered in our country within organized psychoanalysis.

I was trained in psychoanalysis in an American institute in the early 1950s. One course, eight sessions in all, included Balint, Winnicott, Jung, Adler, Melanie Klein, and some others who have since faded from my memory. It was entitled "Controversial Concepts in Psychoanalysis," which still seems an exercise in whimsy since it could hardly be said that within the wider community psychoanalysis itself was noncontroversial. Of course, the most important fact signalled by the contributions we

---

2. For a current historical review see Steiner (1985).

were to study was precisely that the concepts of the more traditional psychoanalysts had become controversial to a growing number of their colleagues.

A prospective discussion of Melanie Klein was introduced with the assurance that it was unnecessary to read her work as it had been admirably summarized in an assigned critique by Edward Bibring. Like so many of the psychoanalytic teachers of that day and this, ours regarded Freud's concepts as a legacy to be cherished, protected, and passed on relatively intact to a new generation. It was only by sheer chance that I was exposed to a maverick teacher, who openly admitted that he could not make much clinical sense out of what he could glean in his reading of Hartmann, Kris, and Loewenstein.[3] On his own he had managed to familiarize himself with the work of Fairbairn and had found it extremely helpful. On the strength of his recommendation I began to read Fairbairn and attempted to test some of his ideas in my practice, in that way first crossing the great divide. I soon recognized that Fairbairn's work could only be understood in the context of Melanie Klein's work. So, with three others from my class I began to study her work and that of other object relations theorists in 1956. Subsequently I made regular trips to London to investigate these developments further, consulting with Rosenfeld, Segal, Winnicott, Bion, and, briefly, Heimann. All those with whom I consulted had been primarily stimulated through their contact with Melanie Klein, and I found them to possess a very high order of intelligence, conviction, and, unlike what I had been given to believe, an unmistakable dedication to psychoanalysis. I was, in consequence, drawn increasingly to that particular school of object relations, studying it intensively and teaching it over the dozen years that followed.

From time to time I have returned to my reading of object relations theorists. I believe that the encompassing perspective supplied by Kohut's self psychology contributes substantially to an enhanced understanding. Kohut's persistent focus on the organization and structuralization of self experience led him to describe a specific and fundamental object relationship, that to selfobjects, a unique contribution to psychoanalytic thought about the nature of the tie to objects as well as to the continuing evolution of psychoanalytic ideas. The essence of this view of object relations rests upon the conviction Kohut came to hold that the primary goal of development is the establishment of a cohesive

---

3. The teacher referred to here is Dr. Ivan McGuire to whom I am deeply indebted.

nuclear self and the maturational consolidation of an individualized and differentiated pattern of goals, purposes, and ideals. The primary and continuing psychological importance of (self) objects lies in the crucial functions they serve in maintaining, restoring, consolidating, and transforming the structures of experience, the self.

Kohut's (1977, 1984) consistent focus on the self as central to normal and impaired development and its supraordination in psychological theory is a second major distinguishing contribution. It provides a unique focus that integrates Balint's repudiation of the theory of primary narcissism and of the then-accepted role of infantile sadism as a developmental force; Fairbairn's observations of the significance of early schizoid splits in the ego (self); and Winnicott's seminal contributions regarding the role of good-enough mothering, the impact of the analyst's conceptual framework upon the analytic process, and his differentiation between "false" and "true" self organizations. Kohut's description of selfobject transferences in which defective or otherwise arrested and pathological self configurations become engaged in the analytic process, together with his account of the analysis of these transferences, provides a bridge uniting the methods of investigation traditionally employed in psychoanalysis and the revised concepts of developmental pathogenesis insistently advanced by individual object relations theorists.

> The essential therapeutic conclusion of all my contributions to the understanding of the self and its development can be formulated as follows: it is the defect in the self that brings about and maintains a patient's selfobject (narcissistic) transference, and it is the working through of this transference which, via transmuting internalization, that is, via a wholesome psychic activity which has been thwarted in childhood, lays down the structures needed to fill the defect in the self. Indeed, I take the emergence of this process, and especially its persistent engagement, as evidence that the treatment situation has reactivated the developmental potential of the defective self. (Kohut, 1984, p. 4)

Kohut and the British object relations theorists came by different paths to share their dissatisfaction with traditional psychoanalytic theories. Kohut's mentor, his link to Freud once removed, was Hartmann with whom the British theorists had little contact. His chief theoretical London connection was Edward Glover, whom Kohut characterized as one of his great heroes and from whom he "benefitted more than from [the writings] of any other psychoanalyst with the exception of Freud" (Kohut, 1984, p. 93). Glover, after an initial interest in Melanie Klein's work, became her chief antagonist. He was so estranged by her emphasis on object relations and by the threat he felt her popularity posed for psychoanalysis that for a time he resigned from the British Psychoanalytic Society and joined first the Japanese then the Swiss societies in protest.

It was from this background that Kohut's first questionings took shape. Ornstein (1978) has traced the development of Kohut's thinking in cogent detail. He takes note of Kohut's initial preoccupation with the psychoeconomic point of view that first led to his focus on alteration of tensions and functional disturbances within a psychic apparatus and then impelled him to consider psychoanalysis as first and foremost the investigation of experience, that is, of complex mental states. This focus on subjective experience took Kohut away from the mechanistic stance of an external observer of events taking place in an isolated intrapsychic apparatus. He was drawn ever more deeply by his commitment to introspection and empathy as the primary tools defining and limiting the field of psychoanalytic inquiry into the realm of patients' subjective experience of their analysts as the primary data of analysis. That remained his singular focus and his psychology became preeminently and increasingly a depth psychology of subjective experience of self and objects and its personal meanings, conscious and unconscious. The transference analysis of self–selfobject experience is distinguished by its emphasis on the investigation of inevitable and codetermined selfobject failures from within the organizing framework of the patient's subjective experience. Acceptance of and attunement to these recurring episodes of hurt and disappointment and their associated affects of pain, anxiety, rage, depression, despair, and withdrawal makes possible a subsequent exploration of the hierarchies of personal meanings and developmental significances that lie embedded within them. Such a procedure avoids reliance upon presumably "therapeutic" enactments, such as described by Ferenczi and Balint, for example, in response to archaic demands upon the analyst, or the alternatives of superimposing theories of unconscious "resistance" upon the patient's own framework of experience.

Thus, it is a distinguishing feature of Kohut's work that it has made possible an analytic approach and resolution requiring neither from the patient the repudiation of his archaic yearnings nor from the analyst the abandonment of analysis in favor of attempts at direct satisfaction. The analysis of subjective experience from a stance consistently within the patient's perspective makes possible the transformation of such needs from concrete psychotherapeutic enactments into a matrix of verbal and affective communication and understanding. In extending the psychoanalytic procedure as a preeminent therapeutic tool beyond its previous boundaries it averts the danger of lifelong addiction to analysis by facilitating the development of psychological resilience and growth.

Kohut's attempt to differentiate himself from the forms of his own background resulted in his repudiation of the dominant theories of *his* time and place. He rejected the theory of development from autoerotism through narcissism to object love, or development from dependence via neutralization and sublimation of instinctual drives to independence; the theory of the drives as supraordinate motivational forces was abandoned in favor of a theory of the maturational transformation of the self and selfobject experiences throughout life. He specifically rejected the theory that it was the pleasure priniciple that governed the first stages of infantile development, recognizing that this theory superimposed an adultomorphic subjectivity upon the experiences of archaic levels of development. What was urgently needed, he insisted, was a renewed effort to understand early experiences and their analogs in analysis by focus not on the "instinctual" phenomenology but rather on the underlying sense of an ill-formed, weakened, defective, derailed, or compromised and frequently heavily defensively armored self.

Kohut's 1959 papers "Introspection, Empathy and Psychoanalyis," marked his own momentous step from a mental apparatus psychology toward a psychology of experience, his break with the ritualistic and concretized forms of psychoanalysis and embrace of its essence-expanded observation of the conscious and unconscious roots of subjectivity of man's inner life. "The observational method defines the contents and the limits of the observed field . . . and thereby also determines the limits of an empirical science," Kohut said (1959, p. 212). From this starting point he provided a singular and enduring methodology that offers protection that the theories of self psychology or any other set of theoretical constructs will not become a dogma of their own; and for their ongoing emendation, elaboration, or correction where the data of observation indicates. His methodology explained the limits of his own theories, for example, as applied to borderline and psychotic disorders.[4] It also explained the limitations of the object relations theorists.

III

By contrast, the towering influence to which object relations theorists responded was that of Melanie Klein. Her apostasy made their own

---

4. See Brandchaft and Stolorow (1984) for an application of self psychological principles to borderline conditions; Stolorow, Brandchaft, and Atwood (1985) on psychosis.

departures from classical analysis less significant than their attempts to differentiate themselves and what they observed from her influence and from her theories. From the background of her own experience with her analysts, Ferenczi and Abraham, she led the way in insisting that the events that resulted in the foundation of basic normal and pathological structure took place in early infancy. She emphasized the significance of more deeply lying configurations, states of mind, and affects than those that had been uncovered by Freud's revolutionary discoveries. She established the centrality of object ties, instinctual she believed, in pathological and healthy development. She opened the door to further advances in our science by making diversity possible and enriching. Her example and her teaching influenced a generation of psychoanalysts outside the United States in the conviction that the key to the understanding and amelioration of basic psychological disorders lay in the activation, observation, understanding, and explanation of archaic transference configurations together with their displacements and disavowals, as entities in their own right and not simply evasions of or regressions from too intense oedipal rivalry. Her overriding thesis, stripped of its concreteness, that the secure establishment of a bond to a good internal object is the key to a useful, productive, creative, and generative life, can hardly now be faulted, if her description of the process by which that bond is established and maintained is now open to serious question and revision. As truly pioneering as were her efforts in her day, she retained her single-minded focus on the vicissitudes of early destructive drives in determining the course of the development of the self and its object relations. She was more Freudian even than Freudians in her support of Freud's proposal that an intrapsychic destructive force "beyond the pleasure principle," the death instinct, accounted for the most relentless resistances to analytic success and to failures in life.

It was Klein's unquestioning acceptance of the death instinct and its universally basic primacy that lent support to the theory of projective identification by which she accounted for unwelcome affective states stimulated in the analyst by aggressively demanding, frustrating, or extremely anxious patients. She maintained that it was the projection of the death instinct that gave rise to the fear of persecutors, and the reintrojection that led to the installation of internal "bad" objects and a persecutory superego. It was her adherence to these theories that limited her exploration of the subjective experiences of her patients in the face of protests of harm and fear of harm and led to her conceptualization of a "paranoid" attitude in her patients and in the reconstruction of a "paranoid position" as fundamental in normal infantile development. As Segal (1979) recounts, Klein attempted to modify her original insistence on the primacy of the destructive instincts through her emphasis upon the ultimately prevailing role of the life instincts in the "depressive position" (pp. 78–79). She regarded the "depressive position" in which the infant comes to integrate split-off configurations of libidinally determined "good" and aggressively determined "bad" objects as central to development, together with the infantile acceptance of responsibility over destructive instincts. In this, however, she minimized the influence of the intersubjective context in which these events occurred, the contribution of caretakers to faulty integration and to the development of "good" and "bad" self concepts in the child, for example. The insistence that the analyst's subjective ordering of the patient's experience of him was objective truth removed a crucial area, the influence of the observer on the observed, from analytic investigation. It thereby precluded consideration of the patient's vulnerability and weakened structures of self experience as the central pathology to be engaged directly in the analytic process. It foreclosed the recognition of the core of truth in the patient's subjective transference experiences and its dynamic and genetic (conscious and unconscious) significance for the patient.

A detailed explication of the clinical observations of archaic transferences that led Kohut to conclude that Klein was in error in equating mental health with the attainment of the specific early developmental psychological task of the capacity for post-paranoid–depressive object love is set forth in his last work (Kohut, 1984). Reports of clinical cases illustrating some of these differences are contained in papers by the present author (Brandchaft, 1983; Brandchaft and Stolorow, 1984).

IV

Michael Balint's career, as his influence in psychoanalysis, was overshadowed by that of Melanie Klein. As he recounts (Balint, 1953, p. 244), he began his studies in Budapest where she had already become an outstanding teacher much admired by him. Later he was instrumental in sponsoring and supporting her when she came to London.

It is impossible in a short review to give the Balints' (Michael and Alice) work the credit it deserves for the originality, courage, and creativeness that distinguished their efforts. For a more comprehensive summation, the reader is referred to Masud Khan's elegant essay (Khan, 1969). A half century ago, the Balints began a systematic reappraisal of accepted psychoanalytic theories. In this effort they brought clinical observations and formulated theoretical concepts that were to differentiate them clearly from both the classical tradition of the Viennese and the Kleinian school then becoming established in London. In a series of papers they anticipated the methodological principle that was to be spelled out explicitly some 30 years later by Kohut, namely that the empathic–introspective mode of observation defines and limits the domain of psychoanalytic inquiry. No penetration by analytic technique, they asserted, reveals a psychological configuration that is not object related (1953, p. 59); all so-called autoerotic expressions are revealed in analysis "as consolations for or defiance against, objects which had been lost or led the child into severe conflicts" (1953, p. 59). From these observations they argued cogently against the concepts of primary narcissism and against regarding the narcissistic pathology of so-called "secondary narcissism" as denoting a regression from or defense against object relations at an oedipal level, as classical analysts maintained, or excessive sadism or envy in preoedipal part-object relations as put forward by the Kleinians. Rather, they proposed, such narcissism is always a protection against an excessively frustrating object. "If the world does not love me enough, I have to love and gratify myself (Balint, 1953, p. 63).

Similarly they took issue with the emphasis of the Freudians on the destructive instincts, as set forward in *Beyond the Pleasure Principle* and its purported appearance in the form of negative analytic transferences stressed in the clinical work of the Kleinians. Anticipating Winnicott's later work, especially on delinquency (Winnicott, 1965, pp. 134–135), they wrote that observation in an analytic setting discloses that "illnature, malice, wickedness and sadism . . . have their antecedents. It is suffering that makes one wicked. Grown ups as well as children, if they are spiteful, aggressive, sadistic, have a reason for being so. And if one removes the cause, this trait disappears" (Balint, 1953, p. 62).

Thus, as early as 1930, Dr. Balint, with a growing body of colleagues, approached a type of disorder that had hitherto not been systematically studied as a psychoanalytic entity in its own right, and that was later to emerge in Kohut's classifications, first of narcissistic personality and behavior disorders (1971, 1978) and later in a broader concept of self disorders (1984). The Balints departed from psychoanalysts who, following Abraham (1919), viewed the phenomenology as a "resistance" to analysis, the strength of which had become the leading criterion of unanalyzability. "These patients" wrote Balint, "are difficult to place under any diagnostic heading. Their chief complaint is that they cannot find their place in life. Nothing is actually wrong with them or, at most, they have some quite insignificant neurotic symptoms; but they take no pleasure in anything" (1965, p. 159).

Balint's ability to pay attention to the accounts of his patients without attempting to fit them into existing metapsychological concepts persuaded him that the illness of these patients was largely the result of early environmental factors in the patient's life. In an early and seminal observation, by no means sufficiently appreciated even today, he wrote that all those "defects of development which we group under the collective name 'the repressed' were originally forced into that state by external influences. . . . That is to say, there is no repression without reality, without an object relation" (1953, p. 196). Balint went even further in delineating the nature of pathogenic environmental influences on development by recognizing that particularly noxious was the use of the child to satisfy a parent's unconscious needs, in this anticipating a cardinal element in Kohut's investigations into the nature of pathological self–selfobject ties.

In their clinical work, the Balints confirmed what other and especially Kleinian analysts regarded as the essence of the infantile psychological organization,

> loss of security, the feeling of being worthless, despair, deeply bitter disappointment, feelings [of mistrust]. Mixed with these came . . . venomous aggression, wildest sadistic phantasies . . . the most cunning tortures and humiliations for the analyst. Then again fear of retaliation . . . contriteness, for one had spoilt forever the hope of being loved by the analyst. . . . (1953, p. 97.)

However, the Balints noted that these reactions invariably followed occasions in which their patients expected and often demanded "certain primitive gratifications from their analysts or others in their environment" and when the analyst "stuck strictly to the rule of analytic passivity" (p. 97).

From repeated and painstaking observations Balint was led to reconsider the role of the analyst's contribution to the psychoanalytic process, and to conclude that analyzability itself and the results of analysis were as much the product of the analyst's understanding and the concepts he used (determined to a greater or lesser extent also by his own unconscious needs) as they were attributable to the disorders of his patients. Such ideas were received with little greater enthusiasm in Great Britain than were to be their fate when they were similarly proposed by Kohut (1971, 1977). Nonetheless Balint insisted that the then predominant psychoanalytic emphasis on the role of the superego was misplaced and that it overlooked and distorted the period of development before such structures could be formed. Balint argued forcefully that "orthodoxies and factional rigidities in the psychoanalytic movement. . . . [create a] bias in our technique especially where training analyses [are concerned]" and he persistently maintained that in such analyses "perhaps dependency and superego pedagogy plays the operative role and goes against a creative and independent discovery of self and one's own mind" (Khan, 1969, p. 239).

The Balints' core theoretical constructs were (1) "the basic fault," (2) primary or primitive object love, and (3) the basic developmental progression from passive primitive object love to interdependent mature love. Their distinctive contribution to technique was "the new beginning."

If patients are permitted to regress in the psychoanalytic situation, the Balints found, the area of "basic fault" will become exposed. Such regression frequently is interfered with by the analyst's "irresistable urge to organize their patient's complaints into an illness" (1968, p. 108). Again Balint anticipates Kohut's (1971) similar injunction concerning the need to abstain from premature interpretations of resistance or defense. The characteristics of "the basic fault" are that it is exclusively dyadic, not triadic; the relationship is not oedipal; and it is not motivated by conflict. In this experience in which feelings of deadness and emptiness may be strong, the patient feels there is a "fault within him" that must be repaired and that this fault was brought about because someone failed him. Balint noted that this experience is accompanied by great anxiety and usually by a "desperate demand that this time the analyst must not fail him" (1968, p. 21).

The therapeutic relationship that then ensues Balint describes as "very primitive and peculiar, different from those usually observed between adults" (1968, p. 23). Only the wishes and needs of one of the parties matters and must be attended to, the other counts only insofar as he gratifies or frustrates. His own interests, wishes and needs do not exist (1968), p. 23). There can be no doubt that Balint was clearly observing the same phenomenology as Kohut described 3 years later similarly following the rules of noninterfering facilitation (Kohut, 1971). However, Kohut in response developed his core concept of selfobject when he recognized the essential pathology here as a defect in the cohesiveness of the self and the "peculiar" relationship as one in which the patient was attempting to revive with the analyst a period of development of the self at the point at which it had been arrested. In this experience, the analyst was not perceived subjectively as separate but rather as a part of the patient. This object relationship was characterized not by the analyst gratifying or frustrating desires and needs of the patient, according to Kohut, but by being looked to for his unquestioned and unquestionable provision of essential functions that the patient could not provide for himself. Within the actuating matrix of the psychoanalytic situation, Kohut proposed, the archaic needs that appear are those for narcissistic sustenance, that is, the need for mirroring and the need to merge with an ideal, not provided for in childhood. The reactivation of these needs signals an incompleteness in the structuralization of the self with the result that the patient reacts to frustration with narcissistic injury in the form of a temporary break-up, enfeeblement, or disharmony. Kohut emphasized,

> the essential importance of such patients re-experiencing and working through the lethargies, depressions and rages of early life via the reactivation and analysis of their archaic traumatic self–selfobject relationships in the transference. (1984, p. 5)

The functions that Kohut described were in the service of maintaining, restoring, and consolidating self cohesion, and then later in the facilitation of establishing the self as the center of initiative and in the consolidation of the child's individualized array of aims and ideals. Thus the goal of analysis for Kohut is the reestablishment of the interrupted developmental process, the sine qua non of psychological health or "cure," leading to the structural completeness of the self (1984, p. 7).

For the Balints, the concept of basic fault representing an arrest in the developmental course of object love was inextricably linked with an older core concept, that of "primary object love," "The aim of human striving," Balint wrote, "is to establish or re-establish an all-embracing harmony with one's environment, to be able to love in peace" (Balint, 1968, p. 69).

The central aspect of the Balints' developmental scheme was the progression in object love from a primary dependent passive archaic object relation to a mature interdependent form of love. Beginning with a stage in the development in which subject and object were felt to be indistinguishable, the "work of conquest" transforms the object relationship to one of "mutuality" in which the object can no longer be taken for granted, its own independent and interdependent needs must be recognized and respected. One comes to realize that

> our needs have become too varied, complicated and specialized, so that we can no longer expect automatic satisfaction by our objects; we must be able to bear the depression caused by this realization; and we must accept that we have to give something to our object (Balint, 1968, p. 146)

in order for the object to be a "co-operative partner." The Balints insisted that the development and transformation of object relation in an infant from primitive to mature requires an optimal caretaker.

Primary object love they described as "a primary archaic object relation without reality sense" (1968, p. 125), a "relation in which only one partner is entitled to make demands, the other treated as an object" (1968, p. 146).

> This form of love works according to principle: what is good for me, is right for you, i.e., it does not recognize any difference between one's own interests and the interests of the object: it assumes as a matter fact that the partner's desires are identical with one's own. Claims of the object which go beyond this harmony are intolerable, and call forth anxiety and aggression. (1968, p. 100)

The Balints objected strongly to the then current psychoanalytic practice of regarding the more flagrant manifestations of this object relation as evidence of "oral greed." That, they wrote, was a subjective impression in adultomorphic language. In this peculiar form of love proper, timely satisfaction of all needs was crucially important because of the infant's (or patient's) almost absolute dependence on the object. In it, they observed, again anitcipating Kohut, the object must be, and is, simply taken for granted, very much like the adult's attitude to the supply of air (1953, p. 145). In this state, the Balints suggested, "Hate is the last remnant, the denial of and the defense against the primitive object love (or the dependent archaic love)" (1953, p. 148). Under analysis, they declared, hate always reveals itself as a derivative of frustrated love.

Familiarity with the psychoanalytic setting in the Balints' Great Britain makes it easy to understand their central concern with the failure to recognize and appreciate the infant's inherent capacity for love. In an historical era when psychoanalysts were becoming increasingly transfixed upon the infant's presumptive sadism and with their patients' presumptive "destructive instincts" from which apocalypse they had to be rescued, the restoration of balance through emphasis on "basic archaic object love" made good sense and would be likely to produce better results. The theory of man's primal destructiveness, one dimension of self and object experience, in its time illuminated some important aspects of human experience. However, fidelity to this theory continues today widely enough to constitute an article of faith, an analytic pledge of allegiance that is relatively unaffected, sad to say, by the work of Balint, Winnicott, and Fairbairn, all of whom addressed this point with intelligence and wider vision. Perhaps the explanation for its persistence now is more a practical than a theoretical matter. Theories of innate destructiveness in the historical forms in which they have been cast from infantile sadism, to negative transference, to moral masochism and unconscious guilt, to more contemporary theories of "highly pathological (and destructive) grandiose self" continue to serve a useful purpose. For those who believe and apply them in the consulting room, they delineate where the problem lies whenever an analysis is not proceeding as favorably as might be hoped.

However, from the current vantage point it does not seem that the errors of excessive weighting of archaic destructive forces are to be corrected by insistence on the primacy of the infant's archaic love, or in clinical practice, as Balint proposed, that behind the rage of a narcissistically injured patient lies his love. Kohut has enabled us to recognize the more salient factors of a defective, weakened self. When an infant (or patient) in distress is relentlessly exposed to an insufficiently attuned selfobject, assertiveness as a signal will proceed to chronic, unreflecting, and relentless rage. In acknowledging the truly significant contributions of the Balints, pioneering in their own historical era and setting, we should also acknowledge that there is a theoretical and clinical gulf that divides Kohut's psychology from that of the Balints.

The Balints were able to recognize and define the methodological errors and the clinical cul-de-sac inherent in the classical concepts of an intrapsychic progression from "autoeroticism" to "primary narcissism" without psychological object attachment and with a presumed subsequent withdrawal from object attachments to a "secondary narcissism"; this was a decisive contribution. That they were also able to recognize that the persistence of archaic narcissistic claims represented a reaction to severe maternal failure and were not defensive structures arising from a primary envy of the nourishing maternal breast, as Melanie Klein hypothesized, was also noteworthy.

The Balints' success in actuating the emergence in analysis of regressed and archaic states was a similar notable achievement. Their description of what is required from the side of the analyst in order to expose the experience of "basic fault" and engage it therapeutically toward a "new beginning" is the work of empathic clinicians. The analyst must be there, pliable to a high degree, not offer much resistance, must be indestructible "and he must allow his patient to live with him in a sort of harmonious interpenetrating mix-up" (1968, p. 66). These, they proposed are the conditions necessary for the establishment of an object relationship similar in structure to the primary relationship.

In much of this, the Balints' observations parallel or are duplicated in Kohut's writings. However the Balints' innovative concepts did not carry them a sufficient distance to maintain an analytic procedure with which to bring about the transformations they sought. Instead they openly proposed that there was an indispensable role for the analyst at certain points in the analytic procedure to lend himself to the patient's reactivated needs for physical contact and/or holding of a hand.[5] Whatever merits or demerits might be and have been assigned to such a course, it represented an abandonment of the analytic procedure and therefore a limitation into the inquiry of the experience being concretely communicated (and responded to) in the request. It derailed an investigation into the complex nature and multiple meanings of the hopes being concretely mobilized as well as the experience averted.

Kohut's concept of selfobject and selfobject transferences made possible an extension of the analytic procedure beyond these limits. With these concepts it becomes possible to broaden our understanding of contexts of subjective experience in which urgent needs for oneness may arise and become concretized. In addition, Kohut's concepts have led us to appreciate that the basic fault includes not only severe narcissistic injury but inevitably also includes failures on the part of important caretakers to become attuned to the discrepant affect states resulting from such injuries and so to assist in the integration of such affect states and so promote the process of healing. The implications for analysis of these findings are profound and include an appreciation of the greater potential for the analytic procedure precisely at the point at which the Balints had to relinquish it in favor of direct responses and exhortations to abandon narcissistic object relations.

---

5. The Balints found that only about one patient in five responded favorably to this procedure and acknowledged that further experience was necessary in this area (1968, pp. 246–247).

V

The work of W. R. D. Fairbairn was summarized contemporaneously in a review by Winnicott and Khan (1953). Guntrip (1968) integrated it with the work of Winnicott and refined and advanced it in an important contribution. Bacal (1984) has advanced an illuminating essay on the relationship of self psychology to the prior work of Fairbairn, as well as an integration of the works of object relations theorists Suttie, Balint, Fairbairn, Winnicott, and Guntrip with that of Kohut. The interested reader would do well to consult this latter reference as a comprehensive auxiliary to this chapter.

In his preface to Fairbairn's *An Object Relations Theory of the Personality* (1954), Ernest Jones wrote:

> Instead of starting as Freud did, from the stimulation of the nervous system proceeding from excitation of various erotogenous zones and internal tension arising from gonadic activity, Dr. Fairbairn starts at the centre of the personality, the ego, and depicts its strivings and difficulties in its endeavor to reach an object where it might find support. All this constitutes a fresh approach in psycho-analysis which should lead to much fruitful discussion.

Fairbairn's focus on schizoid factors in the personality arose directly in relation to Melanie Klein's crucial concepts of the "paranoid position" and defensive splitting of ego and objects in earliest childhood. For Fairbairn, only the exploration of schizoid states could yield the deepest understanding of the origins and foundations of the human personality. "The fundamental schizoid phenomenon is the presence of splits in the ego and . . . the basic position in the psyche is invariably a schizoid position" (1954, p. 8). Although Fairbairn accepted Klein's view that the splitting of the ego occurred in response to conflicts between aggressive and libidinal relationships, he nonetheless emphasized, as did Balint and Winnicott, the contribution to arrests in development and continuing pathogenic effects of persisting internal ties to unsatisfactory caretakers. The schizoid condition, he maintained, is the outcome of an unsatisfactory mother–infant relationship, determined by the failure on the part of the mother "to convince her child by spontaneous and genuine expressions of affection that she loves him as a person" (1954, p. 13).

The Balints visualized the developmental process as centralized in a progression from primary to mature love; Fairbairn's counterpart conceptualization was that infantile immature dependence based on primary identification (by which he meant to indicate a cathexis to an object not yet or only partially differentiated) was gradually abandoned in favor of a state of adult or mature dependence based upon differentiation of object from the self. With the Balints, Fairbairn regarded as a crucial point in development, the infant's acceptance of "reality" and its "abandonment" of archaic object strivings.

Fairbairn's position, which appears sometimes contradictory and often confusing in his earlier work, is set forth in a much more coherent formulation in a paper written near the close of his career (Fairbairn, 1958). There he affirmed that his "chief conscious psychoanalytical interest now lies in promoting a more adequate formulation of psychoanalytical theory" (p. 376). He argued passionately against the tendency to regard existing psychoanalytic theory as objective truth.

> Scientific truth is simply explanatory truth; and the picture of reality provided by science is an intellectual construct. . . . an attempt to describe the various phenomena of the universe, in as coherent and systematic a manner as the limitations of human intelligence permit, by means of the formulation of general laws by inductive inference under conditions of maximum emotional detachment and objectivity on the part of the scientific observer. A special difficulty arises in respect to psychological science, Fairbairn noted, for subjective aspects of phenomena are the most important data being studied and these can only be understood in terms of the subjective experience of the psychologist himself. He therefore is necessarily involved in the difficult task of adapting as detached and objective an attitude as possible to his own experience as to that of those whom he observes (p. 376–377).

Fairbairn characterized his theoretical position as comprising four main conceptual formulations: (1) a theory of dynamic psychic structure, (2) a theory to the effect that libidinal activity is inherently and primarily object-seeking, (3) a theory of development not of zonal dominance but of the quality of dependence, and (4) a theory of the personality in terms of internal object relationships.

In his attempt to find his way to a new theory of endopsychic structure that would address the clinical phenomenology of the schizoid condition, Fairbairn described a self split into three egos, (1) a central ego (the "I"), (2) a libidinal ego, and (3) an aggressive persecutory ego that he first called "the internal saboteur," a term later discarded in favor of "anti-libidinal ego." "Subsequent experience" he wrote, "has led me to regard this classification as having a universal application" (1958, p. 101). These ego structures, he believed, arise from an original, inherent, and unitary ego that becomes split in all cases during the earliest phases of development and each has its own characteristic internal object relationship. The central ego is that which is related to objects in the outer world. It is ambivalent in its attitude toward its objects and this leads to an inner world in which unconscious split relationships exist between libidinal ego and an "exciting" and a "rejecting object." The antilibidinal ego is identified with the rejecting object and is therefore arrayed against the "libidinal ego" in its attachment to "exciting" objects (1958, pp. 102–107). The antilibidinal ego represents the structuralization of attitudes of contempt and hatred for the object-seeking libidinal self, developed in part by identification with such attitudes in the parents toward infantile needs as signs of "weakness" and in part as a reaction to the vulnerability to rejection posed by object-related needs.

Fairbairn's clinical experience, reflected in these concepts, made him especially critical of the requirement of traditional analysts that the analysand should possess a relatively mature, strong, and unmodified ego. He found it impossible to understand what would induce such an individual, if one there were, to seek psychoanalytic treatment. People, he maintained, seek psychoanalytic treatment because they have come to recognize that they are suffering. Even a psychoanalytic candidate's interest in psychoanalysis "must be regarded as ultimately springing from a desire, largely unconscious perhaps, to resolve his own conflicts" (1958, p. 375). Fairbairn was equally critical of the notion that an average patient is interested in the undertaking of a scientific exploration of his personality. Where such a condition exists, he maintained, it reflects obsessional and/or schizoid personality defenses and formidable resistances against emotional involvement, a phenomenon to be investigated, not a motivation to be credited as primary. He considered this claim for its justification on the part of analysts to be an apologia for their lack of therapeutic results.

Fairbairn's passionate commitment to the reestablishment of psychoanalysis in its ultimate raison d'être as the most advanced psychological treatment led him to reconsider the clinical assumptions that had also become regarded as ultimate truths. "It becomes obvious, therefore, that from a therapeutic standpoint, interpretation is not enough," he wrote, "and it would appear to follow that the relationship existing between the patient and the analyst in the psychoanalytical situation serves purposes additional to that of providing a setting for the interpretation of transference phenomena" (1958, p. 377). The disabilities of patients arose, Fairbairn held, not from the distortion of early experiences with objects, but "from the effects of unsatisfactory and unsatisfying object-relationships experienced in early life and perpetuated in an exaggerated form in inner reality" (1958, p. 377). Therefore only the actual relationship between analyst and patient as persons could constitute a new reality and thus an indispensable therapeutic factor. Only such a relationship could provide a means of correcting distorted internal relationships and also provide the patient with the opportunity, foreclosed in his childhood, "to undergo a process of emotional development in the setting of an actual relationship with a reliable and beneficent parental figure" (1958, p. 377). Fairbairn maintained that although such an actual relationship is difficult to reconcile with a psychology of "impulse," it is quite compatible with a psychology of object relations and dynamic structure.

Fairbairn never fully detailed what he had in mind with this recommendation. His recognition that aspects of unsatisfying, distant, and remote parental relations were perpetuated in the analytic situation, with equally unsatisfactory results, led him to subject the whole area of classical technique to reconsideration. He himself abandoned the use of the couch "to great advantage, in my opinion," because he considered that "the stock arguments in favour of couch technique are now largely rationalizations" (1958, p. 378). He suggested that the tendency to adhere rigidly to the details of the classical psychoanalytical technique, as standardized by Freud, is liable to defensive exploitation in the interests of the analyst and at the expense of the patient, "and certainly any tendency to treat the classic technique as sacrosanct raises the suspicion that an element of such defensive exploitation is at work" (1958, p. 379). Theoretical or clinical purism, he insisted, "resolves itself simply into an apotheosis of the method at the expense of the aims which the method is intended to serve" (1958, p. 379). In a succinct passage Fairbairn wrote, "In recent years I have shed enough sophistication to enable me to ask myself repeatedly such naive questions as, 'if the patient does not make satisfactory progress under analysis, how far is this due to some defect in the psychoanalytical method?' " (1958, p. 379).

Much of what Fairbairn wrote is as refreshing and stimulating today as it was 40 years ago. However, as revolutionary as Fairbairn's approach in 1950 it too was simply an important chapter in a continuing evolutionary process within psychoanalysis. Irreverent though he may have been, Fairbairn was not able fully to separate himself from the influence of Klein's thinking that the crucial events of infancy center around conflicts aroused by gratifying and frustrating experiences with objects. Although he came to recognize and describe a fundamental need for objects in order not to "break down," thus approaching Kohut's concept of selfobject, his focus remained on the progression of object ties, in contrast with Kohut's later focus on self experience. For example, Fairbairn believed that masochism, exhibitionism, and so forth, could be explained as "attempts to salvage emotional relationships which have broken down." Focus on the subjective experience in such cases indicates that they are better understood and more effectively treated as experiences in which the person urgently attempts to reconstitute a crumbling sense of self by erotized and concretized enactments, frequently with another individual who has no other importance (Goldberg, 1977). Similarly increased focus on the subjective experience of schizoid individuals seems to indicate that lasting shame and self-hatred in connection with selfobject longings are not primary factors as Fairbairn believed. The more fundamental threat is that to the fragile cohesiveness and the last hopes for empathic resonance still cherished and protected, dangers posed by the engagement of intense selfobject needs. As Kohut observed, it is an understanding, explanation, and acceptance of those underlying fears and their area of subjective validity that are necessary responses to the first selfobject needs of these patients activated in the analytic situation. It is not only the shame for his archaic needs that the patient brings to the analyst but the expectation of the analyst's dislike and contempt for the patient when exposed to the full impact of those unfulfilled primeval needs.

Fairbairn's concepts do not engage the central psychopathology of fragile cohesiveness and precarious boundary formation that lie behind schizoid structures in therapeutic transferences. For Fairbairn, the goal of analysis involved the healing of "splits in the ego" in order to develop the capacity for object relations, not an object relation in order to consolidate a nuclear self so that it could continue its developmental designs. Kohut in his final work demonstrated how pathological defenses such as fit Fairbairn's description of "internal saboteur" are unwittingly reinforced by analysts' failures to appreciate that schizoid defenses are fundamentally in the service of the "primacy of self perservation." "Successful self preservation" Kohut wrote, "is not only compatible with the full flowering of investment in object: it is, for many individuals, though significantly not for all, a precondition for 'object love' " (Kohut, 1984, p. 143).

Fairbairn's clinical focus centers upon the "antilibidinal ego" as the preeminent source of resistance to the emergence of "dependency" needs in analysis, along with the associated focus on patients' reluctance to relinqush ties to their frustrating objects. In my experience the effect of this has been perceived by patients as an attempt to turn them against protective aspects of their own self organization and subsequently to discourage focus on the actual experience of the analyst as a frustrated and frustrating archaic selfobject. When the influence of the analyst is obscured under such circumstances it serves to reinforce the measures the patient employs to preserve the basic integrity of self experience.

VI

Fairbairn was intensely dissatisfied with the quality of emotional experience available in a psychoanalytic procedure in which the analyst regarded himself as a dispassionate and objective observer of events occurring within the psychic apparatus of the patient, with the analyst as a screen for the projection of previously installed images. He recognized that such a posture could itself reflect schizoid characteristics by analysts fearing emotional involvement and in any case contributing to schizoid encapsulation in patients. His understanding led him to attempt to alter the experience through concretized changes in the analytic procedure. Kohut addressed the same problem in the following way.

> In harmony with the popular saying that "half truth is the worst enemy of the truth," the half truth of Freud's early experience-distant formulations about libido regression and fixation allowed analysts to protect themselves against empathic immersion in the analysand's diseased self and prevented them from arriving at the experience-near formulations of self psychology that are relevant to the psychic miseries of our time. Specifically, the availability of the classical theory of fixation and regression . . . has been able to cover up the fact that one of the most important clusters of human psychic disturbance remained de-emphasized. . . . The security that these claims have provided for us has, up to now, prevented us from perceiving what many of our patients have been trying to tell us for a long, time: that the issues they are facing cannot be joined in earnest as long as our theories dictate an ultimate focus either on the drives, genital or pregenital, as the biological bedrock of our personalities, or on the ego, mature or infantile, as the central organ of a mental apparatus that mediates between biological drives and the curbs imposed upon them by reality. (1984, pp. 221–222)

Kohut's understanding led him to an increasing immersion into his patients' subjective experience. In departure from the practices endorsed by classical and Kleinian concepts, he advocated a continual focus on the patient's experience, always from a stance within the framework of that experience. In the maintenance of an experience-near empathic psychoanalytic milieu so dedicated, Kohut found the possibilities for the "new relationship" that Fairbairn, as Balint, sought by other means.

I turn now to Winnicott for whose immensely valuable contributions psychoanalysts are in debt. Winnicott, too, was a creature of his times. In his paper, "A Personal View of the Kleinian Contribution" (Winnicott, 1965) he describes the "period in which my own psycho-analytic growth was taking root and stem," and "the soil in which I had become planted" (p. 171). No one can understand Winnicott's contributions without reference to that soil. In the London of that day, Jones was Winnicott's towering hero. It was Jones who invited Melanie Klein to London to treat a member of his family. And it was Jones who recommended to Winnicott that he have analysis with James Strachey. Strachey steered him into supervision with Melanie Klein out of which eventually evolved an analysis with Joan Rivière, then a most prestigious follower of Klein.

Of his work with Melanie Klein, Winnicott recounts that he consulted her on the one analysis he had done on the basis of his own Strachey analysis and "went on to try to learn some of the immense amount she knew already. . . . This was difficult for me," he wrote "because overnight I changed from being a pioneer into being a student with a pioneer teacher" (Winnicott, 1965, p. 173). Within the context of those times, it is easy to understand how he gradually came to focus increasingly on the contribution of environmental factors in development, when all around him the focus was so heavily on the biological and innate. His contributions reflect his personal attempt to return to his pioneering course and to free himself from some of the influences that undoubtedly governed his personal analysis with Riviere and his supervision in training under the formidable influence of Klein. His declarations that "there is no such thing as a baby" and that "infant and mother together form an indivisible unit" (Winnicott, 1965, p. 39) were the most emphatic challenges to the edifice Klein had built that an unshackled mind could proclaim. The unique and brilliant contributions that marked the last years of his life seem to me to reflect his own personal voyage from what was for him a false self to more singular, unique, and creative true self. They signalled the end of a journey he well might have characterized as from selfless dependence via relative dependence to mature independence. He cast these personal experiences into a theoretical model in which these concepts were elaborated. As lasting as his contributions are likely to be, one cannot read his works without being aware that he was never quite able to separate himself fully from the earlier influences (see, e.g., Winnicott, 1965, pp. 231–232, on depression; see also case report, pp. 252–253).

It is fascinating to read in Winnicott's work in 1962 the discovery that decisively marked his departure from the influence of Klein. "I must refer to the fact," he writes, "that in many cases the analyst displaces environmental influences that are pathological, and we gain insight of the kind that enables us to know when we have become modern representatives of the parent figures of the patient's childhood and infancy, and when by contrast we are displacing such figures" (pp. 167–168). It was the same discovery in very similar terms by Heinz Kohut 8 years earlier that decisively marked his effort to emancipate himself from ego psychology. "Here," he wrote, "analysis is not the screen for the projection of internal structures . . . but the direct combination of an early reality that was too distant, too rejecting or too unreliable to be transformed into solid psychological structures" (1978, pp. 218–219).

After this parallel, however, the paths diverge. Kohut was able to recognize the conditions necessary to set in motion an analytic process based upon the establishment of selfobject transferences. Winnicott took a different course. "I find myself working as a psychoanalyst rather than doing standard analysis when I meet certain conditions that I have learned to recognize" he wrote. "In this sense, I do psychoanalysis when . . . this individual . . . wants psychoanalysis . . . but, by and large, analysis is for those who want it, need it and can take it. . . . [W]hen I am faced with the wrong kind of case I change over into being a psychoanalyst who is meeting the needs, or trying to meet the needs, of this special case" (Winnicott, 1965, pp. 168–169). It was the selfobject concept and the recognition of selfobject transferences that had already enabled Kohut to extend the psychoanalytic process where Winnicott felt obliged to abandon it.

The distinctive contributions of Winnicott are too important to be considered in the limitations of depth in this discussion. His insistence that psychosis could be treated and that a self can be formed out of what Kohut termed as "prepsychological chaos" in a proper therapeutic environment mark an important difference from Kohut's view. His view of transitional space with its emphasis on the harm done by intrusion in development and in analysis, and his contributions on the development of "true" self structure as a materializiaton of an intrinsic individualized design are of lasting significance. Their importance is not diminished if today we might observe that the preservation of transitional space and emergent selfhood may require more specific selfobject facilitating functions and experiential transformations than he was able to describe. However, our debt to Winnicott is not the less on that account nor should we fail to be reminded that we still have much to learn from Winnicott and the other British pioneers. Together they wrought a revolution in psychoanalytic thinking the end of which is nowhere to be seen.

Aside from the broadened and increased precision of our theories and clinical observations, what else can we learn? This surely, that every analyst and psychoanalysis itself can only develop in an environment in which the widest diversity is encouraged. It is the encouragement of such diversity that provides the firmest link to a tradition that illuminates and frees, just as it is the most precious of parenthoods that provides the security and wisdom that enables each child to have his own experiences that will free the creativity that particular child needs to determine truly along what course his own unique interests lie. It is the insistence that the child follow a path predetermined by the parents in order to maintain that bond that shackles the development of the child or turns it into a hollow victory. The object relations theorists and Heinz Kohut together made it possible for succeeding generations of psychoanalysts to see more than had before been visible. What they shared was the determination to continue the tradition of Freud not by the celebration and reaffirmation necessarily of his concepts but of his ideals. They had a passionate commitment to stretch themselves in order to expand man's understanding of his experience and better be able to heal what is damaged and change and revitalize what has become stagnant. Perhaps the most significant of the many facets of their commonality in this continuing quest is expressed in the following quotations:

> Suppose we were really steadfast, one would wonder what was the matter with us. Time passes, we grow older, and if our ideas remain the same there must be something wrong.

> Even the most convincing conclusions seemingly self-evident beyond question, may ultimately come into serious question.

The first quotation is taken from the final work of Wilfred Bion (1980, p. 37), the second from the final work of Heinz Kohut (1984, p. 57).

REFERENCES

Abraham, K. (1919). A particular form of neurotic resistance against the psycho-analytic method. In *Selected Papers of Karl Abraham* (pp. 303–311). London: Hogarth Press, 1927.

Bacal, H. (1984). *British object relations theorists and self psychology.* Paper presented at the 7th Annual Self Psychology Conference: Questions and Controversies. Toronto, Ontario, October 20.

Balint, M. (1953). *Primary Object Love and Psycho-Analytic Technique.* New York: Liveright.

Balint, M. (1968). *The Basic Fault.* London: Tavistock.

Bion, W. (1980). In F. Bion, ed., *Bion in New York and Sao Paolo.* Perthshire, Scotland: Clunie Press.

Brandchaft, B. (1983). The negativism of the negative therapeutic reaction and the psychology of the self. In A. Goldberg, ed., *The Future of Psychoanalysis,* pp. 327–362. New York: International Universities Press.

Brandchaft, B., and Stolorow, R. (1984). The borderline concept: Pathological character or iatrogenic myth (pp. 333–372. In J. Lichtenberg, M. Bornstein, and D. Silver, eds., *Empathy* (Vol. 2). Hillsdale, NJ: Analytic Press.

Fairbairn, W.R.D. (1954). *An Object Relations Theory of the Personality.* New York: Bane Books.

Fairbairn, W.R.D. (1958). On the nature and aims of psychoanalytical treatment. *International Journal of Psychoanalysis,* 39:374–386.

Freud, S. (1914). On narcissism. *Standard Edition,* 14:69–102.

Freud, S. (1937). Analysis, terminable and interminable. *Standard Edition,* 23:216–253.

Goldberg, A. (1977). A fresh look at perverse behavior. *International Journal of Psychoanalysis,* 56:335–342.

Guntrip, H. (1968). *Schizoid Phenomena, Object Relations and the Self.* London: Hogarth Press.

Khan, M. (1969). On the clinical provision of frustrations, recognitions and failures in the analytic situation: An essay on Dr. Michael Balint's researches on the theory of psychoanalytic technique. *International Journal of Psycho-analysis,* 50:237–249.

Kohut, H. (1959). Introspective, empathy and psychoanalysis. *Journal of the American Psychoanalytic Association,* 5:389–407.

Kohut, H. (1971). *The Analysis of the Self.* New York: International Universities Press.

Kohut, H. (1977). *The Restoration of the Self.* New York: International Universities Press.

Kohut, H. (1984). *How Does Analysis Cure?* A. Goldberg, ed., with P. Stepansky. Chicago & London: University of Chicago Press.

Kohut, H., & Wolf, E. (1978). The disorders of the self and their treatment: An outline. *International Journal of Psycho-Analysis,* 59:413–425.

Ornstein, P., ed. (1978). *The Search for the Self: Selected Writings of Heinz Kohut, 1950–1978.* New York: International Universities Press.

Segal, H. (1979). *Klein.* Glascow: William Collins and Son.

Steiner, R. (1985). Some thoughts about tradition and change arising from an examination of the British Psychoanalytical Society's controversial discussions (1943–1944). *International Review of Psychoanalysis* 12:27–73.

Stolorow, R., Brandchaft, B., & Atwood, G. (1986). Symbols of Subjective Truth in Psychotic States. In A. Goldberg, ed., *Progress in Self Psychology.* Hillsdale, NJ: Analytic Press.

Winnicott, D.W. (1965). *The Maturation Processes and the Facilitating Environment.* London: Hogarth Press.

Winnicott, D.W., & Khan, M. (1953). Review of *Psycho-Analytic Studies of the Personality* by W.R.D. Fairbairn. *International Journal of Psycho-Analysis,* 4:329–333.

20

On Experiencing an Object: A Multidimensional Perspective

ROBERT D. STOLOROW

Dualistic thinking has been characteristic of psychoanalytic theory since its inception. In the development of Freud's ideas, such dualism became enshrined in the doctrine of instinctual drive and the psychoeconomic point of view: self-preservative instincts versus sexual instincts, Eros versus Thanatos, libidinal drives versus aggressive drives, narcissistic libido versus object libido. This dualistic tradition has persisted in psychoanalytic self psychology as well. From Kohut's early papers on narcissism (1966, 1968) to his final theoretical statement (1984), human subjective worlds have been pictured as populated by two distinct types of psychological objects—selfobjects, experienced as part of oneself and/or serving to maintain the organization of self, and "true" objects, firmly demarcated from oneself and targets of passionate desire. Such dualities, like all typological systems, lend themselves to the irresistible temptation to substantialize the products of human thought, transforming psychological categories into static, immutable entities—reifications that necessarily obscure the complex, ever-shifting flux of human psychological life. These typological reifications lead inevitably to the encrustation of false dichotomies that, in turn, become sources of endless ideological controversy, as in the current heated debate over the centrality of developmental deficit *versus* psychic conflict in psychoanalytic theory.

The selfobject–true object dichotomy that pervades Kohut's thought originated in the Procrustean bed of classical drive theory. Narcissistic libido and object–instinctual energies each followed their own distinct developmental pathways, cathecting their respective targets of investment (Kohut, 1971). However, even after Kohut abandoned both classical metapsychology and the idea that selfobject relations evolve into true object relations, claiming instead that one never outgrows one's need for selfobjects and that such relatedness undergoes development from archaic to mature modes, the essential dichotomy was still retained, forming the basis for a theoretical complementarity between self psychology and conflict psychology (Kohut, 1977). Moreover, statements about self–selfobject relationships, selves seeking psychological nourishment from their selfobjects, and selfobjects responding empathically to selves all entail reifications that transform organizations of subjective experience and psychological functions into palpable entities and existential agents performing actions. Such reifications can all too readily be seized upon by critics who would trivialize Kohut's monumental clinical and theoretical contributions by reducing them to a prescientific soul psychology or crude interpersonalism (e.g., Oremland, 1985).

These theoretical pitfalls can be avoided if the term "selfobject" is used in accord with its strictly psychoanalytic meaning. "Selfobject" does not refer to an environmental entity or caregiving agent. Rather, it designates a class of psychological *functions* pertaining to the maintenance, restoration, and transformation of self experience.[1] Thus, when we use the term "selfobject," we refer to an object experienced subjectively as serving selfobject functions (Socarides & Stolorow, 1984/1985). We refer, in other words, to a dimension of experiencing an object (Kohut, 1984, p. 49), in which a specific bond is required for maintaining, restoring, or consolidating the organization of self experience.

With this conceptual clarification we are thus led away from the selfobject–true object dichotomy and its attendant reifications toward a multidimensional view of human experience in general and of experiencing an object in particular. Our listening perspective becomes thereby focused on the complex, continuously shifting figure–ground relationships among the selfobject and other dimensions of experiencing another person (Atwood & Stolorow, 1984, Chap. 2; Stolorow & Lachmann, 1984/1985). It is in these shifting figure–ground relationships that the experiential meaning of Kohut's principle of complementarity between self psychology and conflict psychology can be found (Stolorow, 1985). From this perspective, selfobject failure and psychic conflict are seen not as dichotomous, but as dimensions of experience that are indissolubly interrelated. Indeed, it can be shown that the formation of inner

---

1. Similarly, the term "self," as a psychoanalytic construct, should not refer to an existential agent (a person) but to a psychological structure—that is, an organization of experience characterized by varying degrees of cohesion and continuity (see Atwood & Stolorow, 1984, Chap. 1).

conflict, whether in early development or in the psychoanalytic situation, always takes place in specific "intersubjective contexts" of selfobject failure (Stolorow & Brandchaft, in press).

As an example of this multidimensional perspective, let us consider some of the many meanings and functions that may be involved in a sexual act. Sexual union with another person may include a prominent selfobject dimension, serving mirroring and/or idealized soothing functions, lending cohesion, continuity, and positive affective tone to the subject's self experience. On the other hand, the sexual act may be required when the selfobject functions of the tie to the object are experienced as absent, insufficient, or endangered. Here the object is *not* experienced as a reliable source of selfobject functions, and the sexual enactment, often perverse in quality, serves as an eroticized substitute for the missing or unsteady selfobject experience (Goldberg, 1975; Kohut, 1971; Stolorow & Lachmann, 1980). If the object is experienced not only as failing to provide needed selfobject functions but also as potentially rejective or hostile, the sexual act may serve the purpose of pacifying the object, fending off anticipated responses that would be destructive to the subject. Sexual union may also serve the purpose of reassuring against the danger of separation from an object, whether the selfobject dimension of the tie is figure or ground. The sexual act binds the object to the subject, preventing an inner experience of object loss. Finally, the selfobject functions of the bond may be present only as a reliable background feature of the experience, with the object being perceived as clearly demarcated from the subject and passionately desired primarily for its own exciting and pleasurable qualities.

I am suggesting that a multiplicity of such dimensions coexist in any complex object relationship, with certain meanings and functions occupying the experiential foreground and others occupying the background, depending on the subject's motivational priorities at any given moment. Furthermore, the figure–ground relationships among these multiple dimensions of experience may significantly shift, corresponding to shifts in the subject's psychological organization and motivational hierarchy, often in response to alterations or disturbances in the tie to the object. For example, the conflictual dimension invariably comes to the fore in reaction to anticipated or experienced selfobject failure (Stolorow & Brandchaft, in press).

These considerations hold critical implications for the understanding and analysis of analytic transferences. In certain transference configurations—for example, those elucidated by Kohut (1971, 1977)—the selfobject dimension is clearly in the foreground, as the restoration or maintenance of self experience is the paramount psychological purpose motivating the patient's specific tie to the analyst. In other transference configurations, the selfobject dimension operates silently in the background, enabling the patient to confront frightening feelings and painful dilemmas (Atwood & Stolorow, 1984, ch. 2; Stolorow & Lachmann, 1984/1985). In still other situations, the analyst is perceived as significantly failing to provide requisite selfobject functions.[2] Here the analyst is *not* experienced as a selfobject, but as a source of painful and conflictual affect states, in turn engendering resistance.[3] When, in such instances, the patient is resisting the emergence of central selfobject needs, it makes no theoretical sense to speak of the analytic relationship as a self–selfobject unit,[4] because the selfobject dimension of the transference has become temporarily obliterated or obstructed by what the patient has perceived as actual or impending selfobject failure from the side of the analyst, and the analysis must focus on the patient's fears of a transference repetition of traumatically damaging childhood experiences (Kohut, 1971; Ornstein, 1974). When such fears or disturbances are sufficiently analyzed and the broken bond with the analyst is thereby

---

2. There has been a tendency in clinical discourse to reify such experiences of selfobject failure by introducing such unfortunate phrases as "negative selfobjects" or "bad selfobjects." In such expressions, the term "selfobject" is again being employed erroneously, as if it referred to people rather than to a dimension of experience. If "selfobject" is defined, as I believe it should be, as a class of functions, then the notion of a "negative selfobject" is a contradiction in terms. An object not experienced as a source of selfobject functions is simply not a selfobject—good, bad, or indifferent. If a person uses painful experiences with an object for the purpose of self-restoration, as in certain forms of masochism, this is best conceptualized as a substitute for a missing selfobject experience, *not* as a relationship with a "negative selfobject."

3. In two earlier contributions (Socarides & Stolorow, 1984/1985; Stolorow & Brandchaft, in press), it was argued that the specific intersubjective contexts in which conflict originally takes form are those in which central affect states of the child cannot be integrated because they fail to evoke the requisite, attuned responsiveness from the caregiving surround. Such unintegrated affect states become the source of lifelong inner conflict because they are experienced as threats both to the person's established psychological organization and to the maintenance of vitally needed ties. Thus, affect-dissociating defensive operations are called into play, which reappear in the analytic situation in the form of resistance. Such resistance must be understood as being rooted in the patient's expectation or fear *in the transference* that his emerging selfobject needs and feeling states will meet with the same faulty responsiveness that they received from the original caregivers.

4. It is for this and other reasons that I prefer the broader, more inclusive concept of an "intersubjective field" (Atwood & Stolorow, 1984; Stolorow & Brandchaft, in press), referring to the interplay between the differently organized subjective worlds of patient and analyst.

mended, then the selfobject dimension of the tie becomes restored, either to its position in the foreground or to the silent background of the transference. The analyst's empathic grasp of these shifting figure–ground relationships among the selfobject and other dimensions of experience, as they oscillate between the foreground and the background of the transference, determines the content and timing of transference interpretations (Stolorow & Lachmann, 1984/1985).

What is meant, from this multidimensional perspective, by the maturation of selfobject relations from archaic to mature, either in healthy childhood development (Wolf, 1980) or in analytic treatment? What this means is that both the requisite selfobject functions and the subject's predominant mode of acquiring these from an object undergo developmental transformation.

With regard to requisite selfobject functions, in the more archaic states the tie to the object is required for the maintenance of fundamental self-regulatory capacities—that is, for sustaining the basic structural integrity and stability of self experience. In these states, dimensions of experience other than the selfobject one may recede or be unavailable, since the need for psychological survival is overwhelmingly preeminent. In such instances, significant selfobject failure produces profound experiences of self fragmentation or self dissolution. In more mature states, by contrast, in which a nuclear sense of self cohesion has become more or less reliably structuralized, the tie to the object is required primarily for the affective quality of self experience, not for its essential coherence. Hence, dimensions other than the selfobject one can become salient or predominant. Disturbances in the bond produce only fluctuations in self-esteem, with no significant experiences of structural disintegration.

With regard to the mode of acquiring needed selfobject functions, in the more archaic states such modes ordinarily require experiences of merger or oneness with the object, together with an illusion of more or less continuous union. Hence, intrusions of the object's separateness or disruptions in the continuity of the bond can have a profoundly disintegrative impact on the subject's psychological organization. In more mature states, on the other hand, there is greater recognition and tolerance of the distinctness of the object as an independent center of initiative. Here experiences of separateness and discontinuity do not obliterate the bond to the object as a source of selfobject functions and, hence, produce at most only mild disturbances in the organization and affective quality of the subject's self experience.

This multidimensional perspective on experiencing an object thus highlights a critically important area for further investigation, namely, the mutual interaction between the evolving selfobject dimension of experience and other developmental progressions, including especially the consolidation of cognitive–affective structures. It seems apparent that while attuned provision of requisite selfobject functions contributes vitally to the formation of psychological structure, such structuralization, in turn, makes possible more mature modes of selfobject experience, along with increasing complexity in one's experiencing of the object world.

ACKNOWLEDGMENT

The development of this chapter benefitted greatly from discussions with Dr. Michael F. Basch.

REFERENCES

Atwood, G., & Stolorow, R. (1984). *Structures of Subjectivity: Explorations in Psychoanalytic Phenomenology*. Hillsdale, NJ: Analytic Press.

Goldberg, A. (1975). A fresh look at perverse behavior. *International Journal of Psycho-Analysis*, 56:335–342.

Kohut, H. (1966). Forms and transformations of narcissism. *Journal of the American Psychoanalytic Association*, 14:243–272.

Kohut, H. (1968). The psychoanalytic treatment of narcissistic personality disorders. *The Psychoanalytic Study of the Child*, 23:86–113.

Kohut, H. (1971). *The Analysis of the Self*. New York: International Universities Press.

Kohut, H. (1977). *The Restoration of the Self*. New York: International Universities Press.

Kohut, H. (1984). *How Does Analysis Cure?* A. Goldberg, ed., with P. Stepansky. Chicago & London: University of Chicago Press.

Oremland, J. (1985). Kohut's reformulations of defense and resistance as applied in therapeutic psychoanalysis. In A. Goldberg, ed., *Progress in Self Psychology* (Vol. 1, pp. 97–105). New York: Guilford Press.

Ornstein, A. (1974). The dread to repeat and the new beginning. *The Annual of Psychoanalysis*, 2:231–248.

Socarides, D., & Stolorow, R. (1984/1985). Affects and selfobjects. *The Annual of Psychoanalysis*, 12/13:105–119.

Stolorow, R. (1985). Toward a pure psychology of inner conflict. In A. Goldberg, ed., *Progress in Self Psychology* (Vol. 1, pp. 193–201). New York: Guilford Press.

Stolorow, R., & Brandchaft, B. (in press). Developmental failure and psychic conflict. *Psychoanalytic Psychology*.

Stolorow, R., & Lachmann, F. (1980). *Psychoanalysis of Developmental Arrests: Theory and Treatment*. New York: International Universities Press.

Stolorow, R., & Lachmann, F. (1984/1985). Transference: The future of an illusion. *The Annual of Psychoanalysis*, 12/13:19–37.

Wolf, E. (1980). On the developmental line of selfobject relations. In A. Goldberg, ed., *Advances in Self Psychology* (pp. 117–130). New York: International Universities Press.

21

On Working Through in Self Psychology

HYMAN L. MUSLIN

In his posthumous work, *How Does Analysis Cure?*, Kohut remarked that

> whereas self psychology relies on the same tools as traditional analysis (interpretation followed by working through in an atmosphere of abstinence) to bring about the analytic cure, self psychology sees in a different light not only the results that are achieved, but also the very role that interpretation and working through play in the analytic process. (1984, p. 75)

This chapter elaborates, beyond Kohut's commentaries in *How Does Analysis Cure?* and in other writings (1971, 1977), a self psychological conception of "working through." Before turning to this task, however, we must briefly review the way Freud and his successors utilized this notion, thereby showing in stark contrast the "different light" to which Kohut drew attention.

Among Freud's earliest technical guidelines to analysts was the admonition that merely calling attention to resistance on a single occasion would not promote therapeutic change. He observed,

> One must allow the patient time to become more conversant with this resistance with which he has now become acquainted, to "work through," to overcome it by continuing, in defiance of it, the analytic work according to the fundamental rule of analysis. Only when the resistance is at its height can the analyst, working in common with the patient, discover the repressed instinctual impulses which are feeding the resistance; and it is this kind of experience which convinces the patient of the existence and power of such impulses. (1914, p. 155)

Freud's emphasis on the need to overcome resistance to repressed instinctual derivatives was, of course, integral to his theory of analytic cure. He propounded this perspective on resistance to great effect in the case histories of Dora, the Rat Man, and the Wolf Man, and, in theoretical papers of this same era, continued to stress the importance of overcoming resistances to instinctual derivatives and "awakening" memories (1914, p. 154) as central to the treatment of neurosis (Muslin and Gill, 1978). In a variety of works, Freud stressed that only repeated interpretations could eventually diminish the analysand's resistiveness, and that the analytic cure that resulted from such repeated interpretations (working through) was embodied in the ego's access to repressed contents, whether in the guise of instinctual derivatives, pathogenic memories, or oedipal fantasies. It was in this context that Freud initially approached the interpretation of transference–resistance. In the case of the Rat Man, for example, Freud (1909) broached transference interpretation as a strategy for gaining access to repressed memories (see Muslin, 1979). Transference interpretations focusing on the analyst in the here and now were irrelevant to the analytic enterprise, since the transference was merely one vehicle for uncovering repressed memories.

In his monograph of 1926, *Inhibitions, Symptoms and Anxiety*, Freud broadened his earlier perspective somewhat by conceding "that the analyst has to combat no less than five kinds of resistance emanating from three directions—the ego, the id, and the superego" (1926, p. 160). Even here, however, Freud emphasized that it is with respect to the id resistances that the term "working through" had special relevance:

> For we find that even after the ego has decided to relinquish its resistances it still has difficulty in undoing the repression; and we have called the period of strenuous effort which follows after its praiseworthy decision, the phase of "working through." . . . It must be that after the ego-resistance has been removed the power of the compulsion to repeat—the attraction exerted by the unconscious prototypes upon the repressed instinctual process—has still to be overcome. (1926, p. 159)

Succeeding generations of analysts have elaborated, refined, and, in certain instances, altered Freud's basic notion of working through. Among the elaborators, I would single out Fenichel (1939), who broadened Freud's notion so as to provide for "the inclusion of the warded off components in the total personality" (p. 304). For Fenichel, whose concerns were primarily clinical, working through simply designated resistance analysis, independent of the nature of the resistance or the nature of the warded-off content. Both Alexander (1925) and Lewin (1950) compared working through to mourning, stressing that working through aims at, and eventually culminates in, the renunciation of complexes of early memories and wishes. Greenacre (1956), for her part, observed that, among the repressed memories eventually overcome via working through, those of actual traumata occupy a place of importance. Stewart (1963), summarizing Freud's viewpoint, observed that working through should be conceived as the time required of the patient "to change his habitual patterns of discharge" (p. 496). Adhering to Freud's belief that such change involved the overcoming of id resistance, Stewart pointed out that the resistance in question could be equated with libidinal fixation, libidinal "adhesiveness," and/or psychic inertia.

Among contributors who have proffered definitions of working through that dispense with Freud's continuing emphasis on id resistance, I would single out Greenson (1965), Kris (1956), and Loewald (1960). Greenson, who introduced the notion of the therapeutic alliance into the theoretical consideration of working through, redefined the latter as "the analysis of those resistances and other factors which prevent insight from leading to significant and lasting changes in the patient (1965, p. 282). Predictably, he held that only patients able to maintain a therapeutic alliance throughout the analysis of the transference neurosis were able to complete the "work" of working through and successfully terminate. In place of Freud's emphasis on the analysis of id resistances followed by release of pathogenic material in the unconscious, Greenson's definition of working through focuses on the reliving of early wishes and fears in the transference and—when the therapeutic alliance is intact—the curative insight that follows this reliving. Kris (1956) explored working through from the standpoint of the integrative functions of the ego, claiming that the working-through phase of analysis released countercathectic energies that energized the integrative functions of the ego, as confirmed by the emergence of insight. Finally, Loewald (1960), in another contemporary reformulation of working through, looked at this process from a view of the therapeutic action of analysis that focused not on the overcoming of id resistances and the entering of the repressed into consciousness, but on the resumption of ego development. The latter, for Loewald, derived from the analysand's relationship with a new object, the analyst, as mediated by and through the transference.

A SELF PSYCHOLOGICAL PERSPECTIVE ON WORKING THROUGH

I submit that self psychology provides a new perspective on the working-through processes of analysis by virtue of its elevation of the self—

selfobject transferences to a supraordinate status in the theory of therapy. In my view, working through means that the impediments to the potentially curative self–selfobject transference are engaged and the work of dismantling these resistances is undertaken analytically. Like Loewald (1960), Kohut equated the goals of working through with a resumption of development, but unlike Loewald, who understood such development in terms of the growth of secondary-process ego functions, Kohut viewed it in terms of the self's ultimate readiness for empathic interaction with its selfobject surround (1984, p. 77).

Kohut perceived the essential process of cure to consist of a sequence of events: the formation of a selfobject transference that then becomes disrupted through nontraumatic empathy failures—optimal failures or so-called optimal frustration:

> In response to the analyst's errors in understanding or in response to the analyst's erroneous or inaccurate or otherwise improper interpretations, the analysand turns back temporarily form his reliance on empathy to the archaic selfobject relationships (e.g., to remobilization of the need for merger with archaic idealized omnipotent selfobjects or remobilization of the need for immediate and perfect mirroring) that he had already tentatively abandoned in the primary selfobject transference of the analysis. In a properly conducted analysis, the analyst takes note of the analysand's retreat, searches for any mistakes he might have made, nondefensively acknowledges them after he has recognized them (often with the help of the analysand), and then gives the analysand a noncensorious interpretation of the dynamics of his retreat. In this way the flow of empathy between analyst and analysand that had been opened through the originally established selfobject transference is remobilized. The patient's self is then sustained once more by a selfobject matrix that is empathically in tune with him.
>
> In describing these undulations, the researcher must show how each small-scale, temporary empathic failure leads to the acquisition of self-esteem-regulating psychological structure in the analysand—assuming, once more, that the analyst's failures have been nontraumatic ones. Having noticed the patient's retreat, the analyst must watch the analysand's behavior and listen open-mindedly to his associations. By listening open-mindedly, I mean that he must resist the temptation to squeeze his understanding of the patient into the rigid mold of whatever theoretical preconceptions he may hold, be they Kleinian, Rankian, Jungian, Alderian, classical-analytic, or, yes, self psychological, until he has more accurately grasped the essence of the patient's need and can convey his understanding to the patient via a more correct interpretation. (1984, pp. 66–67)

The outcome of this aspect of analysis is that the patient is now able to identify and seek out appropriate selfobjects and to be sustained through empathic resonance with them. Further, psychological structure is acquired and the self becomes firmer (1984, p. 77). In my view, working through, which paves the way for the curative aspects of the therapeutic self–selfobject transference, is to be separated from other aspects of self psychological analysis, such as the progressive unfolding of the curative self–selfobject transferences and their analytic resolution via optimal frustration and transmuting internalization. Thus understood, it is the successful resolution of the working-through aspect of analysis that ushers in these transferential developments and their therapeutic sequelae. As Kohut stated in describing a clinical impasse that was overcome through the work of working through: "It was with the aid of analysis of the tranference—the working through of his feeling rejected by me versus his drawing idealized vitality from me—that the old developmental stalemate was ultimately overcome" (1984, p. 159).

How, from the self psychological perspective, do we construe the resistances that are to be worked through? For the analysand, they amount to archaic approaches to the human encounter that, over the course of a lifetime, have become essential to his self equilibrium. These "resistances" ensure the analysand psychological and experiential safety, albeit a safety characterized by emptiness, feelings of worthlessness, hypochondria, and the like. It follows that the revived archaic self–selfobject experience only appears to be a "resistance" from the viewpoint of the analyst, who sees the self of the analysand seeking to reestablish an archaic bond. For the analysand, the transposition of this search to the analytic situation does not represent a "transference distortion." Rather, it represents a realistic response to what is viewed, albeit unconsciously, as a replica of the environment of early childhood. To the extent that this initial experience serves the analysand's resistance to the therapeutic self–selfobject relationship, we may refer to it, in analogy to the "defense transference" of traditional analysis, as the "self–selfobject defense transference" (Daniels, 1964).

Let us elaborate further on the experiential nature of this resistance. It is a constant source of wonder to the uninitiated that patients who present with depleted selves, feeling worthless and distressed, should prove resistant to the analyst's human concern, determined to persist in patterns of relationship in which their needs can be neither recognized nor gratified. These are the patients who, in the early stages of treatment, continue to experience deprivation; they invite neither the nurturance of a mirroring selfobject nor the invigoration of an idealized selfobject. Immersed in the archaic dyads of childhood, they persist in loneliness, convinced that their longings can never be recognized, much less addressed. Why should this be the case? For these analysands, there can be no guarantee that the expression of their human neediness— however cautiously—will not result in repetition of early insults. They therefore have no choice but to opt for the safety of entrenchment in the withdrawn world of the enfeebled and depleted self. The analyst, from his point of view, sees this entrenchment in terms of persisting archaic self–selfobject patterns that preserve a status quo that forestalls the growth of the analysand's stunted self.

The working-though phase of analysis is set in motion by the analyst's empathic understanding of the analysand's unconscious structuring of the analytic relationship as a revival of an archaic bond. Interpretations at this phase represents attempts to ally the analysand's self-observing functions with the analyst in order to make the striving for the archaic bond a "foreign body," analogous to the interpretive rendering of the transference neurosis as a "symptom." The success of these interpretations is signalled by the analysand's willingness and readiness to enter into a basic selfobject transference—whether of the mirroring, idealized, or alterego variety—that spontaneously unfolds in a manner determined by the analysand's major self deficits.

As early as 1971, Kohut indicated that working through as a process in analysis might have as its initial task the "overcoming of a resistance against the establishment of the narcissistic transference":

> The first task in the working-through process may be the overcoming of a resistance against the establishment of the narcissistic transference (the mirror transference in the present example), i.e., the remobilization in consciousness of the infantile wish or need for parental acceptance. In the next phase of the analysis it is the therapeutic task to keep the mirror transference active, despite the fact that the infantile need is again in essence frustrated. It is during this phrase that the time-consuming, repetitive experiences of the working-through process are being confronted. Under the pressure of the renewed frustrations the patient tries to avoid the pain (a) by re-creating the pre-transference equilibrium through the establishment of a vertical split and/or of a repression barrier; or (b) through regressive evasion, i.e., by a retreat to levels of psychic functioning which are older than that of the pathogenic fixation. (p. 198)

Following Kohut's lead I have divided the working-through aspects of analysis into (1) a working-through *phase* prior to the establishment of a curative self–selfobject transference and (2) a working-through *process* that continues after a selfobject transference is in place. The usefulness of these divisions, clinically and heuristically, is seen in several

ways: The designation of the working-through phase denotes and highlights the work done to overcome resistances during the initial and
ubiquitous period of analysis that precedes the emergence of the selfobject transference(s) and is terminated when the patient enters into
the basic selfobject transference. In cases where the therapeutic self–
selfobject transference emerges spontaneously shortly after analysis has
begun, this phase may be short-lived. In cases where a protracted struggle against a basic selfobject transference pattern ensues, it may be quite
lengthy or unsuccessful.

The working-through *process*, which of course continues throughout
as an integral part of the analysis, signals that the analysand's emergence
from the working-through phase of analysis has been as always incomplete, and that, as the analysis proceeds, additional work will have to
be done to overcome the analysand's intermittent propensity, in response to either real or imagined narcissistic injuries (pursuant to empathic failure, separation, etc.), to reenter the archaic self–selfobject
dyad of early life at the expense of the therapeutic self–selfobject transference (Kohut, 1984, p. 66). Like the working-through phase, the working-through process is quite variable in duration and significance; there
are analyses in which the bond of the therapeutic transference is disrupted frequently and for minor failures of empathy or other imperfections in the analyst. In other analyses, disruptions of the therapeutic
bond, which of course will transpire in any analysis, occur less frequently; the bond of the therapeutic transference once established in
these analyses is more resistive to being dismantled.

The variability of both the working-through phase and working-
through process reflects the special nature of the self fixations and, by
implication, of the self trauma to which the analysand has been exposed.
There are instances in which the working-through phase or process is
never successfully negotiated, resulting in either a continuing stalemate
or premature termination. This is to say that there are patients for whom
growth away from the security of being what Dostoyevski called an
"Underground Man" never becomes a viable option. For these individuals, the memory traces of early experiences of insult or abandonment
are too alive, resulting in an intractable adhesiveness to the seemingly
minimal rewards of an archaic self–selfobject relationship characterized
by loneliness and withdrawal. These individuals never acquire the ability
to "turn their backs" on potential abusers and abandoners; they cling
to their archaic dyads as their only security.

We may summarize to this point by observing that just as analytic theories over the past 60 years have expanded and emended Freud's original concept of working through, so self psychology, via the notion of the therapeutic self–selfobject transference, has expanded and emended the more recent perspectives of ego psychology and object relations theory. For analysts of classical bent, working through continues to betoken the struggle against id resistances (Greenacre, 1956; Novey, 1962; Stewart, 1963) aimed at the recovery of "warded off" material (Fenichel, 1939). For analysts drawing on the perspectives of ego psychology (Kris, 1956) or invoking a concept of the therapeutic alliance (Greenson, 1965), working through corresponds to the development of insight. Only Loewald, it would seem, anticipates Kohut in linking working through to the resumption of developmental potential, although Loewald apprehends such potential only from an object relations standpoint that consigns the analyst to the status of a contemporary "object" who offers himself to the analysand's unconscious. It fell to Kohut to enlarge this developmental framework by calling attention to the analyst's more basic status as a "selfobject" and to the "working through" that had to transpire in order to mobilize and maintain the therapeutic self–selfobject transference so as to allow the patient ultimately to fill out his depleted self through the acquisition of structure. The emphasis of this chapter is on the analysand's resistance to the emergence of this curative self–selfobject dyad, which is to be overcome in the working-through *phase* of a self psychological analysis in my view, just as it is the analysand's tendency to forsake this new therapeutic relationship for the security of the depleting self–selfobject patterns of early life, which must be addressed by the working-through *process* that continues throughout treatment.

These remarks on working through are to seen as an addition to Kohut's views on the essential work in an analysis. They represent an attempt to call attention to the work done in the early stages of analysis on the resistance to the formation of the therapeutic self–selfobject transference (the working-through phase) and the work done on the analysand's urges to retreat to the archaic selfobject bonds once a transference has been established (the working-through process). These remarks proceed from the definition of working through proposed here: Working through refers to the work done in engaging and removing the impediments to the potentially curative self–selfobject transference.

WORKING THROUGH: A SELF PSYCHOLOGICAL CASE STUDY

History

The patient, a slightly built, fragile woman of 32, presented several years after a previous analysis from which she had derived considerable benefit. She had, in the aftermath of this analysis, married, had two children, and achieved a comfortable life style in an attractive home. Yet, these accoutrements of middle-class security notwithstanding, she reported distressing inner experiences, specifically, an unremitting feeling of being unloved and, owing to her pervasive sense of inferiority, a preoccupation with being harshly criticized by all those with whom she had relationships. These concerns and anxieties, well known to her since childhood, had not been alleviated during her previous analysis.

At the time she presented, the patient was experiencing what she termed a "depression," which had persisted for over 6 months. She was still in mourning for her father, then dead for a year, and had given birth to her second child 4 months prior to her initial visit. She reported a 12-year history of analysis and psychotherapy, for which she held her relationship with her mother responsible. Her mother had been seriously depressed since her daughter's high school days. On entering college, the patient had become depressed and agitated in response to her mother's intensifying distress, and had thereupon arranged for psychotherapy. When the mother died of breast cancer during the patient's senior year, she went into an analysis that lasted until her marriage at age 25, ending with what she termed "good results." By way of explaining this outcome, she appealed to her ability to socialize more easily, culminating in the overcoming of her fear of an intimate relationship with a man. The first analysis, she opined, had been "all about my Oedipus complex, my wish to dethrone my mother."

The anamnestic data eventually coalesced around the tragic absence of an adequate mirroring presence throughout her life. Her mother, she recalled, had never been able to calm her; in fact, the latter's ministrations had routinely distressed and agitated her to the point of tears. She recalled being told that she had been a colicky infant, to such an extent that she was evaluated for surgery (in the belief that her colic was due to a pyloric stenosis) in her first year. Early memories revolved around her fear of being picked up and held by her mother; she recalled a vivid scene from her third birthday party when, on being picked up by her mother, she panicked and would not be calmed. She noted that her mother only picked her up when she seemed to be in dire distress, putting her down as soon as she calmed down. At the beginning of treatment, the childhood pattern reasserted itself both inside and outside the analysis: She continue to be distressed at the possibility of anyone spontaneously reaching out to touch her or embrace her.

It was only through reconstructions in the 3rd year of analysis that the basis for her anxiety became clear: She associated her mother's presence and touch with the psychic pain of enforced isolation. To be picked up by her mother was to experience the threat of being ultimately rejected by her. Such rejection took the form of being abruptly put down without any further contact, usually via the crib. This pattern was aggravated by the fact that the mother's "holding" presence was only associated with the patient's physiologic distress, that is, with acute discomfort that could not be alleviated. Whereas we can only surmise the impact of this unsoothable infant on her mother, we can be certain that neither the patient nor her mother experienced a gratifying relationship. For the patient, her mother had never been a source of warm acceptance or nurturance; on the contrary, she had, from early childhood, been vigilant and fearful around her mother, lest the latter find something objectionable in her behavior and become hurtfully critical. Such rejecting maternal criticism, as we learned in the analysis, had as its infantile precursor the patient's experience of being momentarily held and then rejectingly cast into the crib of isolation, where she was left to cry without any prospect of succor.

The major instigator of the patient's lifelong psychic distress was thus revealed to be her experience of her mother as an imprisoner. Although she clamored for interest and acceptance throughout her life— and in her analysis as well—her capacity to accept the calming and soothing ministrations of others, and thereupon to build self-calming and self-soothing self structures, were seriously compromised by the fearful prospect of dismissal. So she could do nothing but verbalize empty complaints that she was not being given adequate attention. In actuality, she placed herself on the "outside" in all her relationships, a victim of her unconscious equation of closeness with imprisonment.

By the time the patient reached latency, she ceased viewing her mother as a source of any assistance whatsoever; she became isolated in her own home, always lonely, always the outsider. In school and in most interpersonal encounters outside the classroom, she was manifestly agitated. Whether by herself or with others, she found it impossible to sit for any length of time, and was therefore unable to sink comfortably into books, movies, or conversations. The only stimulation she received followed from the fact that her mother, until becoming ill when the patient was 12, ran the household like a military installation, replete with rules and fines for infractions. The patient reported that her siblings were somewhat less awed by the mother and therefore less anxious in her presence. But the atmosphere in the home was cold for all of them, no one touched, hugged, or kissed or, perhaps even more significantly, smiled at one another when Mother was around.

The patient's father, toward whom she had more positive feelings, was depicted as a warm and humorous person who took the family on occasional boating and hiking trips that the patient thoroughly enjoyed. These outings, however, dated from her early adolescence. During her childhood, the father's business kept him on the road throughout the week; he returned home mainly on weekends. Thus, he failed to become a major selfobject presence for the patient. In her self experience, he remained a vaguely idealized persona, but not a concrete presence in any of the major events in her life. Even during the occasional outings, he did not entertain any type of special relationship with her; she had enjoyed herself only as a member of the family. Of course, the patient's subjective experience of her father may not do full justice of his status as a strong, calming influence in the family. In the aftermath of her rejection by her mother, she became vigilant with her father as well, and may simply have been unable to tolerate an intimate relationship with him.

The patient's secondary-school experiences paralleled those at home. She became superficially attached to a group of young women toward whom she adopted the persona she had learned at home: To be the accommodating friend who never displays self needs. Unfortunately, her inability to "take in" the emotional availability of others generalized to her school work, where she experienced an analogous inability to "take in" the offerings of her instructors or the contents of her books. In high school, she neither dated nor participated in any social activities. This social isolation was aggravated by her mother's intensifying depression, which, in conjunction with the mother's regular psychotherapy, left the patient and her siblings relatively unattended in the home. Neither the patient nor her siblings ever brought friends into the house. The mother's depression, as we have noted, worsened throughout the patient's college years, leading her to begin her own psychotherapy at the age of 18. When the mother died of metastasized breast cancer during the patient's senior year, she reacted with a mixture of sadness and relief that the mother's suffering was at an end; the latter had received neither physical nor emotional relief for many years.

Following moderately successful analysis that focused on the patient's oedipal competitiveness with her mother for her father's interest, she met her future husband at a dance; he was her first beau, and they married a month later. Although she respected his serious approach to life and devotion to high ideals, their relationship was marred by her continuing inability to accept his emotional availability; we may speak of her refusal to let herself be cherished by him as the major obstacle to their romantic relationship. This difficulty extended to her children as well; she could not enjoy merger experiences with them, and her maternal ministrations were dutiful at best. As noted, the equilibrium that resulted from her first analysis was disrupted when her father suddenly died of a cerebrovascular accident. Although she had seen her father infrequently in the years following her mother's death, she experienced his passing as a catastrophe engendering a sense of intolerable loneliness. As we later came to understand, his death signified the end of her belief that she could ever have her archaic merger needs recognized and accommodated.

The Analysis

The analysis began with the patient articulating a fear of allowing me to enter her psychic life that, she believed, was identical to her feeling at the outset of her first analysis. She added that not only her behavior but even her voice seemed to be the same as it had been in the former treatment. To me, she presented as a person remarkably responsive to my own bodily movements, to which she reacted with intense anxiety. Indeed, her agitation during the first years of analysis occasionally became so intense that she would shriek in the sessions. I quickly understood that my initial task was to foster a safe holding environment, free of any unwitting "controlling" on my part. The provision of this milieu meant keeping overt interventions to a minimum.

Little by little, the manner in which she structured her life—as summarized above—emerged: how she managed to keep everyone, emotionally speaking, at bay, and how her complaints of emptiness and loneliness proved unavailing, given her inability to be receptive to the emotional availability of others without feeling panic. Predictably, this defensive pattern reemerged in the early phase of the analysis: Her complaints of being lonely elicited defenses against allowing herself to experience intimacy. These defenses were expressed both verbally, via her accusations of my indifference and summary rejection of my interpretive comments, and nonverbally, via her tendency to arrive late and/or leave early. At this juncture of treatment, we had not recovered the history of her early deprivations, and were thereby limited to the here-and-now material of her fear of my potentially intrusive presence. Retrospectively, of course, we can understand these early anxieties as emblematic of the archaic self–selfobject relationship that the patient sought to reinstate in the analysis, and we can see the analytic work of the time as the engagement of the working-through phase of treatment. This is to say that the patient began her analysis with a selfobject defense transference in the service of preserving her manifestly frozen self state; it was the task of the working-through phase to illuminate this transference via interpretation. Well into the 2nd year of treatment, the selfobject defense transference continued to unfold, and she continued to resist any interpretive exploration of her need to maintain barriers in the analysis. Interpretations of her complaints about being lonely were invariably followed by rejection of my remarks and emotional withdrawal.

It was only at the end of the 2nd year that she finally responded to these interventions—and the analytic ambience in which they had been undertaken—by recounting her early relationship with her mother, especially her pervasive fear of closeness with the latter. It was at this juncture that we reconstructed her early fear of being cast away and imprisoned in her crib. Her persistent pattern of self-protection via isolation began to wane, and her continuing complaints about my indifference were joined by new wishes that I provide her with more comfort and support.

As we entered the 3rd year of analysis, the patient's selfobject defense transference gave way to a selfobject transference of a predominantly idealizing type. Over the course of the next 4 years, the analytic sequence of optimal frustrations followed by transmuting internalizations resulted in the acquisition of new self structures subserving her self-calming and self-soothing capabilities. As in any analysis, these gains were interrupted by periodic retreats from the therapeutic selfobject transference to the old defensive constellation in which I was again experienced as an untrustworthy tyrant capable of imprisoning her in the crib of her childhood. At these junctures of treatment, the working-through process was activated to alert the patient, via interpretations, to her defensive need to freeze me out in order to avoid exposing herself to the hurt of fantasied rejection.

These interruptions in the idealizing selfobject transference were typically evoked by situations in which her need for nurturance was temporarily heightened—for example, by separations, physical illness in herself or her children, or the need to make important decisions bearing on the welfare of her family. The working-through process that addressed and resolved these exigencies was of varying duration, ranging from several interpretations within a session to 2 weeks of interpretation addressing her resumption of the old defensive pattern. It should be noted again that the periodic activation of the working-through *process* during the course of an analysis stands in contrast to the working-through *phase* that typifies the beginning of self psychological analyses, in my view. Whereas the working-through phase is a prerequisite for the unfolding of the therapeutic self–selfobject transference, the working-through process presupposes that the basic self–selfobject transference has been engaged and that all further disruptions of the selfobject transference, once recognized and studied, become a vital part of the analytic cure. As Kohut noted:

> Time and time again in the course of analysis, the basic therapeutic unit is brought into play when a disruption of the selfobject transference, be it of the mirroring, twinship, or idealizing variety, is understood and explained and a potential trauma is transformed into an experience of optimal frustration. And, in consequence of these optimal frustrations, the needs of the analysand gradually change as, via imperceptible accretions of structure, his damaged self is increasingly able to feel enhanced and supported by those selfobject responses that are available to adults. (1984, p. 206)

In the analysis in question, the working-through process successfully countered the patient's regressive tendencies, and, by the 6th year of treatment, the transmuting internalizations had led to significant adaptive gains. She became able more easily to touch and hold both her children and her husband; from the latter, she also became capable of asking for warmth. In addition, she resumed contact with siblings whom she had previously avoided for many years.

Concomitant with these gains was a new enthusiasm for the work of analysis since, as she observed, she was no longer preoccupied with the "putdowns" that had blocked her in the past. The latter phase of treatment followed a recurrent, cyclical pattern: Exploration of the patient's emergent need for mirroring of her assertive strivings was quickly followed by a psychological "looking backward" to make sure I was still there as an approving selfobject. This maneuver usually engendered a temporary reactivation of her empty complaining, followed by her re-engagement of the empathic milieu of the analysis. Experientially, this pattern might begin with the patient's recounting a romantically satisfying weekend with her husband, followed by anxious associations to an impending separation from the analyst and hence to poignant early memories of sharing a homework assignment with her mother, only to have the latter "take over" her project. Finally, she would "wake up" and remind herself of the distance between such early experiences and the present.

The patient's announcement of her wish to terminate, broached after 6 years of analysis, seemed reasonable enough. For the preceding 2 years, she had been able to pursue major activities with enthusiasm, free from her previous shackles. As mother, wife, and friend, she had achieved a new equilibrium. Recent analytic work betrayed little evidence of either her defensive proclivities or her tendency to reactivate the archaic patterns in response to impending separations or empathic errors.

Having confirmed the patient's assessment of her readiness to approach termination, the termination phase of treatment began and, with it, her relationship to me underwent a dramatic, regressive transformation: She returned to the defensive patterns that typified her early relationship to her mother and to me in the early phase of treatment. In fact, directly after announcing that she had arrived at a termination date, she had an anxiety attack and, in the next session, reported a self-state dream centering on a fearful reaction to separation. In the dream, the patient began a new life with an analyst who ultimately rejected her. The sequel to this anxiety attack and dream was a reactivation of the selfobject defense transference that had preoccupied us in the early years of treatment. For a time, I again became the withholding and unempathic mother of her early years, in response to whom she withdrew, mobilizing an archaic self state in which isolation, however painful, defended against the far greater pain of exposing needs that would not be gratified by the unreliable mother–analyst.

As the patient reexperienced the archaic self–selfobject relationship with her mother, we had one final opportunity to explore both its hurtful dimension and the more subtle security that it had provided. The analytic material of the time involved the patient's simultaneous experience of me as someone she could not leave, and someone who had never been adequately involved with her and was dismissing her out of disappointment. These transference perceptions predictably evoked associations to the mother, who had only become manifestly interested in the patient during crisis states, as when she screamed for attention or fought with her siblings. In this same context, she recalled once more how uneasy she had been around her mother, with whom she had feared physical contact. The interpretations that followed these termination-phase developments focused on the patient's need to structure the analytic relationship in such a way that I would either abandon the termination plans or, alternatively, *make* her continue with treatment. Subsequent associations confirmed the accuracy of these interpretations.

Via a final recourse to the working-through process, we resolved this dying flicker of the selfobject defense transference. After several months, the patient once more became receptive to my words and my presence, and once again experienced the calming effect of her previous analytic bond. As we worked toward termination, this cycle of retreating to the selfobject defense transference and then, via interpretation, re-accepting my empathic interest, recurred several times.

DISCUSSION

It has been my contention that working through is best conceptualized, from a self psychological perspective, as the analytic work performed in dissolving the patient's resistances to entering a new self–selfobject relationship. These resistances represent attempts to preserve archaic childhood bonds that, however stifling to growth, have heretofore provided the primary type of security known to these individuals.

In the patient we have described, both the working-through phase with which we commenced analytic work and the working-through process that was reinvoked throughout the analysis, centered on her experience of me as a potential imprisoner who was to be kept out of her life at all costs, and whose empathic overtures mandated even greater vigilance. In the termination phase, when the selfobject defense transference was reactivated, she rationalized her withdrawal by claiming that I had never provided adequate assistance and had, in any event, simply lost interest in her as an analysand. At those junctures of treatment when her defensiveness was at its height, her bearing, affect, and words revealed that she was now in a veritable panic state, her shrieking that I keep away form her alternating with futile crying for help. At such times, she *became* the threatened youngster whose mother was so distant as to make her feel abandoned, and whose occasional "holding" gestures were only preludes to imprisonment in the crib. In the selfobject defense transference, she was equally convinced of my lack of interest in her and my readiness to censure her.

It was the initial task of this analysis to transform the self of this child in distress into an observing self capable of accepting the therapeutic rapport that is a precondition for the unfolding of the curative self–selfobject transference. It fell to the working-through phase of treatment—and the working-through process that was sporadically invoked in its aftermath—to enable the patient to overcome her resistance to embracing a new type of self–selfobject relationship, and to do so by facilitating her "rediscovery" (Fenichel, 1939) of the childhood anlagen of her ingrained defensiveness toward any offer of human contact.

I believe the foregoing remarks, premised on the vicissitudes of the patient's experienced self states, point out the relevance of self psychology to an experiential understanding of working through. In the case under discussion, the patient not only experienced the vicissitudes of her self states, as documented above, but reported on these vicissitudes with growing articulateness as the analysis progressed. It was her alternating experience of the analyst, as shaped by modulations in her experience of the archaic self–selfobject dyad of childhood, that was unique to her, and that provides the uniquely experiential vantage point for understanding the course of her analysis.

We may generalize and say that it is the *reexperience* of the archaic self in analysis that signals the engagement of the working-through aspects of analysis. It is the task of the working through in analysis to illuminate interpretively the archaic neediness characteristic of this self, thereby enabling the patient to relinquish the security entailed in the selfobject defense transference and to become immersed or reimmersed in the therapeutic self–selfobject transference. Finally, it is the achievement of the working-through aspects of analysis at any stage in the treatment to have subjected the archaic self to yet another defeat—this time in relation to the analyst—in its quest for a world of archaic selfobjects.

I conclude with some tentative reflections on the role of the analyst's presence and the analyst's interventions in the resolutions of the working-through phase of treatment. I have already alluded to the empathic ambience that typifies any properly conducted analysis, allowing the patient to retell the dramas of his life without fear of censure. Certainly, the basic experience of safety that occurs within this ambience plays an important role in the patient's ability to relinquish the security associated with the archaic self–selfobject relationship of the past and enter the therapeutic self–selfobject relationship.

The impact of the analyst's dynamic and genetic interpretations is more problematic to assess. It is always difficult to state unequivocally that accurate interpretations were the major force in a given patient's repudiation of the archaic self and its investments. Accurate interpretations, as Freud first discovered in his treatment of the Wolf Man (Freud, 1918), rarely dissolve the patient's need to maintain resistances. How, then, do certain interpretations prove to be effective? One useful way of addressing this problem is provided by self psychology: It is the patient's growing investment in the analyst as a major source of self-sustenance that, in the course of analysis, mobilizes the patient's receptivity to the analyst's interpretations and enhances his ability to respond to these interpretations. It would seem that the patient cannot fully overcome his resistance to the therapeutic self–selfobject relationship until he experiences—via displacements from the original selfobjects of early life—the analyst as the provider of psychological oxygen (Kohut, 1977). It is only at this point that the patient can follow the analyst's lead and direct his attention to genetic reconstructions that enable him to see the past in the present.

References

Alexander, F. (1925). A metapsychological description of the process of cure. *International Journal of PsychoAnalysis*, 6:13–34.

Daniels, R.S. (1964). Some early manifestations of transference. *Journal of the American Psychoanalytic Association*, 17:995–1055.

Fenichel, O. (1939). *Problems of Psychoanalytic Technique*. Albany, NY: Psychoanalytic Quarterly.

Freud, S. (1914). Remembering, repeating and working-through. *Standard Edition*, 12:145–156.

Freud, S. (1909), Notes upon a case of obsessional neurosis. *Standard Edition*, 10:153–318.

Freud, S. (1918). From the history of an infantile neurosis. *Standard Edition*, 17:3–243.

Freud, S. (1926). Inhibitions, symptoms and anxiety. *Standard Edition*, 20:77–174.

Greenacre, P. (1956). Re-evaluation of the process of working through. *International Journal of Psycho-Analysis*, 37:439–444.

Greenson, R.R. (1965). The working alliance and the transference neurosis. *Psychoanalytic Quarterly*, 34:155–181.

Kohut, H. (1971). *The Analysis of the Self*. New York: International Universities Press.

Kohut, H. (1977). *The Restoration of the Self*. New York: International Universities Press.

Kohut, H. (1984). *How Does Analysis Cure?* A. Goldberg, ed., with P. Stepansky. Chicago & London: University of Chicago Press. 1984.

Kris, E. (1956). On some vicissitudes of insight in psycho-analysis. *International Journal of Psycho-Analysis*, 37:445–455.

Lewin, B.D. (1950). *The Psychoanalysis of Elation*. New York: Norton.

Loewald, H.W. (1960). On the therapeutic action of psycho-analysis. *International Journal of Psycho-Analysis*, 41:16–23.

Muslin, H.L. (1979). Transference in the Ratman case. *Journal of the American Psychoanalytic Association*, 27:561–578.

Muslin, H.L. & Gill, M.M. (1978). Transference in the Dora case. *Journal of the American Psychoanalytic Association*, 26:311–328.

Novey, S. (1962). The principle of "working through" in psychoanalysis. *Journal of the American Psychoanalytic Association*, 10:658–676.

Stewart, W. (1963). An inquiry into the concept of working through. *Journal of the American Psychoanalytic Association*. 11:474–499.

22

Alterego Phenomena and the Alterego Transferences: Some Further Considerations

DOUGLAS W. DETRICK

Heinz Kohut's final contribution of major importance to self psychological theory was determining that the alterego or twinship transference formed from a disturbance in a third major selfobject developmental line. He no longer considered the alterego or twinship transference to be a subspecies of the mirroring transference. He also suggested that there may be an intrinsic relationship between alterego experiences and the acquisition of skills and talents.

Kohut introduced his discussion of the twinship developmental needs in *How Does Analysis Cure?* (1984) by describing a particular phase in the analysis of a middle-aged woman. This phase was ushered in by a disruption in the transference that resulted from the announcement of Kohut's upcoming vacation. This patient's transference disruption brought about the emergence of a highly valued fantasy that had been important to her from early in life. It was the fantasy of a genie in a bottle, and, as Kohut was eventually to discover, this genie was experienced as a twin, an essential likeness of the patient to whom she could relate whenever she felt unsupported and alone. Further association and the analysis of particular resistances motivated by shame, brought forth the memory of the normal alterego counterpart of the genie-in-the-bottle fantasy. The patient remembered a time when she was a little girl, perhaps 4 years old, and she was standing in the kitchen alongside her grandmother, kneading dough. On the basis of such observations as this, the primary experience of likeness and the learning of a particular skill, in this instance, kneading dough, Kohut came to link these two phenomena (Kohut, 1984).

In a recent essay (Detrick, 1985) on the alterego or twinship developmental line, I focused on sexualizations, addictions, borderline

states, and the interpretive process, and concluded that alterego experiences are in some sense more basic to human experience than either
those of being mirrored or idealizing (p. 251). I also concluded that the
structure of the group nuclear self is not analogous but reciprocal to the
individual's nuclear self (p. 254).

In this chapter I hope to make some further theoretical progress
by inquiring into the apparent necessity for Kohut of having two terms,
"alterego" and "twinship," cover the same ground. When I asked Kohut
how he would distinguish them, he stated, "The relationship to a twin
is that of an alterego." I have reached a different conclusion on this
issue and make a sharp distinction between the twinship and alterego
phenomena: *Twinship* phenomena are those in which an experience of
sameness or likeness serves the central function of the acquisition of
skills and tools. *Alterego* phenomena are those experiences of sameness
or likeness that anchor the individual in a group process.

In regard to the twinship phenomenon I offer a short clinicla vignette. This is from a session that a colleague described; this was a one-
time consultation so it is lacking in background information and description of the clinical process. The therapist described a session with
a gay woman who had became intensely angry at her lover. From what
the therapist related, it seemed that the relationship was based on twinship needs. The two women had the same interests, the same values,
similar family backgrounds, and apparently even looked very much alike.
The patient had become enraged because her lover had established a
sexual relationship with a man. I was not able to determine whether
this threatened the relationship of the two women fundamentally. I was
interested to hear that the patient had related other similar experiences,
which she characterized as abandonment. Her rage was the result of a
disrupted twinning experience. A need for static sameness is sometimes
seen in twinship relationships, which may be a pathological, regressive
variant of the healthy, joyful need to learn and to grow together. This
particular woman had felt her lover's step toward heterosexuality to be
a developmental achievement that would leave her behind.

As described earlier, I believe we should see the group nuclear self
as reciprocal to the individual nuclear self. Whereas in the individual
the nuclear self is bipolar, constructed of the ambitions at one pole and
the ideals at the other, with the skills and talents mediating between
them, the group nuclear self is unipolar (Detrick, 1985, p. 254), with
the alterego dimension of experience central and essential to group
cohesiveness and the so-called group boundary. Following this line of

reasoning, I suggest that the motivational core of the group is the experience of sameness among the group members as a function of the group process as it is directed by the ambitions or ideals of the leader. Or, to put it differently, there are two dynamic relationships that make up the group process. One is the relationship among the group members in which the alterego experience is primary. The second dynamic is among the group members in their relation to the leader. The group is moved in a particular direction by the leader's initiative and goal-setting activity.

The healthy group is characterized by the pursuit of productive goals as directed by the behavior of the leader, in the context of a cohesive group process as organized by the alterego sameness experience of the members. This conceptualization of the group self allows us several advantages. The first is that we may replace the metaphorical concept of the group boundary with the psychologically more precise idea that the group is defined by the alterego experience of its members. This is the result of placing the empathic point of view at the center of our exploration of group phenomena. The second advantage is that it underscores the function of leadership as a defining characteristic of the group process. (See Detrick, 1985, for a discussion of the two types of leadership behavior, designated *a potiori* as charismatic and messianic.)

An excellent place to study leadership is at Tavistock group conferences (Colman & Bexton, 1975; Lawrence, 1979). The conference format is such that the participants divide into groups, each group having a "consultant." Everyone arrives with the expectation that the consultant is really the leader. Yet this person does the one thing that groups find intolerable, he reflects upon and interprets the group's behavior. In my view, forcing the group to look at its own behavior is the one thing the group cannot tolerate and maintain its cohesiveness. Why should this be so?

There are two reasons why this "leadership" behavior is so disruptive. The first is that the group members have an expectation, perhaps better described as an unconscious expectational set, that they are about to engage in a healthy group process in which the leader provides a direction and motivation. Second, the interpretation of group process disrupts the group because it forces all of the group members to be introspective. By the very fact of this individual introspection by each of the members, the alterego experience of sameness is rendered impossible, and the group fragments of necessity.

The foregoing theoretical conclusions require us to make a relatively sharp distinction between individual and group psychotherapy. In individual psychotherapy the patient can remobilize and deal with any number of issues in the transference to the therapist. The therapist, following Kohut, is able to see the multifarious transference manifestations, fragmentations, and regressions, related to the developmental vicissitudes of the patient. This cannot happen in a group setting. On the one hand, the presence of group members makes it highly unlikely that specific archaic transference needs can be mobilized and sustained so that working through can take place. On the other hand, being in a group draws participants into a particular process. The unconscious expectations that they bring to this group are, for the most part, different from those a person brings to individual psychotherapy.

Be that as it may, I believe we can offer an explanation of the change process as it is rendered by group psychotherapy. In individual psychotherapy the essence of the curative process is the healing of deficits in the nuclear self via transmuting internalization in the context of optimal frustration (Kohut, 1984). The working-through process involves primarily the mirroring and/or idealizing developmental needs that were functionally impaired. I suggest that the process of change in group psychotherapy is the acquisition of skills via transmuting internalization in the context of optimal gratification. To use the metaphor that Kohut (1971) relied on in *The Analysis of the Self*, individual psychotherapy cures as a result of the structure building that takes place when the archaic transference is disrupted. Change in group psychotherapy takes place with the acquisition of skills in the context of an interpretation that evokes an experience of twinship.

The step from the consideration of the alterego aspects of small group dynamics and group psychotherapy to the consideration of civilization and the sociocultural processes that comprise it is a large one, yet here, too, self psychology has something of fundamental importance to offer. On one level, it can deepen our comprehension of societal processes to the extent it formulates a valid group psychology. This would involve such tasks as researching the psychological essence of and interaction between such sociocultural institutions as the family, schools, the criminal justice system, churches, and the creative literary–art community, among many others. One important aspect of this research is mapping how each of these sociocultural groups either supports and enhances or undermines and destroys the genesis and growth of the individual's nuclear self.

I believe that we can also observe the expression and influence of these social institutions in the clinical situation. I'll discuss just one of the various manifestations: group or ideological countertransference. This type of countertransference is caused by an unwarranted intrusion into the therapeutic situation of the dynamics, values, and goals of sociocultural institutions leading to various psychological or psychotherapeutic schools mimicking these institutions. The therapist, in effect, becomes the tacit representative of a particular group, and cure then becomes unconsciously equated with the acceptance of the group's values and goals.

Ego psychology, archetypal or Jungian psychology, and self psychology all have equally valid claims to scientific respectability and therapeutic effectiveness. However, each school of thought may give rise to an ideological countertransference in which certain ideas of Freud, Jung, or Kohut are taken out of context and emphasized, sacrificing a more accurate and balanced view, and resulting in a distortion of each seminal thinker's point of view. Yet, I would contend that even though the corrupting of the therapeutic process by an attempt at a covert ideological conversion is almost always deleterious, each of the various cultural institutions and associated group values form a healthy and necessary part of society.

For example, an ideological countertransference that could derive from ego psychology would be in certain respects analogous to the "sin morality" of certain religious traditions. Utilizing a dynamic centered around guilt and authority, the patient might experience therapy as a seeking out of moral transgressions, real and imagined, allowing for the self-esteem enhancing effect of confession and absolution.

An ideological countertransference based on Jung's work might create a dynamic that could be characterized as "inspiration and the collective." Combining the therapist's unwarranted personal revelations with a reluctance to interpret *any* of the patient's material as transference related to experiences early in life replaces an effective Jungian therapy with an intense and exciting mutuality that neglects the patient's more centrally located feelings of emptiness or depression. More precisely, the ideological transference "inspiration and the collective" is a regressively altered distortion of the normal function or role that art and the humanities may play in society.

As for self-psychology, its ideological countertransference may be derived from the dynamic, "empathy and personal growth." In such instances the therapeutic situation is no longer oriented toward the basic therapeutic unit of empathy followed by interpretation. Instead the therapist sees the patient as a distressed, helpless child and himself as the benign parent. Interventions intended directly to provide the patient what the parents did not, replace interpretation, and the therapeutic process as a whole is replaced by a family dynamic that interferes with the optimal mobilization and working through of the pathognomonic transferences.

In this chapter the terms "alterego" and "twinship" instead of being used synonymously, have been differentiated. Twinship phenomena are those in which an experience of sameness or alikeness serves the central function in the acquisition of skill. Alterego phenomena are experiences of sameness or alikeness that anchor the individual in a group process. A distinction between the curative process in individual and group therapy was offered, the former stressing the healing of deficits via transmuting internalization, and the latter, skill acquisition via transmuting internalization in the context of optimal gratification, particularly in the context of interpretations evoking twinship experiences. Finally, a particular type of countertransference was suggested based on the intrusion of certain groups' (alterego) values and goals into the psychoanalytic situation.

REFERENCES

Colman, A. & Bexton, H., eds. (1975). *Group Relations Reader*. Sausalito, CA: GREX.
Detrick, D.W. (1985). Alterego phenomena and the alterego transferences. In A. Goldberg, ed., *Progress in Self Psychology* (Vol. 1, pp. 240–256). New York: Guilford Press.
Kohut, H. (1971). *The Analysis of the Self*. New York: International Universities Press.
Kohut, H. (1984). *How Does Analysis Cure?* A. Goldberg, ed., with P. Stepansky. Chicago & London: University of Chicago Press.
Lawrence, W.G., ed. (1979). *Exploring Individual and Organizational Boundaries*. New York: Wiley.

Index